advanced
JAVA

Idioms, Pitfalls, Styles and Programming Tips

CHRIS LAFFRA

To **join** a Prentice Hall internet mailing list, point to http://www.prenhall.com/register

Prentice Hall PTR
Upper Saddle River, New Jersey 07458
http://www.prenhall.com

Acquisitions editor: *Paul W. Becker*
Editorial assistant: *Maureen Diana*
Production supervision: *Mary Sudul*
Cover design: *Anthony Gemmellaro*
Cover design director: *Jerry Votta*
Copyeditor: *Barbara Danziger*
Manufacturing manager: *Alexis R. Heydt*

© 1997 Prentice Hall PTR
Prentice Hall, Inc.
A Simon & Schuster Company
Upper Saddle River, New Jersey 07458

The publisher offers discounts on this book when ordered in bulk quantities. For more information, contact Corporate Sales Department, Prentice Hall PTR, One Lake Street, Upper Saddle River, NJ 07458. Phone: 800-382-3419; FAX: 201-236-7141; email: corpsales@prenhall.com

Printed in the United States of America

10 9 8 7 6 5 4 3 2 1

ISBN 0-13-534348-8

Prentice-Hall International (UK) Limited, *London*
Prentice-Hall of Australia Pty. Limited, *Sydney*
Prentice-Hall Canada Inc., *Toronto*
Prentice-Hall Hispanoamericana, S.A., *Mexico*
Prentice-Hall of India Private Limited, *New Delhi*
Prentice-Hall of Japan, Inc., *Tokyo*
Simon & Schuster Asia Pte. Ltd., *Singapore*
Editora Prentice-Hall do Brasil, Ltda., *Rio de Janeiro*

Contents

Foreword

As one of the authors of the Java compiler and the Java Applet APIs I was both surprised and intrigued by "Advanced Java." In the book many interesting aspects of Java and the Java APIs are uncovered which have not been addressed anywhere else in this much detail. The book not only demonstrates the power of Java but it also highlights potential problems that a Java programmer should watch out for.

The LTK toolkit is an example of a sophisticated toolkit which is built on top of the standard AWT classes. It successfully addresses some of the drawbacks of the AWT in an elegant manner and is surprisingly complete. Although this won't be the last of the Java toolkits, it is certainly one of the more interesting ones, and if I could do it again, the AWT would certainly be a lot more like the LTK.

It must be said that the AWT was developed in only a few months and some of the design decisions were made under time pressure, and as a result there are a number of imperfections which are uncovered in detail in this book. Fortunately, the LTK solves some of these and it is better to know the pitfalls before you stumble upon them yourself.

For Java junkies that want to know Java inside and out, this book is required reading. I certainly had trouble putting it down after the first few pages.

Have fun,

Arthur van Hoff

Preface

Java is an immensely popular programming language. It can be used to develop small applications that can be embedded into otherwise static World Wide Web (WWW) pages. Whenever a Java-enabled browser encounters a page with a reference to such an applet, it is automatically retrieved over the Internet by the browser and executed locally on the user's display. In this fashion, Hypertext Markup Language (HTML) pages can be host to a wide variety of interactive applications ranging from displaying a simple image, showing various animations, implementing a game like solitary or chess, performing client-based manipulation of data without needing a round-trip to a server, to retrieving live stock quotes from an external data source.

Java was initially designed as a language for programming embedded consumer electronics. Its syntax is inspired by C++, but it is simpler in quite a number of aspects. Removed from the language are pointer arithmetic, templates, multiple inheritance, and a lot of other things that were considered too complicated by the language designers. Added to the language are multithreaded programming support, garbage collection, interfaces, and Internet awareness. This makes the language a perfect vehicle for efficient compilation, distribution, and execution of enhanced WWW pages.

History and Background of Java

Java has attracted a lot of attention over the past year, and some people might perceive Java to be a revolutionary language. However, the strongest aspect of the language is that it is inherently evolutionary. The design of the language incorporates a lot of constructs and paradigms that are borrowed from previously defined languages. In particular, Java borrows its syntax from C++, its single inheritance and garbage collection from Smalltalk, its interface construct from Objective C, and its multiple threads from Modula 3. Of course, each of these languages again borrowed from languages like Simula, Algol, and C. The runtime environment of Java resembles the main design of the NeWS windowing system, allowing executable code to be distributed over the network (in the case of the NeWS system in the form of postscript). This familiarity with existing languages makes the learning curve for Java very easy to climb. This assumes we can ignore the time it takes to learn standard libraries that are shipped with Java.

Language design is the ultimate art of finding compromises. Often, one given design criterion conflicts with others, or needs to be compromised (or completely ignored) due to less idealistic and more pragmatic reasons. The ``ideal'' programming language does not exist and probably never will. Simply put, a programming language has one goal: to tell the computer what to do. Such a language could be geared towards a very specific domain (like Structured Query Language (SQL), to access relational databases), or be a general purpose language (like the C programming language). Java ended up to be a general purpose language, yet it was designed with a specific use in mind: an embedded description language for adding behavior to things such as smart TV set-top controllers or WWW browsers. Therefore, the design of Java was driven by a couple of clearly identifiable design goals, amongst others:

- *Platform independence.* Software developed in Java should run on a large set of hardware platforms without needing to recompile code or maintain different versions.

- *Easy to learn.* The language should look familiar to users (i.e., C++) but at the same time be less complex than existing languages. This requirement ruled out constructs that were perceived to be too difficult to understand, or that were deemed unnecessary for the scope of the language.

- *Efficiency.* How can one design a programming language that is directly executable on multiple platforms, yet at the same time is efficient enough to compete with natively compiled C, for instance? The approach taken is to distribute the code in the form of bytecodes, which are interpreted on the user's local display. To gain performance, these byte codes can be compiled on demand into native machine instructions by the local Java enabled browser.

- *Ease of software distribution.* Software developed with Java should be easily transportable over the network to facilitate its use in a local browser. The producer and the consumer of the code may be located at remote nodes of the world wide web.

- *Abstraction.* One of the most serious problems programmers face is complexity. Abstractions provide a way of developing a smaller part of the application first, and use the resulting abstraction to put together the larger whole. In the times of structured programming, functions and modules were the abstraction mechanism. The current fashion is to use objects. Therefore, Java is an object-oriented language, where the main building blocks are objects.

Scope of This Book

This book does not give an introduction to Java for novices. Do not expect to find a description of how to set your class path on Windows 95, or what special relationships Jim Gosling has with oak trees, nor expect to find in this book how to make a simple applet run both with the applet viewer and with Netscape. Those basic topics are dealt with enough in any of the dozens of Java books currently available on the shelves at your local bookstore. Instead, this book tries to concentrate on more advanced features, some of which are:

- object-oriented analysis and design (OOAD) aspects of Java programs

- how to implement programming idioms, such as callbacks

- how to enhance the Java AWT toolkit

- the range of meta-programming techniques in Java

- security aspects

- Java pitfalls and "gotchas"

- how to debug Java programs

- automatically translating C++ code to Java

Much of this book is based on experiences that I gained during my formal education. After receiving a Master's degree in Computer Science from the Free University of Amsterdam, the Netherlands, I codesigned and implemented PROCOL, a parallel object oriented language as part of my Ph.D. research at the Erasmus University of Rotterdam, the Netherlands. In the summer of 1992, I started a postdoc position at the IBM T. J. Watson Research, where I worked on a compiler and a development environment for the Oberon programming language. Furthermore, I developed HotWire, a platform independent visual debugger for C++ and Smalltalk. Some of the ideas in HotWire can now be found in commercial versions of the IBM Smalltalk system, VisualAge.

In the summer of 1994, I moved to the information technology department of Morgan Stanley in New York City, one of the ten best U.S. companies to work for, confirmed by a survey done by *Money* magazine. At Morgan, I continued working with OO languages as a member of the MStk development team. MStk is a proprietary multiplatform C++ toolkit providing support for firm-wide infrastructure and user-interface aspects of financial applications used by Morgan Stanley at Wall Street. I have also been actively involved in evaluation and pilot projects of the Java language inside Morgan Stanley, and lead a porting effort of MStk from C++ to Java, which was done to get more familiar with the strengths and limitations of the language.

This book was written while I was employed by Morgan Stanley. However, it does not represent any opinions or official statements from my employer. Any opinions stated in this manuscript are mine alone, and I am solely responsible for the contents.

Structure of This Book

This book talks about "advanced topics". It is split up in four major parts:

Chapter 1. Idioms, Pitfalls, and Programming Tips

This chapter discusses topics like common programming practices and idioms. Examples are variable naming guidelines, performance considerations, and incremental compilation of Java programs. Furthermore, some common *pitfalls* are addressed (things to be aware of). Most of the topics in this chapter are based on my experiences while translating existing C++ code to Java. Therefore, Chapter 1 may read to some people as a "Java for C++ programmers" section. It was not planned to be written as such. Namely, I was targeting any Java developer that wanted to read about more "advanced" topics. However, this chapter may be of particular interest for C++ developers as well.

Chapter 2. LTK—The Little Toolkit

This chapter discusses the design and implementation of LTK, a GUI toolkit which so far has seen four host OO languages: Procol, Oberon, C++, and now Java. To contrast the design of LTK, some time is devoted to a short discussion on the design of AWT. Then each of the classes in LTK is described, and a list of examples is discussed. This chapter may be of interest to anyone who wants to learn more about how to write a GUI toolkit. Obviously, the market for GUI toolkits is small. But, most lessons can be applied to a more general class of Java programs and libraries. The source code is enclosed.

Chapter 3. Visual Debugging of Java Programs

This chapter discusses different techniques for debugging Java programs, such as using plain-old print statements, using the Java debugger API (as *jdb* does), using instrumentation of Java code, and enhancing the Java Virtual Machine. Once information about the executing Java program is obtained, a visualization is created of the objects that execute inside it. This chapter describes an implementation of one such visual debugger, developed especially for this book. The source code is enclosed on the diskette.

Chapter 4. C2J—A C++ to Java translator

This chapter could be particularly interesting for C++ developers. Differences between C++ and Java are highlighted, such as stack declarations, the "delete" statement, multiple inheritance, (the lack of) overloaded operators, callback functions, and pointers vs. references. A description of C2J, a C++ to Java translator is given (source code is provided on diskette). Furthermore, a list of possible enhancements is discussed.

Acknowledgments

The question I have been asked most often the last half year has undoubtedly been, "Hi Chris, how is your book doing?" This genuine interest in my writing, expressed by friends, relatives, and colleagues alike, has been very instrumental for me to continue finding the time and energy to write this book, next to my already busy job at Morgan Stanley. I guess every writer goes through extreme mood-swings. One end of the spectrum is feeling guilty about doing fun things such as going out with friends, doing anything remotely social, watching TV, or simply not working on "the book". The other end of the spectrum is feeling the anticipation of holding the finished book in your hands, being proud of ones accomplishments, and dreaming of becoming a best-seller. Only the never-ending support and interest from my friends ensured that I could keep my sanity.

"Wise men are not wise at all times", Emerson wrote as early as in 1860. This translates into "an author always needs help to repair his/her mistakes". That has also been the case for my book. Various persons have provided feedback and guidance to its contents. Invaluable suggestions were provided in particular by Arthur van Hoff, Roger Hoover, Kenny Zadeck, Cliff Berg, Gary Entsminger, Jeff Birnbaum and Vadim Strizhevsky. Together, they pointed out inconsistencies, shortcomings, and blunt errors in this book and the enclosed software. I have carefully tried to include all of their remarks, but some of their suggestions could not make it to this version of the book, and of course, I take full responsibility for the final content. A lot of the technical topics in this book have been brought to the surface in discussions with colleagues at Morgan Stanley, including Vadim Strizhevsky, Jeff Birnbaum, Kevin Luo, Ben Fried, and Andy Lowry.

LTK has seen a number of different host languages, and the initial version has benefited a lot from input from Peter van Oosterom, Anco Smit, Frans Heeman, and Vincent Schenkelaars. Jan van den Bos, my advisor during my PhD study, regretfully never lived to see how far at least one part of the Procol language has come, although he of course had more grandiose plans for the actual language.

Putting words to paper, or better said, typing words into a computer, is only a small part of the process of developing a book. First of all, thanks go to Paul Becker from Prentice Hall, for, in his own words, setting a personal record of signing a book contract within one day of receiving the proposal. His enthusiasm and support makes him the perfect editor. Thanks also go to Bertrand Meyer for initially getting me in contact with Paul, three years ago. The production team at Prentice Hall has been extremely competent and efficient. In particular, compliments are in place for Mary Sudul.

Finally, special thanks go to Carla, my wife, for enduring my compulsive habit of having to visit every bookstore we ever came close to the last half year, and count the number of Java books already on the shelves. In the winter of 1995, after I came up with the idea for the book, she completely supported me to start working on this project. This, despite the numerous promises I made myself earlier never to start another book, after the long delays on the first book I was involved with. In bad times, coming back from a busy office day, she even made sure I spent my required quota on the book, while she ran the household. Carla, this one is for you.

Chris Laffra,
White Plains, New York

CHAPTER 1

- Idioms
- Pitfalls
- Programming Tips
- Lessons Learned

Idioms, Pitfalls, and Programming Tips

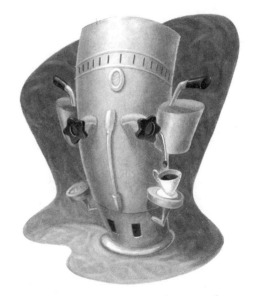

This chapter discusses topics such as common programming practices and idioms. Examples use variable naming guidelines, performance tips, and incremental Java compilation. Furthermore, some common pitfalls are addressed. This chapter should be interesting for people with a C++ background, but also to advanced Java programmers with a different background. Each section describes an idiom or topic which is in principle unrelated to the others. The sections get increasingly "advanced" towards the end of this chapter.

1. Boolean Expressions

The following type of expression, abusing the infamous invisible = operator, has lead to numerous bugs in C++ programs. I have been caught by it enough times myself.

```
if (n = 0) { ... } else { ... }
```

The else branch is never, ever executed, because the expression always evaluates to 0, indicating false (in C and C++). Of course, the intention was to use (n == 0), but something magical happens to programmers that make this small typo, compile their program, and keep running it with a different behavior than expected. I more than once had to call a colleague over to point out the mistake, and embarrass me for the rest of the week. In Java, this mistake will never occur, as there is no automatic conversion from int to `boolean`. Therefore, the assignment expression will not be recognized as a boolean expression, and the compiler will not compile our code successfully. There is one special case that may go undetected, when the operands are already of type boolean

```
if (stop = true) { ... }
```

which will always execute the if-branch. Really defensive programmers use the following style

```
if (true == stop) { ... }
```

A typo in this case results in the compiler error: invalid left-hand side of assignment. For some reason, I think it reads funny, though. But, I guess that is a matter of taste.

1.1 Composite Boolean Expressions

An if-statement that contains a compound boolean expression, using & or && operators could lead to another nasty "gotcha." The following example has a typo, and will always result in a NullPointerException, when `vector` is equal to `null`, although we explicitly test for it

```
if (vector!=null & vector.length()>0) { ... }
```

This is correct Java, following the current language definition. The behavior is also to be expected, as the semantics of the & operator is to not short-circuit. If the && operator would be used, and `vector` would be null indeed, the second part of the condition is never checked, similar to C and C++ rules. No null pointer exception is generated then. Adding the & operator for boolean operands to Java was a mistake, in my opinion, as its use is bizarre and confusing. It certainly may create subtle bugs in Java programs, especially when the compiler does not generate a warning.

1.2 Compiler Optimization of Constant Expressions

The Java compiler will optimize test conditions that involve constant boolean expressions. Therefore, the following method declaration will not generate code for the else-branch

```
public void foo() {
    if (true) {
        System.out.println("true");
    } else {
        System.out.println("false");
    }
}
```

The generated byte-codes are

```
Method void foo()
0 getstatic #7
        <Field java.lang.System.out Ljava/io/PrintStream;>
3 ldc #1 <String "true">
5 invokevirtual #8 <Method
        java.io.PrintStream.println(Ljava/lang/String;)V>
8 return
```

This knowledge can be used to implement conditional debugging/testing statements. A final static boolean variable could be used as a test variable, as the following example

```java
final static boolean debug = true;

public void foo() {
    if (debug) System.out.println("someone entered foo!");
    bar();
}
```

The if-statement will be optimized away when the variable is set to false and will have no overhead when it is set to true. Therefore, it is equivalent to using the following, less readable, solution with macros in C++

```cpp
#define debug 1

public void foo() {
#if debug
    cout << "someone entered foo!" << endl;
#endif
    bar();
}
```

2. System Properties

System properties are system-specific properties that can be read using a call to `System.getProperty(String)`. The Sun Security FAQ mentions the system available properties at

> `http://www.javasoft.com/java.sun.com/sfaq/index.html`

The following system properties can be read by Java applets and applications:

key	meaning
java.version	Java version number
java.vendor	Java vendor-specific string
java.vendor.url	Java vendor URL
java.class.version	Java class version number
os.name	Operating system name
os.arch	Operating system architecture
file.separator	File separator (e.g., "/")
path.separator	Path separator (e.g., ":")
line.separator	Line separator (e.g., "\r\n")

Java applications can also read the following properties, while applets cannot, due to security reasons:

key	meaning
java.home	Java installation directory
java.class.path	Java CLASSPATH variable setting
user.home	User home directory
user.name	User account name
user.dir	User's current working directory

There has been considerable debate on allowing *applets* access to the local file system, limited to a certain area on the user's local file system. Applets would be allowed to save temporary files and cache images or setups for future executions. That could make applets much more efficient and intelligent. Of course, it is hard to enforce applets to stay in one single segment of the file system (although http servers have no problems limiting access to a certain area). Malicious applets will undoubtedly try and fill up (the special section of) the file system, or interfere with other information left in this publicly accessible section of the user's local file system.

3. Array Initializer Lists

Unbeknownst to many Java programmers, the syntax for array declarations is a lot richer than it looks at first sight. Most Java programmers are already accustomed to using the following syntax

```
String array = new String[2];
array[0] = "Hello";
array[1] = "World";
```

and most know that these statements are equal to the more compact

```
String array = { "Hello", "World" };
```

which also creates an array of two strings and initializes both elements. However, the syntax for the individual elements includes any expression rendering an object of the appropriate type. Therefore, the following code

```
String array[] = {
    "abc"+"def", null, new String("123"), getString()
};
```

is valid Java, and it creates an array of four strings and initializes each element.

3.1 Declaring an Array of Objects

Java is based on C++, takes away some of its complexity, and adds some features. For programmers that are used to C++, there is one thing to be aware of when declaring arrays. The following declaration in C++ creates an array of four objects and properly initializes them

```
MyObject array[4];                // C++ array of 4 objects
```

In Java, arrays are objects, and they need to be explicitly created.

```
MyObject array[] = new MyObject[4]; // Java array of 4 refs
```

However, that is not yet enough to get an equivalent result. The elements need to be created also. Therefore, the equivalent to creating 4 objects on the stack is the following

```
MyObject array[] = new MyObject[4]; // Java array of 4 refs
array[0] = new MyObject();
array[1] = new MyObject();
array[2] = new MyObject();
array[3] = new MyObject();
```

Typically, this incompatibility is difficult to understand for C++ programmers, but you can get used to it.

4. Packages

Packages group together related classes. They provide a useful mechanism for controlling the global name space. Classes can be implemented that have the same name, yet are accessible from different packages. Classes are added to a package by inserting a special statement at the beginning of the source file. Here are two examples:

file myWholePackage/subPackage1/test.java

```
package myWholePackage.subPackage1;
public class test { ... }
```

file myWholePackage/subPackage2/test.java

```
package myWholePackage.subPackage2;
public class test { ... }
```

There is a direct relationship to the place where the `javac` compiler expects the two Java files to exist in the files system. There is a similar relationship while loading classes. When classes are loaded directly from a file (and not from a zipped archive), the class file has to have a relative path corresponding to its package structure. In this example, the two `test.class` files need to be installed in two directories myWholePackage/subPackage1 and `myWholePackage/subPackage2`, both accessible from one of the directories mentioned in the CLASSPATH environment variable.

When a class wants to use a class from another package, it needs to be explicitly imported in the Java source file, or properly scoped. The following Java code gives an example

```
import java.lang.String;                // line 1
import java.awt.*;                      // line 2
class test {
    java.util.Vector vector;            // line 4
}
```

The import statement at line 1 explicitly names the String class. Technically speaking, all classes in the package `java.lang` are included implicitly by the Java compiler, so this statement is superfluous. However, it demonstrates a good programming technique. It explicitly names the classes that are used in this class, allowing users to quickly determine the external dependencies of this class. That is also why the statement at line 2 shows a bad style. Other than explicitly naming the classes from `java.awt` that are used by this class, a wild card is used. It simply says, "I am using some classes from this package, you figure out which ones yourself." Finally, the statement at line 4 explicitly names the class by using its fully scoped name. This style is particularly bad, as it hides the use of external classes deep into the client's implementation. Concluding, the best style is to explicitly name each class in one single import statement.

4.1 Loading Classes over the Internet

Every time a class is used from a package the has to be loaded over the network, a separate connection is set up, the class is downloaded, and the connection is closed again. For any realistic system, this may result in dozens, if not hundreds, of separate connections being set up. This is not acceptable. A different technique is to download the whole package in one single sweep, unpack the package locally, and extract the classes from it. In that case, only one connection needs to be set up, and that dramatically improves the load time of an applet. For the first releases of Java, there did not exist a standard way for archiving classes. Experimental *ziploaders* have been developed, and Netscape already uses a zipped file for all standard Java classes to be loaded from the file system directly. Collecting classes into one archive will also make adding digital signatures a lot easier, as it may be impractical to authenticate every single class.

5. Java Coding Standards

This section describes one particular Java coding style, and gives suggestions and tips for how to program in Java.

5.1 Packages

First of all, put all classes that can be grouped together into their own package. Use sub-packages for smaller components of a big project.

5.2 Versions

Use a version management system to manage changes made to your source code. This is particularly important where multiple people access the same code.

In lack of a general, agreed-upon, and standardized class versioning mechanism, you may perhaps include a version number in the *name* of your package.

5.3 One Class per File

Put every class in a separate file, even when the class is not public. This will make it much easier to locate the class and to manage a system.

5.4 Indentation

Use a consistent indentation style throughout your program. Choose a style and adhere to it. Often, styles are culture- and organization-dependent. Most of the Java libraries place the starting brace of a block on the same line as the owning statement, and uses 4-character indentation.

```
switch (n) {              if (true) {           void foo(int x) {
    case 0: break;            always();             function1();
    default:              }                         function2();
}                                               }
```

Alternative indentations place the left curly brace on the next line, and use 2-character indentation.

```
switch (n)                if (true)             void foo(int x)
{                         {                     {
    case 0: break;            always();             function1();
    default:              }                         function2();
      }                                         }
```

Notice the braces are always aligned in this indentation style. Choose any of these styles and be consistent in your indentation, and people will find it much easier to read your Java code.

5.5 Documentation

Use `javadoc` style comments for each class and method in your Java system. An example

```
/**
 * class Rectangle
 *
 * This is a <b>very</b> useful class!
 *
 * Copyright 1995/1996, I-me-and-myself, All rights reserved
 *
 * @version 0.1
 * @author me.
 * @see someString
 * @see http://www.some.domain
 * @see classname#methodname
 */
public class Rectangle {

    /**
     * overlapsWith checks whether two rectangles overlap
     * @param rect the other rectangle
     * @return whether this rectangle overlaps with another
     */
    public boolean overlapsWith(Rectangle rect) { ... }
}
```

5.6 Importing Packages

Never use the import-on-demand syntax for importing classes. Always specifically mention the class that is used from a package. Example:

bad style	good style
`import java.awt.*`	`import java.awt.Component`
	`import java.awt.Rectangle`

5.7 Naming

Use sensible names for variables and class names. Use long names where appropriate. Prefer names like `printField` to `prtFld`. Choose names that reduce the need for comments (write self-documenting code). Use a consistent naming strategy for variables, fields, methods, classes, packages, and constants:

type of element	naming strategy
package	all lowercase letters and numbers
class	start with uppercase, rest mixed, no underscores
method	start with lowercase, rest mixed, no underscores
fields	only lowercase letters, avoid underscores
local variables	only lowercase letters, avoid underscores
function parameters	only lowercase letters, avoid underscores
constants	only uppercase letters and underscores

For accessor methods (methods that set or get a variable), use the prefix *set* or *get*. Example:

```
public final void setSize(int size) { this.size = size; }
public final int getSize() { return size; }
private int size;
```

5.8 Class Ordering

Collect all public, private, and protected methods and fields, and place them logically in your class definition. This will make it easier for others to maintain your code. Use the following order

1. constructors
2. public methods and fields
3. unspecified methods and fields (public to classes in same package)
4. protected methods and fields
5. private methods and fields

5.9 Variables

Declare variables as close as possible to where they are used. Do not declare the variables at the top of a method. Declare index variables that are only used in a for-loop, inside the for-loop: for (int n=0; n<100; n++). Do not add a variable to the class definition, when a local variable would suffice. Use logical names for the variables, even when the use may be "obvious."

5.10 Encapsulation

Avoid exposing implementation details of a class. Define a public interface and hide the implementation. This will allow future versions of the class to change the implementation without bothering any clients of the class. Make instance variables nonpublic. Declare public methods to get and set their value. Enforce the "Demeter Principle": Do not return a reference to a locally maintained object. Instead, increase the interface of the encapsulating class to hide the local implementation.

5.11 *Synchronization*

Only use synchronization when a class needs to be made thread-safe. Obtaining a monitor is relatively expensive.

5.12 *Testing*

Write test code for all classes that you write. Add a `main` method to your class definition that tests the class. In that way, the class can be tested in isolation, from the command-line. This main method can also function as a "how-to-use" section. When developing a class library, also develop test programs that live outside of the package (to test access qualifiers).

6. Some Inconsistencies in the Standard Java Libraries

Some of the most important properties of good class libraries are an intuitive overall design, availability of the right kind of abstractions, not too complex, not too simple, and consistency in the application programmer's interface (API). It is there that the Java libraries expose a certain degree of immaturity. It shows that the designers did not have the time to carefully check the large number of classes supported in the current Java distribution. In most cases, the result is a surprised programmer. However, the surprise can easily turn into frustration, when time is wasted with extra recompilations, simply because parameters are inadvertently reversed. For example, the Vector class has a method

```
setElementAt(Object obj, int index);
```

whereas StringBuffer has

```
setCharAt(int index, char c);
```

Of course, Java's behavior here is much better than that of C++. Because there is no automatic conversion between the types int and char, the following incorrect use would be caught by the (strongly type-checked) compiler

```
myBuffer.setCharAt('a', 36);
```

In C++, this would be silently accepted (setting element 33 to character 'd').

There are more examples. Namely, there are quite a number of classes in the Java libraries that somehow have a "size." They contain a given number of other elements, and these elements can be counted. Each of the classes has an interface to this number of elements; however, there is no consistency. The complete list of public classes in Java JDK 1.0 that export an interface to inquire the "size" of its instances are:

java.net class	how to get its "size"
java.net.DatagramPacket	int getLength()

java.io class	how to get its "size"
java.io.File	long length()

java.awt class	how to get its "size"
java.awt.Choice	int countItems()
java.awt.Container	int countComponents()
java.awt.List	int countItems()
java.awt.Menu	int countItems()
java.awt.MenuBar	int countMenus()
java.awt.Polygon	int npoints

java.util class	how to get its "size"
java.util.BitSet	int size()
java.util.HashTable	int size()
java.util.Dictionary	int size()
java.util.Vector	int size()

java.lang class	how to get its "size"
java.lang.String	int length()
java.lang.StringBuffer	int length()
java.lang.ThreadGroup	int activeCount()
java.lang.Thread	int activeCount()
arrays	int length

Of course, there is a clear difference in functionality for some of these classes, hence the different sort of interface. However, the most obvious cases are the three most often used classes, java.lang.String, java.util.Vector, and arrays. Especially the use of those three may lead to confusion. Personally, I frequently made a mistake with those three, where I try to obtain the length() of a vector, or get the size() of a string. A string is really a specialization of the more abstract vector (or array). Therefore, one would have expected their interfaces to be more similar.

6.1 Months and Weeks

When someone is born on January 4, 1964, the corresponding U.S. style short-write is 1964/01/04. When creating a java.util.Date object to represent this date, the appropriate constructor is: new Date(1964, 0, 04).The value 0 for the month parameter is not an error, because months are counted starting at zero. This confuses a lot of people (even fellow Java book writers). To convert a string representation of a date into a Date object, a special parse routine is provided. It parses "1994/01/04" into the date Fri Feb 04 00:00:00 1994. It will not parse "1964/01/04", complaining that the year is out of range. The reason is that the date class is intended to reflect CUT, Coordinated Universal Time, which is based on an "epoch" of Greenwich Mean Time (GMT), of January 1, 1970. No date prior to that date can be specified. This limitation has generated numerous threads on the on-line Java newsgroups to fix the "broken" Date class.

7. Communicating Applets

Although this book concentrates mainly on the Java language and does not discuss Applet programming in any much detail, I thought the following topic is of enough general interest to devote some time on it.

In order to compose applets together on one HTML page, a mechanism needs to be devised for these different applets to communicate together directly. There are two main ways of communication, where one is less reliable than the other.

7.1 Communicating Through the Applet Context

The first (and suggested) way is to use the applet context. The applet context lets an applet control the applet's environment that is usually the browser or the applet viewer. The applet class implements the following method

```
public AppletContext getAppletContext();
```

Once we have a handle on the applet's executing context, we can inquire on all the applets currently contained in the context. The applet context class implements the following method to enumerate the applets in a context. The documentation specifies that only applets that are accessible will be returned. It is unclear what that means. The returned list always includes the applet itself.

```
Enumeration getApplets();
```

One of the applets could be selected, and methods on the applet can be called. Only methods that are implemented in the Applet class can be called, because all others will fail due to the mechanism by which classes are loaded and then checked for security.

7.2 Communicating Through Static Variables

Another technique exposes an underlying implementation detail of some browsers. When classes are loaded into a VM, all the class variables are initialized. When a second applet wants to load the same class, and the VM determines that the class is already loaded, or is still cached in memory, it will *not* reload the class and also not initialize the class variables. This causes applets that have nothing to do with one another to share the same static variables. This may either break an otherwise perfectly fine running applet when another applet is loaded on the same page. Furthermore, the feature is not documented and is rumored to be a bug in the class caching mechanism. People are not supposed to take advantage of the feature, as in future versions of the VM, this behavior will undoubtedly be repaired. It is also an indication that loading multiple applets on one single browser page is still not in common practice enough to have highlighted the problem at an earlier stage.

The following applet shares memory with another applet running inside the same appletviewer session

```
import java.applet.Applet;
public class test extends Applet {
    static int sharedVariable = 0;
    int privateVariable = 1;
    public void start() {
        while (true) {
            if (privateVariable != sharedVariable) {
                sharedVariable += 2;
                privateVariable++;
                System.out.print(this.hashCode() + " ");
                System.out.println(privateVariable);
            }
            try { Thread.sleep(200); } catch (Exception e) { };
        }
    }
}
```

The printed output from two of these applets loaded in one single HTML file is
as follows

```
17063624  2
17065032  2
17063624  3
17065032  3
17063624  4
17065032  4
17063624  5
17065032  5
17063624  6
17065032  6
17063624  7
17065032  7
. . .
```

Smart (and malicious) applets that abuse this technique in another form could
create "covert channels," to communicate information from one server to
another, using the end user's browser as a gateway. This may make it hard to
trace information flow, when several malicious applets work together to move
information around.

8. Exception Handling in Java

Exceptions form a powerful programming paradigm by allowing the freedom to separate program logic from error handling logic. Exceptions are more flexible than using special return values of a method. Furthermore, there is no way to indicate a certain failure in the case that the method is declared type void. Additionally, how do we indicate an error in the execution of a constructor? Because of the perceived importance of exceptions in Java, they form an integral part of the language. Exceptions are actually "first class citizens," and are represented by object instances of a special type, accessible by whoever catches the exception. Users can extend the exception handling type system by declaring their own new exception classes.

However, the language support does not stop there. When a method potentially throws an exception, the method needs to be declared to indicate this behavior. If a user accesses a method that throws an exception, it cannot simply be ignored, and the user is forced to deal with the possible exceptions that it may run into. The method call involved needs to be enclosed within an appropriate try-catch clause, or the method in which the call is made must be declared to also throw the exception. The error generated by the compiler explains that rather well.

```
SliderDemo.java:47: Warning: Exception ltk.EEE must be caught,
or it must be declared in the throws clause of this method.
slider1.setValue(value);
                ^
```

An example of catching an exception would be to enclose it in a try-catch clause

```
try { slider1.setValue(value); } catch (Exception e) { }
```

Notice that the catch body does not do anything at all. This is the typical usage of exception handling in most of the applets I have seen so far. Typically, Java programmers experience exception handling to be a nuisance, rather than a powerful programming mechanism. A better approach is given in the AWT toolkit where a certain exception is caught and dealt with more sensibly.

```
public static synchronized Toolkit getDefaultToolkit() {
    if (toolkit == null) {
        String nm = System.getProperty("awt.toolkit",
                                    "sun.awt.motif.MToolkt");
        try {
            toolkit = (Toolkit)Class.forName(nm).newInstance();
        } catch (ClassNotFoundException e) {
            throw new AWTError("Toolkit not found: " + nm);
        } catch (InstantiationException e) {
```

```
          throw new AWTError("Could not instantiate Toolkit: " +
                                                             nm);
      } catch (IllegalAccessException e) {
          throw new AWTError("Could not access Toolkit: " + nm);
      }
  }
  return toolkit;
}
```

Notice the different kinds of exceptions that are caught. In fact the multiple catch clauses act as a switch statement on the type of the exception. All different types of exceptions that `classForName` and `createInstance` may throw are caught in one try clause. A really defensive programmer could add another catch clause for exceptions not in any of the three categories, by using

```
catch (Exception e) {
    throw new AWTError("Unknown Exception");
}
```

This would catch the case where someone would inadvertently change the underlying implementation of the classes that we use to throw more exceptions than before. If we do not recompile our client class, it will never become aware of this change. Although the compiler thoroughly checks your code to see if it catches all exceptions that may be thrown, the class loader and byte code verifier do no such checking. Other class incompatibility problems *will* surface (like removed methods), but uncaught exceptions just trickle up until they reach the unsuspecting user.

8.1 System Exceptions and User-Defined Exceptions

There are two main types of exceptions in Java:

- Those that indicate unforeseen runtime or system exceptions or errors. These exceptions are a subclass of `RuntimeException` or `Error`. They indicate the fact that although the user called a method with parameters in the correct range of values, something really bad happened inside the method. An example could be that the system ran out of memory, or the `AWTError` thrown in the previous example, or that an I/O error occurred (e.g., file system full or socket problems). Because exceptions of this kind can in principle be thrown by any called code, it makes no sense in practice to enclose every statement in a try-catch clause. Therefore, these types of exceptions need not be explicitly caught by users. Exceptions of type `RuntimeException` are exceptions that can reasonably occur, whereas exceptions of type `Error` are errors signaling events that should not occur, and that are intended to really bring down the system. Do not catch events of type `Error`, unless you are really sure what you are doing. The system is not assumed to be able to continue execution after this point.

- User-defined exceptions. Declared as a subclass of `Exception`, these classes *have* to be caught by any code using the methods that may throw them. They are used by classes to communicate certain problems that cannot easily be passed through return values.

Be aware that every time a method declares a "throws" clause, the user of the method has to explicitly catch the exception. When too many methods throw exceptions, life as a programmer becomes impossible, as almost everything needs to be enclosed in try-catch clauses. Exceptions should be used in moderation and reserved for the hard cases. Otherwise, you are bound to have some unhappy customers. A naive suggestion would be to declare all user-defined exceptions as a subclass of `RuntimeException`, so that they are ignored by the compiler, and the user does not need to "worry" about them, if he/she would decide to. That suggestion defeats the whole purpose and importance of exception handling supported to such a high degree as done by the Java language designers.

8.2 Throwing Exceptions from Native Code

To throw an exception from user-written native code, the following C function can be used

```
SignalError(0, "package/subpackage/ExceptionName", "description");
```

This is equivalent to the Java code

```
throw package.subpackage.ExceptionName("description");
```

An often generated exception is the following

```
SignalError(0, JAVAPKG "NullPointerException", 0);
```

One major difference between exceptions thrown in C and Java, is that in the C version, control continues after the call to the SignalError function, and the native method does not automatically return. Only when the native method returns, the exception is thrown in the enclosing Java stub. It is undefined what happens when the native code decides to throw more than one exception. In Java, control is not continued after an exception is thrown. Instead, the function returns directly. Therefore, in the native method, a return statement should immediately follow the call to SignalError.

8.3 Exception, Blocks, and Local Variables

Because the `try` and `catch` statements use blocks for containing the statements to be executed, special rules apply for variable scoping. The following example will not compile, because the second reference to n refers to a variable whose scope is declared only within the try block

```
try {
    int n = 10;
} catch (Exception e) {
    n++; // Undefined variable
}
```

Moving the declaration up in scope for the variable will solve the problem, yet resulting in another caveat

```
int n;
try {
    n = 10;
} catch (Exception e) {
    n++; // Variable n may not have been initialized
}
```

The compiler is not able to do complete control flow analysis of the `try` block, so it fears that the n variable may never have been initialized (it's not inside a `try` block for nothing, right?). Although the compiler could be a little smarter, we can do something simple to help it somewhat. Namely, in Java, local variables are not initialized (contrary to instance variables). Therefore, we can get rid of this message by just initializing the variable ourselves

```
int n = 0;
try {
    n = 10;
} catch (Exception e) {
    n++;
}
```

9. Implementing Multiple inheritance

In languages like C++, multiple inheritance enables a software designer to define a new relationship between two logically independent components of a system. The derived class is an extension of both inherited classes, and instances of the derived class can be used wherever objects of one of the inherited types are actually expected.

For example, a MoveableButton may inherit both from Moveable and Button, Now, anywhere where a Button is actually expected, it is perfectly safe to pass a MoveableButton instead. The same is true for those occasions where a Moveable is expected (like the data structure that contains moveable objects in an animated scene). In the case of multiple inheritance, all the instance variables, and all method bodies for both classes are inherited. Multiple inheritance renders a flexible mechanism for mixing behavior into new forms.

Java does not have multiple inheritance for a number of reasons. Problems with multiple inheritance are caused when name collisions occur. When the same variable or method is provided somewhere in the public interface of any of the inherited classes, a decision has to be made which one to take. The definition of the semantics, or facilities to support this would complicate the language unnecessarily, it was deemed.

Another problem with multiple inheritance is that instances of the derived class will have to have one virtual method table for each of the roles it can play as one of the inherited classes. This problem is a runtime system complication, and introduces a higher demand of memory usage and overhead for dynamic method dispatching.

Therefore, having made the choice to use single inheritance in Java, how do we mix behavior from two or more sources? The answer is Interfaces. An interface is a list of static variables and method signatures. Classes that implement a given signature, basically promise to implement each of these methods. The compiler checks to see if these methods are really implemented in the class definition (inherited methods are acceptable also). Interfaces allow the Java developer to inherit a specification, yet no implemented behavior is inherited. Every class that implements an interface, needs to provide its own implementation. An interface works as a type in the language. For instance, an interface could be used as the type of formal parameter in a given method. Then, only those classes that actu-ally are declared to implement that interface can be passed as valid parameters. Simply implementing the required methods is not sufficient. Concluding, as a typing and modeling mechanism the combination of single inheritance with interfaces is equivalent to multiple inheritance.

Interfaces are only a specification of a list of methods. and the actual implementation is not inherited (as is the case in multiple inheritance). Therefore, classes that do implement similar behavior and, consequently, have to use interfaces are faced with a dilemma also of how to actually also share implementation of the methods mentioned in the interface. In small or naive applications, the good old cut-and-paste approach is a favorite one, leading to maintenance nightmares in larger systems. From personal, practical experience, I know how hard it is to maintain copies of code implementing one interface and replicated in three different classes.

For large-scale Java development, a different strategy has to be employed. In order to achieve the intended mixin behavior, each interface should be accompanied by a corresponding class that actually implements the required methods. An example of the basic principle is given here

```
interface Moveable {                    // the specification
    void move(int x, int y);
    int getX();
    int getY();
};
class MoveableImplementation {          // the implementation
    private int x, y;
    void move(int x, int y) { this.x = x; this.y = y; }
    int getX() { return x; }
    int getY() { return y; }
}
class Box extends Graphical implements Moveable { // a user
    MoveableImplementation moveable = new
MoveableImplementation();
    void move(int x, int y) { moveable.move(x,y); }
    int getX() { return moveable.getX(); }
    int getX() { return moveable.getX(); }
}
class Circle extends Graphical implements Moveable { // a user
    MoveableImplementation moveable = new
MoveableImplementation();
    void move(int x, int y) { moveable.move(x,y); }
    int getX() { return moveable.getX(); }
    int getX() { return moveable.getX(); }
}
```

The essence is that we centralize the *implementation* of the moveable interface. This allows us to change the implementation at a later stage, at one single location, without needing to visit every single class that uses this interface declaration to check and make sure if we want to change *its* implementation, also. In the case that an interface has a generic implementation and usage, as in this example, it is advisable to document this in the declaration of the interface (i.e., add a special "typical usage" section).

The disadvantage of this "mixin" implementation is that it is also messy, error-prone, and hard to maintain, especially when, for example, the interface is expanded to include an extra method. Still, having the real implementation code at one single place is a great advantage.

10. Basic Types in Java

The syntax of Java is based on C++, and basic types such as `int`, `float`, and `char` are also used in Java as basic types for representing variables. Unlike languages like Eiffel and Smalltalk, these basic types are not represented by a class, and there are no real instances of type `int`, for instance. Instead, the treatment of these basic types is special, and the compiler and runtime system (i.e., the virtual machine), are aware of these special types. Variables of type `int` cannot be passed to a method expecting a real object, such as when creating a hash table, where the key and contents are both subclasses of java.lang.Object. In order to allow users to create hash tables with a key based on an integer value, classes like java.lang.Integer have been invented. The rationale is also explained in the on-line documentation for the Integer class:

The Integer class is a wrapper for integer values. In Java, integers are not objects and most of the Java utility classes require the use of objects. Thus, if you needed to store an integer in a hashtable, you would have to "wrap" an Integer instance around it.

To enable this, the Integer class has a constructor accepting an int value, which can be used as follows

```
Integer myInteger = new Integer(32);
```

However, the Integer class does not have any parameter methods for changing its value. Subclassing the Integer class and adding a `setValue(int)` method does not work either, because the class is declared final. Apparently, this behavior is intentional, and the class is made immutable with a reason. It makes its behavior and semantics to be as close as possible to the behavior of the corresponding basic type. When objects of type Integer are passed to a method, their value cannot be changed by the recipient, just as is the case for int objects. In the receiving method the value cannot be changed, because there is no appropriate method declared to do this. This breaks the similarity with the underlying basic type, of course.

Basically, the Integer, Boolean, and Character class are an admittance of the fact that the Java language has no *pass by value* semantics for objects. By definition, all objects are passed by reference. Methods that receive an object instance can change its state, assuming appropriate methods are defined. In contrast, variables of basic types, like int, are passed by value. Not being able to pass or return an object by value is a simplification in the Java language, limiting a programmer's creative freedom. Datastructures like hash tables rely on the behavior of its key element to be immutable. If the user would be able to change the underlying state of the key object, the hash table's ordering would become invalid, and its behavior undefined. An example of the intended use of class Integer is given in the documentation for the java.util.Hashtable class.

This example creates a hashtable of numbers. It uses the names of the numbers as keys

```
Hashtable numbers = new Hashtable();
numbers.put("one", new Integer(1));
numbers.put("two", new Integer(2));
numbers.put("three", new Integer(3));
```

To retrieve a number use

```
Integer n = (Integer)numbers.get("two");
if (n != null) {
        System.out.println("two = " + n);
}
```

Another reason for making the Integer class final is to allow compilers to inline all its methods, and make the use of the class more efficient. However, nowhere in the Java distribution is there ever an instance of these special "wrapper" classes created. Because of their immutable behavior, I personally find them really useless (neither would I have made the String class immutable). Who wants to put something in a hash table that cannot be manipulated or extended? Inserting objects of type Integer into a hash table makes no sense. Typically, the nature of object-oriented design is that the elements in a hash table are not as simple as an integer. Instead, objects with a more complex behavior are inserted into a hash table, and after retrieving them with a certain key, they are manipulated as a regular object.

Together with the argument made in Section 11.4, this leads me to the following suggestion: Let's get rid of the wrapper classes. Of course, this would break too much existing code, and this suggestion will never be followed up. Therefore, at best, I can give you the advice to never use them other than for the useful utility functions they provide.

11. Instanceof, equals and ==

11.1 *Instanceof*

The *instanceof* operator is a binary operator that checks whether the first operand (an object reference) is an instance of the second operand (a type identifier), or one of its superclasses. There are some things to be aware of when using the `instanceof` operator. First of all, the object reference `null` is not an instance of any class. Therefore, checking any null reference for being an instance of any type will always render false, even when compared with the universal type `Object`

```
(null instanceof Object)                    → false
```

Some other cases will also result false, regardless of the runtime values. The compiler does no type analysis on the `instanceof` operator. Therefore, although the test in the following example will always fail, it is something the compiler does not check or detect

```
Integer object;
...
if (object instanceof String) ...
```

This test can never succeed, as the object can never be assigned a reference to a String. Basically, if the compile-time type of the object is not a *superclass* of the tested type, the compiler should issue a warning that the expression will always yield false.

Operator precedence places the `instanceof` operator below the ! operator. Therefore, the following expression will not compile (with a rather confusing error message for some people)

```
if (!object instanceof Object) ...
```

Furthermore, there is a limitation for the type expression. Although the compiler apparently does no type checking during compilation and defers all checks to runtime, the type name can only be a real type name, visible during compilation. The type specification cannot be made more dynamic, for instance, by using a string, or a reference to a class. Therefore, the following statements are not valid in Java

```
if (object instanceof "java.awt.Frame") ...
if (object instanceof Class.forName("java.awt.Frame")) ...
```

11.2 *Equality*

In the English literature classic *Animal Farm* all pigs are equal, yet some are more equal than others. In Java, something similar is the case. In order to be able to compare two arbitrary objects, and determine if they are equal (have the same value), class `Object` implements the method `equals()`. The documentation for this method is as follows

---

Compares two Objects for equality. Returns a boolean that indicates whether this Object is equivalent to the specified Object. This method is used when an Object is stored in a hash table.

From a language purist standpoint, the last sentence is rather disturbing. In a multi-purpose language, it is hard to find the validation for placing a method at the top of the inheritance tree, simply because it makes it easier to insert objects in something so specific as a hash table. Namely, this assumes that at the time the language was designed, the designers had complete insight into what kind of data structures would be appropriate for usage in Java. A hash table was deemed important enough to give it the esteemed status of being supported directly in the language. One must realize that because all objects derive from the class `Object`, each method that is declared in this class automatically becomes part of the vocabulary, thereby extending the expressiveness of the language. The following methods are currently implemented in class `Object`:

```
1.   public final native Class getClass()
2.   public native int hashCode()
3.   public boolean equals(Object obj)
4.   protected native void copy(Object src)
5.   protected native Object clone()
6.   public native String toString()
7.   public final native void notify()
8.   public final native void notifyAll()
9.   public final native void wait(long timeout)
10.  public final void wait(long timeout, int nanos)
11.  public final void wait()
```

Method 1 returns the (hardly useful) class representation for this object. Methods 2 and 3 are meant to support the hash table class. Methods 4 and 5 allow for copying and cloning objects (for those occasions where a C++ copy constructor would be used). Method 6 is only used in debugging. Finally, methods 7 through 11 are for multiple thread support.

In order to put objects into a hash table, we need to be able to compute a hash value for the object, and need to be able to compare two given objects for equality. Because hash tables are considered a critical part of the Java runtime system and libraries, the language designers thought it makes sense to support them as well as possible. Adding a hash code and equality method to class Object is not exactly the kind of support I would have in mind. Why not use an interface? The following simple interface is not part of the JDK, but its definition could be

```
interface Hashable {                    // not part of JDK
    public int hashCode();
    public boolean equals(Object obj);
};
```

Then, instead of accepting any object to be added to a hash table, only objects that implement the `Hashable` interface are acceptable. This has the added benefit of forcing the user to think about implementing these two very important methods to guarantee correct behavior of the hash table class. Currently, because the `Object` class already provides an implementation for both of these methods, users are tricked into not overriding its behavior, resulting in bad hash values. Alternatively, objects with the same "value" may not be recognized as equal, because the default implementation simply compares the two references to look at whether the two objects are one and the same.

The approach suggested here, by using an interface, would limit the users of a hash table to classes that implement the interface explicitly. This leads us to the question: "How many classes actually implement the `equals` method?" In the current Java distribution there are only 15 classes (Color, Font, Point, Rectangle, String, InetAddress, URL, BitSet, Boolean/Double/Float/Integer/Long, and Date) overriding its implementation. The impact of using an interface is therefore minimal. It would restrict users from putting any other available object directly in a hash table. Is this good, or bad? It is not directly a limitation for the user-defined element type, but it could be for the object we want to use as a key. If we want to use any predefined class for the key, moreover, it doesn't implement the `Hashable` interface, we can still use it. When the JDK would include the above-mentioned interface, we could simply declare a subclass of the predefined class we want to use as a key as follows

```
class BasicObjectKey extends BasicObject implements Hashable {
    // list all constructors and call super constructors
    public int hashCode() { ... }
    public boolean equals(Object obj) { ... }
}
```

11.3 Efficiency of Hash Tables

The hash table implementation in JDK 1.0 uses arbitrary bucket sizes and is based on *chaining* (an efficient and standard technique to handle hash key collisions). Choosing a hash function that distributes nicely over the size of the hash table is critical, as it reduces the chance of different objects resolving to the same index in the hash table (a *collision*). When the hash function is badly chosen, and the translation of the hash value to indices does not result in a nice distribution, it leads to an effect referred to as *clustering*. In the current Java implementation this may be the case. Namely, as a casual user will typically not override the `hashCode()` function, clustering of values may very well occur (as the default hash codes tend to be based on the address of the object's representation in the Java virtual machine. The only thing happening during the translation of this hash code into an index in the hash table, is to make the hash code an absolute number and use the *division* method to determine an index

```
int hash = key.hashCode();
int index = (hash & 0x7FFFFFFF) % tab.length;
```

Although no sensible programmer would ever use a hash table and make its size not a prime number, there is some information that may be interesting to know. Namely, a naive combination of a bad hash table size and the default hash code function could lead to a severe form of clustering. This is because the default hash code will always be a multiple of the native addressing word size (on Windows NT, a multiple of 8). It is well-known that hash tables that are based on chaining, work best when the hash table size is a prime number, not too close to a full power of 2. When the hash table size is a multiple of 8, 16, or 32, the distribution of the index is particularly bad. Using a prime number (as is understandably the case for the default size of the hash table class) solves all these problems. Even better would be to use a universal hashing technique, based on random hash functions, independent of the key.

A behavior of the Hashtable class is that when the hash table gets too full (or reaches the user-defined threshold), it is automatically *rehashed*. The hash table is resized to two times the old size + 1. If we want to fully optimize a hash table, the hash code function needs to be carefully aligned with the current size of the hash table. When the hash table resizes without telling us, we cannot update our hash function, and the resulting performance may be less than optimal. The problem is with the fact that the current hash table implementation enforces policies. Other hash table implementations typically ask the user to generate a hash value in a given *range*, allowing the user more flexibility in assuring that the hash function has a nice distribution behavior.

11.4 More on Equality
In the language LISP, there are two different ways to find out if two objects are equal. There is one method called `eq` that checks to see if the objects involved are the same physical object (i.e., have the same address in the runtime system). Another method, called `equal`, actually checks to see if two (possibly different) objects are logically equal. The language Python uses "is" for object identity, and uses the == operator for logical equality. In C++ there is no standard function comparable to the latter, but there is a standard way of comparing if two objects are the same object: the == operator. The compiler simply compares the address of the two objects (as is the case in Java). In C++, classes are free to overload the equality operator and give it a different meaning (like doing a logical comparison instead). In Java, there are no overloaded operators, but there

are two diff-erent ways of comparing equality of objects. The first (using the ==
operator) tests for reference equality. The second uses the `equals` method. An
example is given in the following piece of Java code

```
public class test {
    static String s1 = "Hello", s2 = "Hello";    /* line 2 */
    static Integer i1 = new Integer(1234), i2 = new Integer(1234);
    public static void main(String args[]) {
        if (s1 == "Hello") System.out.print("5 "); /* line 5 */
        if (s1 == s2) System.out.print("6 ");         /* line 6 */
        if (s1.equals(s2)) System.out.print("7 "); /* line 7 */
        if (s1.substring(1,5) == "ello")
                        System.out.print("8 ");    /* line 8 */
        // if (i1 == 1234) System.out.print("9 "); /* line 9 */
        if (i1 == i2) System.out.print("10");         /* line 10 */
        if (i1.equals(i2)) System.out.print("11"); /* line 11 */
    }
}
```

When executed, this program will print "5 6 7 11". Let us look at this line by
line, because there are some strange things happening here. First of all, it is good
to remember that any literal string in Java code gets translated into the creation of
a new String object by the compiler. Therefore, at line 2, s1 and s2 are assigned
to two new String objects. To optimize the size of the resulting byte codes, all
occurrences of string objects with the same value are mapped onto one single
instance. As can be seen in the following sequence of byte code (generated by
running `javap -c test2.java`),

```
0 ldc #8 <String "Hello">
2 putstatic #30 <Field test.s1 Ljava/lang/String;>
5 ldc #8 <String "Hello">
7 putstatic #28 <Field test.s2 Ljava/lang/String;>
```

both fields s1 and s2 are assigned to the same local instance stored at #8. All
other occurrences of string "Hello" will also reference the same instance. That
is why lines 5 and 6 in the example generate output, contrary to what one might
expect. The string at line 8 results in a different instance of type String, and is
therefore not the same object that represents the constant string "ello".

Up to JDK 1.0.2, the reuse of string constants *only* happens for usage within the
same *class*. Even if the same string occurs in the same Java source code file
("compilation unit"), but is used inside different classes, the strings do not reuse
the same instance, but have their own unique string instance per class. This

implementation detail is too dangerous to expose to the end user, and may result into many "gotcha" situations.

Reusing the memory used by constant strings is commendable, but the solution taken here introduces a strange side effect. Furthermore, although objects of type Integer, Float, Double, Boolean, and Long are just as immutable as String (their value cannot be changed after initialization), their instances are not reused by the compiler, as this apparently required too complex analysis of the Java code being compiled. Strings are so special that the language and compiler are fully aware of them, yet their numeric and boolean counterparts are ignored. This is a slight inconsistency, resulting in nothing being printed at lines 10 and 11 of the example being discussed. The two Integer objects created at line 3 are really two different objects, reflected in the following snapshot of byte codes

```
10 new #15 <Class java.lang.Integer>
13 dup
14 sipush 1234
17 invokenonvirtual #24 <Method java.lang.Integer.<init>(I)V>
20 putstatic #33 <Field test.i1 Ljava/lang/Integer;>
23 new #15 <Class java.lang.Integer>
26 dup
27 sipush 1234
30 invokenonvirtual #24 <Method java.lang.Integer.<init>(I)V>
33 putstatic #31 <Field test.i2 Ljava/lang/Integer;>
```

Furthermore, there is no automatic casting between integer values. Which is why the following code is invalid in the language

```
Integer i1 = 1234;      // Can't convert int to java.lang.Integer
if (i1 == 1234)         // Can't convert int to java.lang.Object
```

This means that variables of type int *cannot* be directly replaced by objects of type Integer, without needing to change the code that uses the variables.

12. String Performance

The Java compiler tries to implement strings as efficient as it can. In the following program, two optimizations for the String class occur

```
public class test {
    public static void main(String args[]) {
        String world = "World";
        System.out.println("Hello " + "World");    // line 4
        System.out.println("Hello " + world);       // line 5
    }
}
```

The two strings at line 4 are concatenated by the compiler and are replaced by one single string. This is shown in the following generated byte codes

```
3 getstatic #10 <Field java.lang.System.out Ljava/io/PrintStream;>
6 ldc #1 <String "Hello World">
8 invokevirtual #14
    <Method java.io.PrintStream.println(Ljava/lang/String;)V>
```

The two strings at line 5 are concatenated by using a StringBuffer object to append the strings together. In general, creating new objects is much more expensive than calling a method. Therefore, concatenating strings using a StringBuffer is much more efficient than creating a new string object every time two strings are concatenated. The generated byte codes are shown here

```
0 ldc #2 <String "World">
2 astore_1
11 getstatic #10 <Field java.lang.System.out Ljava/io/PrintStream;>
14 new #6 <Class java.lang.StringBuffer>
17 dup
18 invokenonvirtual #13 <Method java.lang.StringBuffer.<init>()V>
21 ldc #3 <String "Hello ">
23 invokevirtual #12
    <Method java.lang.StringBuffer.append(Ljava/lang/String;)
                                    Ljava/lang/StringBuffer;>
26 aload_1
27 invokevirtual #12
    <Method java.lang.StringBuffer.append(Ljava/lang/String;)
                                    Ljava/lang/StringBuffer;>
30 invokevirtual #9
    <Method java.lang.StringBuffer.toString()Ljava/lang/String;>
```

```
33 invokevirtual #14
   <Method java.io.PrintStream.println(Ljava/lang/String;)V>
```

Although the expression is optimized and as many operations are performed on the StringBuffer class as possible, eventually, a String object is created (in the `toString` method). This is also the case for the concatenation. The following example shows two loops where a string is concatenated 10,000 times to another string. Because strings are immutable, the resulting string replaces the old one. Therefore, the first loop effectively creates 10,000 temporary objects. Creating objects is relatively expensive. The second loop uses a method call, and creates no new object.

```
public class test {
    public static void main(String args[]) {
        String s = "Hello";
        long start = System.currentTimeMillis();
        for (int n=0; n<10000; n++)
            s += "World";
        long end = System.currentTimeMillis();
        System.out.println("+ gives: " + (end-start));

        StringBuffer b = new StringBuffer("Hello");
        start = System.currentTimeMillis();
        for (int n=0; n<10000; n++)
            b.append("World");
        end = System.currentTimeMillis();
        System.out.println("append gives: " + (end-start));
    }
}
```

Running this program three times, gives the following timings

```
+ gives: 96079
append gives: 1011
+ gives: 96008
append gives: 1011
+ gives: 96078
append gives: 1001
```

The first loop is almost 100 times slower. Programs that do a lot of string manipulation, such as parsers, compilers, and text editors, will obviously benefit from using the StringBuffer approach for manipulating strings.

Because strings are immutable, another "side effect" of the += operator is that it does not change the string itself (as is normally the case for this operator). Instead, the following expression

```
string += "text";
```

really reads as:

```
string = string + "text";
```

which gets translated by the compiler into

```
string = (new StringBuffer()) .append(string)
                    .append("text").toString();
```

The special semantics of the += operator could generate some unexpected behavior. The following code uses the operator in two different situations

```
public class test {
    public static void concat(String s) {         // line 2
        s += " bar";                               // line 3
        System.out.println("Inside concat: s = " + s);   // line 4
    }
    public static void main (String args[]) {
        String s1 = "Hello", s2 = s1;              // line 7
        if (s1 == s2) System.out.println("equal 1");   // line 8
        s1 += "World";                             // line 9
        if (s1 == s2) System.out.println("equal 2");   // line 10

        String s3 = "foo";                         // line 12
        concat(s3);                                // line 13
        System.out.println("Inside main: s3 = " + s3); // line 14
    }
}
```

Because strings are immutable and the += operator creates a new string for the result, this program prints the following output

```
equal 1                          from line 8
Inside concat: s = foo bar       from line 4
Inside main: s3 = foo            from line 14
```

First of all, a string is created at line 7, and another reference is assigned to it. The first print statement at line 8 works, because both s1 and s2 refer to the same object. After adding another string to s1, the test no longer results to a true value, so the print statement at line 10 is not activated. The operator at line 9 does not change the state of the *object*, but instead creates a new object and changes the *reference variable*. This is the only operator in the Java language that has such a side effect (all other assignment operators only work on basic types, and not on objects).

Because strings are immutable, the call to the concat method does not change the value of the s3 variable at line 13. In Java, *all* objects are passed by reference to a function, except for string objects, which are passed by value. This semantics makes the language unnecessarily more complex. Strings should not have been made immutable. In that case, there would have been no need for a StringBuffer class at all, because all operations on strings could have been implemented efficiently in the string class itself. One reason to make strings immutable, was to be able to share the internal implementation for multiple strings with the same value. But, with a simple reference count mechanism, strings can still share state, even when they are mutable. Anyway, currently strings are immutable, and have the above described behavior, and programmers should be aware of the implications of manipulating and passing strings.

13. Efficiency of Vectors versus Arrays

Vectors are generic data structures, functioning as a replacement for an array, when either the number of total elements is unknown or objects need to be inserted sometimes at the end, the middle, or the start of the vector. Vectors have a certain overhead when compared to arrays, because synchronized methods are used to add and access the individual elements. That makes vectors thread-safe. Some people claim that vectors are *much* slower than arrays; statements are made about them being probably 100 times slower when iterating over elements. The following (not very scientific) timing test indicates that vectors are indeed slower, yet not so dramatically as claimed. First, a dynamically sized vector is used to allocate an array of 100,000 elements, initialize them, and access them. The second loop does the same on a vector that has been "presized." Loop three and four do the same but are now on a copy of the vector class with all synchronization removed. The fifth loop uses an array

```
import java.util.Vector;
public class test {
    public static void main(String args[]) {
        Object object;
        long start, time;
        Vector vector;
        UnsynchronizedVector uvector;

        start = System.currentTimeMillis();
        vector = new Vector();
        for (int n=0; n<100000; n++)
            vector.addElement(null);
        for (int n=0; n<100000; n++)
            object = vector.elementAt(n);
        time = System.currentTimeMillis() - start;
        System.out.println("dynamic vector: " + time);

        start = System.currentTimeMillis();
        vector = new Vector();
        vector.setSize(100000);
        for (int n=0; n<100000; n++)
            vector.setElementAt(null, n);
        for (int n=0; n<100000; n++)
            object = vector.elementAt(n);
        time = System.currentTimeMillis() - start;
        System.out.println("fixed sized vector: " + time);

        start = System.currentTimeMillis();
        uvector = new UnsynchronizedVector();
        for (int n=0; n<100000; n++)
            uvector.addElement(null);
        for (int n=0; n<100000; n++)
```

```
            object = uvector.elementAt(n);
      time = System.currentTimeMillis() - start;
      System.out.println("Unsynchronized dynamic vector: " + time);

      start = System.currentTimeMillis();
      uvector = new UnsynchronizedVector();
      uvector.setSize(100000);
      for (int n=0; n<100000; n++)
            uvector.setElementAt(null,n);
      for (int n=0; n<100000; n++)
            object = uvector.elementAt(n);
      time = System.currentTimeMillis() - start;
      System.out.println("Unsynchronized fixed vector: " + time);

      start = System.currentTimeMillis();
      Object array[] = new Object[100000];
      for (int n=0; n<100000; n++)
            array[n] = null;
      for (int n=0; n<100000; n++)
            object = array[n];
      time = System.currentTimeMillis() - start;
      System.out.println("fixed sized array: " + time);
   }
}
```

Accessing the standard vectors is roughly ten times slower than using an array. Using an nonsynchronized vector is only three times slower than using an array. When recompiling the new code with javac, using the –O compile flag, the time goes down even more, because the methods in the Vector class are almost all final. In that case, vector access is roughly *two times* as slow as arrays.

```
dynamic vector: 12228
fixed sized vector: 8773
Unsynchronized dynamic vector: 3755
Unsynchronized fixed vector: 2263
Unsynchronized dynamic vector compiled with -O : 2814
Unsynchronized fixed vector compiled with -O: 1602
fixed sized array: 751
```

The minimal overhead that is paid at runtime by using a generic data structure like Vectors, over using a basic array is not worth the possible maintenance nightmare for the resize management of dynamic arrays. To make a generic, automatically resizing an array, a user would have to implement a code similar to the following

```
public class test {
    static Object array[] = new Object[8];
    static int arraylength = 8;
    synchronized static void addElement(Object object) {
        if (arraylength >= array.length) {
            Object newarray[] = new Object[arraylength*2];
            System.arraycopy(array, 0, newarray, 0, arraylength);
            array = newarray;
        }
        array[arraylength++] = object;
    }
    public static void main(String args[]) {
        long start, time;
        Object object;
        start = System.currentTimeMillis();
        for (int n=0; n<100000; n++) addElement(null);
        for (int n=0; n<100000; n++) object = array[n];
        time = System.currentTimeMillis() - start;
        System.out.println("dynamic array: " + time);
    }
}
```

When run, this program prints a surprising

```
dynamic array: 4306
```

This is one-third of the standard vectors yet slower than an unsynchronized vector. Removing the synchronization from the last example, brings down the execution time to

```
dynamic array: 1605
```

which only makes it twice as fast as a generic, nonsynchronized vector. Remember that this time advantage may not be at all detectable anymore when this code is embedded in a large system where the overhead of other parts may be much larger.

We should use arrays for their speed but have to use vectors to create maintainable code. Having to add the dynamic array size management code for each single array we use is not acceptable, and this dilemma clearly shows the need for parameterized types, such as templates in C++.

14. Improving Performance of Java programs

The first step in improving performance of Java programs is not to worry about performance at all during initial development. The Java virtual machine can generate performance figures for how many times a method is called, from what other method that call originated, and how much elapsed time was spent inside the method. That information can then be used to analyze the behavior of the program. A sample trace is the following

```
#count callee caller time
935 java/awt/Component.getForeground()Ljava/awt/Color;
                                java/awt/Component.getForeground()Ljava/awt/Color; 20
1 java/awt/Component.getBackground()Ljava/awt/Color;
                                java/awt/Component.getBackground()Ljava/awt/Color; 0
935 java/awt/Component.getFont()Ljava/awt/Font;
                                java/awt/Component.getFont()Ljava/awt/Font; 30
62 java/awt/Component.postEvent(Ljava/awt/Event;)Z
                                java/awt/Component.postEvent(Ljava/awt/Event;)Z 40
3 java/awt/Container.validate()V java/awt/Container.validate()V 160
232 sun/awt/win32/Win32Graphics.drawImage(Ljava/awt/Image;
        IILjava/awt/image/ImageObserver;)Z ltk/DisplayListCanvas.paint(Ljava/awt/Graphics;)V 580
4 sun/awt/win32/Win32FontMetrics.stringWidth(Ljava/lang/String;)I
                                ltk/Label.setFont(Ljava/awt/Font;)V 0
2 java/lang/StringBuffer.append(Ljava/lang/String;)Ljava/lang/StringBuffer;
                                sun/awt/image/Image.<init>(II)V 0
1075 ltk/Area.set(IIII)V ltk/Graphical.setConstrainedArea(IIIII)V 0
7 java/awt/Event.<init>(Ljava/lang/Object;JIIIIILjava/lang/Object;)V
                                sun/awt/win32/MComponentPeer.handleMouseEnter(JII)V 0
5 java/awt/Event.<init>(Ljava/lang/Object;JIIIIILjava/lang/Object;)V
                                sun/awt/win32/MComponentPeer.handleMouseExit(JII)V 0
2 java/awt/Component.addNotify()V java/awt/Container.addNotify()V 0
300 java/awt/Event.<init>(Ljava/lang/Object;JIIIIILjava/lang/Object;)V
                                sun/awt/win32/MComponentPeer.handleMouseMoved(JIIII)V 20
5 java/awt/Event.<init>(Ljava/lang/Object;JIIIIILjava/lang/Object;)V
                                sun/awt/win32/MComponentPeer.handleMouseDown(JIIII)V 0
5 java/awt/Event.<init>(Ljava/lang/Object;JIIIIILjava/lang/Object;)V
                                sun/awt/win32/MComponentPeer.handleMouseUp(JIIII)V 0

. . .
```

When sorted on the fourth column, using `sort -r -k 4 java.prof` the
result is

```
# count callee caller time
1 ltk/LTKApplet.runAppletAsApplication(Ljava/lang/String;II)V
                           ltk/LTKApplet.runAppletAsApplication(Ljava/lang/String;)V 991
1 ltk/LTKApplet.runAppletAsApplication(Ljava/lang/String;)V
                                       Demo.main([Ljava/lang/String;)V 991
254 sun/awt/win32/MComponentPeer.handleMouseDrag(JIIII)V ?.? 91
39 ltk/GUIStyle.getDefaultStyle()Lltk/GUIStyle;
             ltk/Button.init(Lltk/DisplayListCanvas;Lltk/CallBackable;IIIIILjava/lang/String;)V 90
300 java/awt/Component.postEvent(Ljava/awt/Event;)Z
                       sun/awt/win32/MComponentPeer.handleMouseMoved(JIIII)V 90
296 ltk/EventManager.dispatch(Lltk/EventClient;Ljava/awt/Event;)V
                       ltk/EventManager.dispatchEvent(Ljava/awt/Event;)V 90
...
```

This shows the methods where most of the time is spent. It always makes
sense to start from there, fixing the most expensive methods first. After fixing
those, another run can be made, again making the most expensive methods
less expensive.

The file also contains information about the number of objects that have been
created from each class, and how much memory the instances occupy all
together (again sorted)

```
# type count bytes
Lsun/awt/win32/Win32Graphics; 241 5784
[C 158 5288
Ljava/lang/String; 111 1332
Lltk/DisplayListElement; 58 696
Lltk/EventClient; 45 720
Lltk/Button; 39 2652
Lltk/Area; 24 384
Ljava/awt/Color; 17 136
Ljava/util/HashtableEntry; 14 224
[Ljava/lang/Object; 12 520
Ljava/util/Vector; 12 144
...
```

Other possibilities are to use a visual debugger, such as the one described in
Chapter 3.

14.1 Relative Cost of Java Operations

Operations like drawing on the screen, writing to a file, or communicating
through a socket connection, are by far the most expensive things you can do in
a Java program. Minimizing drawing operations, using a buffered stream, and
doing things in memory instead of going to a file, may have the most dramatic

influence on the performance of your Java program. Furthermore, data structures that have $O(n)$ or $O(n^2)$ complexity should, of course, also be avoided.

Apart from these general observations, there are few "hidden" costs to using standard Java constructs. The following program shows some timings for field access (either regular or synchronized), and method calls (regular or synchronized)

```
public class test {
    void f1() { x = 0; }
    synchronized void f2() { x = 0; }
    int x;
    public static void main (String args[]) {
        long start, time;
        int x;
        test t = new test();

        start = System.currentTimeMillis();
        for (int n=0; n<100000; n++) x = t.x;
        time = System.currentTimeMillis() - start;
        System.out.println("access to regular field: " + time);

        start = System.currentTimeMillis();
        synchronized(t) { for (int n=0; n<100000; n++) x = t.x; }
        time = System.currentTimeMillis() - start;
        System.out.println("access to synchronized field: " + time);

        start = System.currentTimeMillis();
        for (int n=0; n<100000; n++) t.f1();
        time = System.currentTimeMillis() - start;
        System.out.println("call to regular method: " + time);

        start = System.currentTimeMillis();
        for (int n=0; n<100000; n++) t = new test();
        time = System.currentTimeMillis() - start;
        System.out.println("object creation: " + time);

        start = System.currentTimeMillis();
        for (int n=0; n<100000; n++) t.f2();
        time = System.currentTimeMillis() - start;
        System.out.println("call to synchronized method: " + time);

        start = System.currentTimeMillis();
        for (int n=0; n<100000; n++) synchronized(t) { x = t.x; }
        time = System.currentTimeMillis() - start;
        System.out.println("access to synchronized field: " + time);
    }
}
```

The timings for this program on a 70Mhz Pentium, running Windows NT, are as follows

```
access to regular field: 271
access to synchronized field: 270
call to regular method: 601
object creation: 1913
call to synchronized method: 3043
access to synchronized field: 3075
```

The numbers have no absolute meaning, because they may be different on any given platform or implementation of the Java virtual machine. What does matter are the values of the timings relative to each other. Basically, direct field access is cheapest, with method calls being twice as expensive. Object creation is roughly eight times as expensive as accessing a field. Really expensive are actions that involve getting a monitor on an object.

Accessing a field or calling a method are equally expensive when the object or method is synchronized. Due to different implementation models, the cost for synchronization varies most between platforms. Although synchronization can be more or less expensive on different platforms, it certainly deserves attention. This is because a synchronized method may be up to *five* times as expensive as a regular method.

When methods or classes are declared `final`, then a client that is compiled with the -O flag will *inline* the body of the function. Therefore, simple accessor functions (which just return a data field) should always be declared final.

One should be careful not to sacrifice sensible object-oriented principles (such as encapsulation and maintainability) to overoptimize Java code. In one big GUI intensive Java system I was involved with, we had a certain run of the application that used to take 43 seconds. After carefully visiting hundreds of methods, making as many methods final as we could, and recompiling the whole system with the optimization flag, we were able to bring the execution time down to 41 seconds. Hardly shocking. This shows that things that may appear to be expensive on the surface, can have irrelevant influence on the overall time consumption. Optimization should always be done with care, and only be done after determining those parts of the system where most of the time is spent.

15. Accessing Methods before Objects Are Constructed

Contrary to common intuition, there is a way in Java to call methods of a class *before* the object is properly constructed and instance variables have been assigned their initial values. The first time I was exposed to this behavior was while I was porting a large collection of C++ classes to Java, together with my colleagues at work. The class library consisted of an inheritance tree of quite a number of classes and methods. Because the code was designed as a reusable class library, most classes had multiple forms of constructors, one for each of the different construction roles it played.

In order to limit code replication through different constructors in the same class, we resorted to a very common technique in C++. We used a member function to share the common behavior and called that method from within each of the constructors. Each constructor did whatever was special to its function and then called the `init()` method, declared especially for its class. In C++, there is no problem when multiple classes in a inheritance tree declare a function with the same name, as we did with our initialize function.

Now, consider the following piece of Java code

```
1.  class A {
2.    A() { init(); }
3.    void init() { System.out.println("init of A"); }
4.  };
5.  class B extends A {
6.    B() { init(); }
7.    void init() { System.out.println("init of B, x=" + x); }
8.    final int x = 5;
9.  };
10. public class bug {
11.   public void main(String args[]) { new B(); }
12. }
```

First of all, when executed, this Java program prints out

```
init of B, x=0
init of B, x=5
```

Observe that both classes implement the `init()` method, and call it from their constructor. In Java, methods are by default virtual and will be overridden (shadowed) by subclasses. When the instance of type B gets constructed (line 11), its constructor is called (line 6). As a result, the constructor for A is called (line 2). Inside the constructor of class A, a call is made to the `init()` method. When we observe class A to be in isolation, it is clear that the intention is for the `A.init()` to be called. However, in Java, overridden methods always shadow methods defined in a superclass, even when that call is made from within a constructor. Therefore, the `A.init()` routine is hidden when the constructor for A gets called, and the call to init() at line 2 will actually call B.init() defined at line 7. After the constructor for A is finished, control returns to the constructor of B. Then, at line 6, another call is made to init(), again resolving in a call to B.init() defined at line 7.

Concluding, the init() method for class B is called twice, once when the object is not yet fully constructed (hence the value 0 for variable x). The init() routine of class A never gets called at all.

In the large system that we were trying to port, we ran into subtle, weird behavior of our code, because the wrong init() function was called multiple times. In other cases, we were saved by the Java runtime system, because we accessed object references, instead of an integer variable (such as x in our example). As the object reference should have been initialized in one of the initializer functions, which now did not happen, we ran into a couple of null pointer exceptions. It did take us close to a day to determine and prove this (for us at the time weird) behavior of the Java language.

Note that it does not matter what we do at line 2. Changing the init() call into an explicit call to A's method, such as ((A)this).init() will not change anything to the virtual method call mechanism. The object instance will still have the same virtual method table, and any call to init() will resolve to the one defined in class B. By the way, if we insert a print statement in both constructors to print out the dynamic class name, it will always resolve to B, even when we are in A's constructor.

In C++, the runtime behavior is different. The C++ Annotated Reference Manual [Ellis & Stroustrup, 1991], states at page 294:

> *Member functions may be called in constructors and destructors. This implies that virtual functions may be called (directly or indirectly). The function called will be the one defined in the constructor's (or destructor's) own class or its bases, but not any function overriding it in a derived class. This ensures that unconstructed derived class objects will not be accessed during construction or destruction.*

The way that this is typically implemented is that multiple virtual function tables for an object instance are maintained at runtime. When a constructor of a base class gets executed, the virtual table for that class is used. In Java, the object will have the same virtual method table. This is an operational simplification, which complicates the design and implementation of object construction, because there is one extra detail users of the language have to worry about.

All of this may seem a complicated, academic, and artificial problem. However, we ran into it a couple of times in a practical setting during our porting efforts. It will come up in any large-scale Java system at one time or another. Especially when people are porting large portions of code from C++ to Java, as it is such a common technique in C++ to call helper methods from within a set of constructors that share common code.

The implication of this behavior in the Java runtime system is that anyone who writes a class in Java, has to ensure that no other methods *are* ever called from its constructors. Or, when methods are called, special care needs to be given to make these methods final, so that subclasses cannot override and shadow them. We will have to choose a unique name, to not limit the freedom of subclass designers to take a similar name. For that reason, the name `init` would be a bad choice, and `initA` and `initB` are more unique names. It doesn't stop there, though. We also have to check all methods that are called from within those methods, and also make them final. Concluding, this is an error-prone task that should be performed by a compiler and not by human beings, which is currently the case.

16. Implementing Callbacks in Java

A callback is the mechanism of calling a method on an object, without knowing the actual type of the object, nor the actual name of the method. It is often used not only in graphical user interfaces, where components such as buttons notify a given object whenever activated but also for connecting other loosely coupled components in a system. To allow a flexible plug-and-play style of composing applications, the intention is to minimize the dependencies between the sender and the receiver of a callback.

16.1 Callback Implementation Techniques in Java

There are various ways of implementing callback behavior, each with its own degree of decoupling of the interface between the sender and receiver.

- Using an event handling mechanism, as is done in AWT. Each component has a special `handleEvent` method that handles the events coming in from all GUI elements that it contains. If the component holds multiple elements, some way of discriminating the source of the callback is required. Additional information is encoded in the event. The *target* field in the java.awt.Event class is used to identify the *sender* of the callback (a small misnomer). The target of the event identifies the element for which the event was originally created. Alternatively, special high-level events can be generated by the components (whose value is defined in the java.awt.Event class). The disadvantage of this mixed approach is that there are two different, and therefore confusing, ways of determining the sender of the callback. The first way results in many if-than-else clauses, whereas the second one is not extensible (new GUI widgets don't have the luxury of having their event being registered with the Event class). Furthermore, users tend to include application logic directly inside the handleEvent method. That makes code hard to understand, structure, extend, and maintain.

- One step towards a better approach is to not implement any application logic in the handleEvent method but separate the logic into more manageable parts. Each callback would have its own implementation, and the handleEvent method is only used for dispatching the event to the right method. This decouples the callback sender-receiver relationship only at the receiver side, though.

- The ideal situation is where GUI elements, like buttons, would not implement the strict protocol of generating a given event that is carried up the component hierarchy. Instead, the intended callback receiver and the notification method could be passed as a parameter while creating or initializing the button. In languages like C++, one can pass an object and the address of any method implemented by the object's class. When the button wants to activate the callback, it simply calls the specified method on the object. In order to implement this, one must be able to store a reference to a method in a variable, and be able to call it later (without knowing its actual name). In Java, it is not possible to take the address of a method or to generate a reference to it.

Therefore, a more symbolic technique needs to be applied. One approach is to represent methods by symbolic *integers.*

- LTK uses an integer value to use as an identification mechanism between the callback sender and receiver. The combination of an object and a method number identifies the intended method to be called. A limitation of this approach is that it may be hard to maintain a unique match between an integer and a given method, especially when one has to ensure that the number is unique for all classes up the inheritance tree.

- A better way is to use a global mechanism for matching numbers and method identifiers (strings). A hash table-based symbol table approach would suffice in that case.

Alternatively, there are two different practical ways of representing methods by a string

- Use a piece of native code to call the method for us. The Java language does not have method references and does not allow an object to call a late-bound method on another object. Surprisingly enough, from native C code, any method can be called, as long as we have a string representation of the name of the method and a reference to the object involved. Let's assume AWT would have implemented the following Java class

```
package java.awt;
public class Callback {
    public native static void call(Object o, String m);
};
```

Then, classes like java.AWT.Button, instead of generating a predefined event, could have used a different technique by implementing code like the following

```
void activateCallback() {
    Callback.call(target, "print");
}
```

The native method's implementation in a DLL would dynamically call the specified method. To make the programmer's life a lot easier, this piece of native code should really have been included in AWT. Right now, if a user would want to implement this technique, it would mean having to distribute and install the corresponding DLL on the client side before an applet using this solution could be run there. This is not acceptable, as the distribution problems directly defeat the whole platform independent success of Java in the first place.

- Instead of using a native method, one could use an elegant hack. Here, the method is also identified by a string exactly matching the name of the method. However, when the callback is created, no call to native code is made, but instead a unique class that implements the call to the identified method is generated on the fly in the form of byte code, and those byte codes are loaded dynamically by the class loader. This does not require any preparation from the client to run applets. For an interesting implementation, look at Sal Cataudella's work at `http://www.panix.com/~rangerx`. One problem is that the technique generates byte codes directly, something that not everyone is capable of doing. An alternative is using incremental compilation techniques, using the Java compiler that is shipped with the JDK (see Section 19 of Chapter 1).

Mapping methods to integers and/or strings suffers from a more or less serious limitation of having a very late binding. If a typo is made in the string, or somehow the integer representations are mixed up, we will not find out until the program is run, and the callback is actually activated. Depending on our recovery mechanism, the problem may be hard to detect, or even go undetected.

16.2 A Proposal for Method References in Java

Of course, implementing callbacks would be so much easier if the Java language had direct support for method pointers (or method references, if you prefer to call them that). Then, the compiler could help and do static typing on the method signatures, and make sure whatever we pass out as the intended reference to a method, really refers to a method of the expected signature. Extending the language to include method references opens up a can of worms, though. Anyone who ever had to prototype a method pointer signature in C or C++ (including the return type and argument specifications), will agree that a simpler syntax would be welcome. Here is an example of declaring and calling a callback method (using a template) in C++

```
template <class T>
class callback {
public:
    typedef void (T::*Method)(void);
    callback(T *obj, Method f) { this->obj=obj; this->f=f; }
    void activate() { (obj->*f)(); }
    T *obj;
    Method f;
```

```
    };
    class callbackUser {
    public:
        callbackUser() {
            new callback<callbackUser>(this, &callbackUser::wakeup);
        }
        void wakeup(void) { ... }
    };
```

Ignoring the server side (which may look like obfuscated C++), the client side is very simple. Instead of referring to `this`, another object could just as well have been specified as the target, separating the "owner" of a component from the one in charge of handling interesting events (this could be used to implement a "Chain of Responsibility," see [Gamma et.al., 1995]).

My personal (limited) proposal for method references in Java is

```
    package java.lang;
    public final class Method {
        private Method() { }                        // line 3
    };
    public final class Callback {
        public native callback(Object obj, Method f);
        public native void activate();
    };
    package myProject;                              // line 10
    class Button {
        public Button (Callback cb) {
            this.cb=cb;                             // line 13
        }
        public void tellClient() {
            cb.activate();                          // line 16
        }
        Callback cb;                                // line 18
    }
    class callbackUser {
        callbackUser() {
            new Button(new Callback(this, print));  // line 22
        }
        public void print(void) { ... }
    };
```

This example creates a button and passes it an instance of the proposed class java.lang.Callback. The intention is for the "print" method to be called every time the button is activated by the user.

Some assumptions and caveats are in order here:

- Two new basic types have to be defined, java.lang.Callback and java.lang.Method. Both are final classes. The Java compiler needs to be aware of these two new types (in particular, Method), as they deserve some special treatment (see next point).

- At line 18, a variable is declared. It is assigned a new value at line 13. So far, so good. No special treatment from the compiler is necessary. The sticky part begins at line 16. The "activate" method is called, and its implementation has to do something special. For now, we will simply assume that the native implementation will do the right trick, and call the stored method. The method may of course be implemented as a string (as suggested earlier in the section).

- At line 22, the compiler has to help out. It has to realize that the Callback class has a special constructor, and it has to ensure that the second parameter refers to a public void method with no parameter. Only when the named method has the right signature, an object of type Callback can be safely created, and the method is guaranteed to exist.

- The language extension sketched here is only necessary to ensure that we can do compile-time checking to see if a named method really exists, and has the right return type and number of parameters. If we can live with a looser binding, the native method approach described earlier would suffice. In both proposals, a simplification is made, because the method signature is restricted to a void function. In practice, this does not impose a limitation though. Any additional information required to correctly react to the callback can always be inquired by the client.

17. Overriding Methods and Hiding Variables

17.1 Dynamic Method Resolution in Java

In Java, methods in a derived class override methods with the same signature declared in one of the superclasses. The original method is really not visible and can never be called even when the object is dynamically cast to the superclass. Consider the following example Java code

```java
class A {
    void foo(int i) { System.out.println("A.foo "+i); }
}
class B extends A {
    void foo(int i) { System.out.println("B.foo "+i); }
}
public class test {
    public static void main(String args[]) {
        A a = new A();
        a.foo(123);                     // line 10
        B b = new B();
        b.foo(456);                     // line 12
        a = b;      // this is a valid implicit cast
        a.foo(789);                     // line 14
    }
}
```

This Java program prints the following three lines

```
A.foo 123
B.foo 456
B.foo 789
```

The "surprising" line could be the third line. Although the dynamic type of variable a at line 14 is class A, the VM uses the virtual method table of class B, and method foo will be resolved into B.foo. This behavior is intended and is according to the language specification. The equivalent C++ program (given below) produces a different output, because in C++ the dynamic type of the variable determines the method resolution algorithm. If the dynamic type of the variable happens to be class A, a call to method foo will resolve into A.foo and not into B.foo, which is the original type of the object when it was created. Here is the equivalent C++ program

```
#include <iostream.h>
class A {
public:
    void foo(int i) { cout << "A.foo " << i << endl; }
};
class B : public A {
public:
    void foo(int i) { cout << "B.foo " << i << endl; }
};
void main(int argc, char **argv) {
   A a;
   a.foo(123);
   B b;
   b.foo(456);
   a=b;
   a.foo(789);
}
```

This C++ program prints the following three lines, where the third line prints something different, because of a difference in method resolution performed in Java

```
A.foo 123
B.foo 456
A.foo 789         ← different from Java!
```

17.2 Method Overriding Compared with C++

In C++, methods in a derived class hide all methods with the same *name* declared by any of the base classes. Therefore, the following legal Java program would not compile in its C++ equivalent, because the call on line 10 is made to a function that is not visible in the scope of DerivedClass. The C++ language has this semantics to reduce conflicts in deeply nested inheritance structures.

```
class SuperClass {
   void foo(int i) { System.out.println("SuperClass.foo "+i); }
}
class DerivedClass extends SuperClass {
   void foo(String s) { System.out.println("Derived.foo "+s); }
}
public class test {
   public static void main(String args[]) {
      DerivedClass d = new DerivedClass();
      d.foo(12345);                           // line 10
      d.foo("Hello");
   }
}
```

Note that in this Java example, it is not necessary to actually scope the method by mentioning the super class. In C++, the equivalent program would not compile. Here follows a C++ example that will not compile, because `B::foo(void)` hides `A::foo(int)`. The compiler will not compile line 13. The call has to be made more specific by saying, `d.SuperClass::foo(78)`.

```cpp
#include <iostream.h>
class A {
public:
    void foo(int i) { cout << "A.foo " << i << endl; }
};
class B : public A {
public:
    void foo() { cout << "B.foo " << endl; }
};
void main(int argc, char **argv) {
    B b;
    b.foo(78); // line 13, causes compile error
    b.foo();
}
```

Another difference is in explicit specification of a superclass. The following program shows how Java effectively makes the `foo` method declared in class A invisible to the user

```java
class A {
    void foo(int i) { System.out.println("A.foo "+i); }
}
class B extends A {
    void foo(int i) { System.out.println("B.foo "+i); }
    A getBSuper() { return super; }
}
class C extends B {
    void foo(int i) { System.out.println("C.foo "+i); }
    B getCSuper() { return super; }
}
public class test {
    public static void main(String args[]) {
        C c = new C();
        c.foo(12);
        B b = c.getCSuper();
        b.foo(34);
        A a = b.getBSuper();
        a.foo(56);
        a = c;              // implicit cast from C to A
        a.foo(78);
    }
}
```

In Java, derived methods hide methods of a superclass, and there is no scope resolution operator (the :: operator in C++). The closest thing to the getting to a superclass is by either using the `super` keyword or by (implicitly) casting an object to one of its superclasses. Before we look at the output of the Java program, we will contrast it with an equivalent C++ program, given here

```
#include <iostream.h>
class A {
public:
    void foo(int i) { cout << "A.foo " << i << endl; }
};
class B : public A {
public:
    void foo(int i) { cout << "B.foo " << i << endl; }
};
class C : public B {
public:
    void foo(int i) { cout << "C.foo " << i << endl; }
};
void main(int argc, char **argv) {
    C c;
    c.foo(12);
    c.B::foo(34);
    c.C::foo(56);
    A &a = c;                    // implicit cast to A
    a.foo(78);
}
```

The previous Java and C++ versions of this example print the following (quite different) output:

Java example	C++ example
C.foo 12	C.foo 12
C.foo 34	B.foo 34
C.foo 56	A.foo 56
C.foo 78	A.foo 78

Note that in Java, in all four cases, C.foo is used. Namely, in Java, it is the *actual type* that specifies which method will be selected, no matter what the *declared type* of the reference is. In C++, overloaded member resolution is based on the actual type of the reference (or can be made explicit with the scope resolution operator).

17.3 Dynamic Variable Access in Java

In Java, methods are *overridden*, and fields are *hidden*. That means that the
declared type of the reference and not the *actual* type of the object implies which
fields are chosen.

```
class A {
    void foo() { System.out.println("Inside A.foo, "+s); }
    String s = "the use of s resolves to A.s";
}
class B extends A {
    void bar() { System.out.println("Inside B.bar, "+s); }
    String s = "the use of s resolves to B.s";
}
public class test {
    public static void main(String args[]) {
        A a = new A();
        a.foo();
        B b = new B();
        b.foo();
        b.bar();
        a = b; // this is a valid implicit cast
        a.foo();
    }
}
```

The equivalent C++ code is

```
#include <iostream.h>
class A {
public:
    A() : s("the use of s resolves to A.s") { }
    void foo() { cout << "Inside A.foo, " << s << endl; }
    char *s;
};
class B : public A {
public:
    B() : s("the use of s resolves to B.s") { }
    void bar() { cout << "Inside B.bar, " << s << endl; }
    char *s;
};
void main(int argc, char **argv) {
    A a;
    a.foo();
    B b;
    b.foo();
    b.bar();
    a=b; // this is a valid implicit cast
    a.foo();
}
```

Interestingly enough, this time the programs print the same output

```
Inside A.foo, the use of s resolves to A.s
Inside A.foo, the use of s resolves to A.s
Inside B.bar, the use of s resolves to B.s
Inside A.foo, the use of s resolves to A.s
```

In both languages, the actual type denotes which fields (data members) are selected.

18. Garbage Collection and Finalization

Java is a language with garbage collection. Whether a language should support garbage collection (as is done in Lisp, Smalltalk, and Java) or use explicit memory management by the programmer (as is done in Pascal, C, and C++), is a topic I would rather not pass a moral judgment on. The topic is extremely sensitive among language lawyers, and I would at least offend half of my intended audience by either blessing garbage collection or by cursing it. OK, I can't escape the discussion, so let's devote some time on it.

First, let's look at memory management in a language that has no garbage collection. Experienced C++ developers hardly have any problems with memory allocation, and the code to do memory management certainly does not waste 30 percent of their applications (I have seen "claims" like this reported). In contrast, inexperienced C++ programmers have more problems. They can have difficulty to understand the differences between creation of objects on the heap and on the stack, or, for instance, what happens when objects are passed by value. Those types of novice C++ programmers easily introduce memory leaks into their programs, simply by misunderstanding the general memory allocation principles of C++. Experienced C++ programmers do not, because they *know* all these principles. Therefore, they generally can generate highly efficient code. The resulting code need not be *obfuscated* code at all, and can be easy to understand and maintain. Explicit memory management is a powerful engineering solution. It can be hard to master, but C++ was explicitly created to be an efficient multipurpose language. Of course, no C++ application needs to contain any memory leak with current-day memory analysis and debugging tools.

Java has no explicit memory management. Objects are *created* explicitly, yet objects are never *deleted* by the user. When a variable leaves scope or is assigned a new variable, there may be one or more fewer references to the object. When there are no references to the object anymore, the garbage collector may reclaim the object's memory at a later stage. The garbage collector runs in a separate thread, and unlike some garbage collected systems, execution of the program need not be completely suspended to do garbage collection. Therefore, garbage collection is unobtrusive. In fact, in Java, I am never aware of garbage collection happening at all. Garbage collection does not necessarily make a language run much slower. It is not true that Java is a slower language than C++, just because it uses garbage collection, instead of *new* and *delete*. However, garbage collection could make programmers lazy. Because their garbage is cleaned up after them, temporary objects may be created at will, some of them without knowing. The more temporary objects are created, the more garbage needs to be collected, the more memory the program uses, and the more time is wasted on collecting it. Tools that demonstrate object creation and how often the garbage collector comes around, may become important to keep Java programs efficient.

18.1 Finalization

Right before an object is garbage collected, its `finalize` method is called by the garbage collector. The finalize method is a protected method called by the garbage collector and allows the object to release critical resources such as open socket connections. Because the method is a *protected* method, access protection ensures that only subclasses can call this method. This is the case for user-defined objects as well as for system objects. Although some classes in the Java distribution declare their finalize method as *public*, this cannot be meant to be so, and these isolated cases could be considered (harmless?) bugs. As advised in the Java language specification, inside their finalize method, subclasses should always call the finalize method of the superclass, before doing whatever they want to clean up themselves. The suggested form is

```
protected void finalize() throws Throwable {
   super.finalize();
   ...                            // clean up resources?
}
```

Although I agree with the necessity of making sure that the superclass also cleans up its resources, it is safer to *first* clean up the derived class, and *then* let the superclass do its cleanup.

```
protected void finalize() throws Throwable {
   ...                            // clean up resources?
   super.finalize();
}
```

Furthermore, there is a little twist in making the finalize method a *protected* method. Namely, the result is that the finalize method can be called any number of times from any place inside the object itself or from one of its subclasses (not necessarily from the finalize method). An example is given in the following Java program

```
class Finalizer {
   void doSomething() {
      finalize(); // Java programs should NEVER call this
   }
   public void finalize() { System.out.println("finalize"); }
}
public class test {
   public static void main(String args[]) {
      Runtime runtime = Runtime.getRuntime();
      Finalizer finalizer = new Finalizer();
      finalizer.doSomething();
      finalizer.doSomething();
      finalizer.doSomething();
      finalizer = null; // no more refs to finalizer exist
      runtime.gc(); // activate garbage collector
```

```
        runtime.runFinalization();
    }
}
```

Because the finalize method can be called from anywhere in the object, this Java
program compiles and runs fine. It prints the following four lines

```
finalize
finalize
finalize
finalize
```

There is no protection mechanism in the language for unwanted calls to the
finalize method. As far as I can tell, none of the system classes that actually
implement the finalize method make an explicit test to ensure that they are not
finalized more than once. Most of the classes release underlying system
resources, and the behavior of releasing a resource more than once may be
undefined. It might actually bring the system down. Therefore, for security reasons, classes that implement a finalize method should always ensure that they
perform their own finalization code only once. This is a little strange, considering the fact that the language ensures in another way that the finalize method is
only called once, namely when the object is "resurrected" in a finalizer. The following Java program explains this behavior

```
class Zombie {
    void printSomething() { System.out.println("alive !!"); }
    protected void finalize() {
        System.out.println("finalize");
        Resurrected.itsAlive = this;        // resurrect object
    }
}
class Resurrected {
    public static Zombie itsAlive;
}
public class test {
    public static void main(String args[]) {
        Runtime runtime = Runtime.getRuntime();
        Zombie zombie = new Zombie();
        do {
            zombie.printSomething();
            zombie = null; // no more refs to zombie exist
            Resurrected.itsAlive = null;
            runtime.gc(); // activate garbage collector
            runtime.runFinalization();
            zombie = Resurrected.itsAlive;
        } while (zombie != null);
    }
}
```

This program prints the following three lines

```
alive !!
finalize
alive !!
```

The program creates an object (`zombie`), does something with it, and makes sure it loses all references to it. Then, the garbage collector is activated, and all finalization code is run. As a result of that, the finalize method for `zombie` is called, which stores a reference to itself in a "global" variable. Although all references to the object were lost and the object already "died," it is herewith "resurrected," as we now have a new reference to the object. The second time we enter the loop, something is printed, and all references to `zombie` are again lost. This time something special happens, because Java calls the finalize only once. Resurrecting objects is not advisable, as it can be done only once anyway.

One last thing is that the Java language specification dictates that inside the finalize method, runtime exceptions can be thrown; however, as there is no one to catch them, any uncaught exceptions will therefore be ignored. In combination with the fact that the finalize method can be called by anyone, that statement should be relaxed a little bit. When called from the garbage collector, all uncaught runtime exceptions thrown from the finalize method will be ignored. This means, when called from the garbage collector, i.e., when the system decides to do garbage collection. If the garbage collector is called explicitly by the user, as is done above, uncaught exceptions are *not* ignored. Furthermore, when the finalize method is called from another place, uncaught exceptions will of course not be ignored either, as is shown in the following program

```
class Finalizer {
   void doSomething() {
      x=0;
      finalize();          // Java programs should NEVER call this
   }
   protected void finalize() {
      System.out.println("finalize");
      int x=0, y=4/x; // throws exception
   }
}
public class test {
   public static void main(String args[]) {
      Finalizer finalizer = new Finalizer();
      finalizer.doSomething();
   }
}
```

When executed, this program throws a runtime exception, and halts the program.

```
finalize
java.lang.ArithmeticException: / by zero
    at Finalizer.finalize(test.java:6)
    at Finalizer.doSomething(test.java:3)
    at test.main(test.java:13)
```

However, when run from the garbage collector, all uncaught exceptions are ignored.

19. Templates

Java does not have templates, although the language specification anticipates its use, and reserves the keyword `generic`. Having generic datastructures like the `vector` class in the `java.util` package is hardly a replacement for parameterized types. Namely, the vector class stores its elements as references to type `Object`. When inserting elements into a vector, and when retrieving them from it, the element needs to be converted into the actual type:

```
MyElement element = (MyElement)vector.elementAt(3);
```

The conversion is happening at run-time, and no compile-time check can be performed. The big advantage of a language that supports parameterized types, such as templates, is that it offers the combination of both an efficient implementation *and* static type checking.

Various ways of obtaining the same effects as parameterized types can be employed. Worst of all is the simple cut-and-paste method, where a copy of a specific class is used as an example, and all references to a given type (e.g., `int`) are replaced by another type (e.g., `float`). Of course, it becomes hard to keep track of the many different copies of the code. A better technique is to use a macro preprocessor, or even a simple text processing tool (such as the Unix tool *sed*). All specific instantiations of the "template" are then manually created (possibly using a tool like *make*). An example how this technique might work is:

```
class __TYPENAME__Vector {
    public __TYPENAME__Vector() { ... }
    public void addElement(__TYPE__ obj) { ... }
    public __TYPE__ elementAt(int index) { ... }
    ...
    __TYPE__ elements[];
}
```

The template instantiation script is the following:

```
cat $1 | sed "s/__TYPE__/$2/" | sed "s/__TYPENAME__/$3/" > $4
```

To generate an instantiation for the types int and float, the script is run twice:

```
instantiate.sh TypeVector.java int Int IntVector.java
instantiate.sh TypeVector.java float Float FloatVector.java
```

This generates two files, IntVector.java:

```
class IntVector {
    public IntVector() { ... }
    public void addElement(int obj) { ... }
    public int elementAt(int index) { ... }
    ...
    int elements[];
}
```

and FloatVector.java:

```
class FloatVector {
    public FloatVector() { ... }
    public void addElement(float obj) { ... }
    public float elementAt(int index) { ... }
    ...
    float elements[];
}
```

Until parameterized types are added to Java, this technique works OK, assuming appropriate makefile rules are provided for automatically regenerating the instantiations if we decide to update the original.

20. Incremental Compilation of Java Code

Advanced Java systems, such as interactive development environments or systems that want to perform some kind of reflective computation, will sooner or later need the capability to dynamically compile and load Java source code. Java applications have access to the Java compiler and can call the compiler and load the class. The following example creates a new Java class on the fly. The file is written in the current directory, and it implements the `printable` interface. While compiling this example, the compiler needs to be able to fully resolve all classes and interfaces. Therefore, as long as the new class implements an existing interface or extends an existing class, we can compile it and call it dynamically from the precompiled example. The test code is generated twice. The second time, the `print` method prints something different.

```java
import java.io.RandomAccessFile;

interface printable { void print(); }

class demo {
  public static void main(String args[]) {
    Class c;
    printable t;
    RandomAccessFile file;

    try {
      file = new RandomAccessFile("test.java", "rw");
      file.writeBytes("public class test implements printable {\n");
      file.writeBytes(" public void print() { \n");
      file.writeBytes(" System.out.println(\"foo\");\n");
      file.writeBytes(" }\n");
      file.writeBytes("}\n");
      file.close();
      c = DynamicLoader.load("test");
      try {
        t = (printable)c.newInstance();
        t.print();
      } catch (Exception e) { }

      file = new RandomAccessFile("test.java", "rw");
      file.writeBytes("public class test implements printable {\n");
      file.writeBytes(" public void print() { \n");
      file.writeBytes(" System.out.println(\"bar\");\n");
      file.writeBytes(" }\n");
      file.writeBytes("}\n");
      file.close();
      c = DynamicLoader.load("test");
      try {
        t = (printable)c.newInstance();
```

```
        t.print();
    } catch (Exception e) { }
} catch (Exception e) { }
}
}
```

For simplicity sake, no exceptions are being dealt with. Nor do we test if the current directory is writeable. When compiled and executed as java demo, this example prints

```
foo
bar
```

The example uses a special class, DynamicLoader. That class tries to find a Java file in the current directory (which is rather limited), and then tries to compile it. To compile the generated code, the standard javac compiler is used. If the file actually compiles (apparently it could also be found), it is loaded using a private class loader. Again, all thrown exceptions are ignored.

```
Import sun.tools.javac.Main;
class DynamicLoader {
    public static Class load(String classname) {
        String file[] = { classname+".java" };
        if (compiler.compile(file)) {
            try { return cl.loadClass(classname,true); }
            catch (Exception e) { }
        }
        return null;
    }
    static Main compiler = new Main(System.out, "javac");
    static DynamicClassLoader cl = new DynamicClassLoader();
}
```

The private class loader is only necessary to eliminate the class caching that the standard class loader does. Normally, when a class is loaded, and it has been loaded before, it may still be available in a cache kept by the class loader. Therefore, the second time a class is loaded, it is retrieved from the cache and not actually loaded from the file system. For this example, that behavior is not appropriate. That is why we use the following class loader. It ignores caches, and always loads the class from the current directory (too limited for general use, but appropriate for this example)

```java
import java.io.File;
import java.io.FileInputStream;

class DynamicClassLoader extends ClassLoader {
    public Class loadClass(String name, boolean resolve)
    throws java.lang.ClassNotFoundException {
        try {
            String fname = name + ".class";
            File file = new File(fname);
            if (!file.exists()) return null;
            FileInputStream f = new FileInputStream(fname);
            byte bytes[] = new byte[(int)file.length()];
            int n = f.read(bytes);
            Class c = defineClass(bytes,0,bytes.length);
            if (resolve) resolveClass(c);
            return c;
        } catch (Exception e) { }
        return null;
    }
}
```

The mechanism used in this example shows how classes can be "reloaded" into an already executing Java program. The approach does not work for applets, as applets cannot write files, and cannot use their own class loaders due to security reasons. Furthermore, the sun packages are not part of the standard Java classes, and are therefore not supported by browsers such as Netscape.

A limitation of this example is that the Java code is written to a file in the current directory, and the file is subsequently read again by the Java compiler (which itself will also write a class file in the current directory). However, the Java compiler can also be configured to read the Java code from a buffer and return the byte codes in another buffer, so that the class loader can load the class out of memory. In that case, no file access needs to be made. Actually, a class that performs this behavior (compile and load Java code out of memory), could have been included in the standard Java release (as is the case for Smalltalk, for instance). It would have allowed the development of much more dynamic and powerful applets.

CHAPTER
2

- The Design of AWT

- The Design of LTK

- LTK Components

- LTK Examples

LTK—
The Little
Toolkit

1. LTK, The Little Toolkit

LTK (the little toolkit) is a response to AWT (the Abstract Window Toolkit), which is part of the standard java API. The toolkit uses a more general approach to handling both the drawing of GUI elements and the handling of user events. It is easy to build your own widgets in LTK, because much of the drawing logic is encapsulated in specialized GUI components that know how to draw themselves.

Initial work on LTK commenced as part of a Ph.D. research project in the Netherlands around 1990. The toolkit has been designed mainly as a test case for an OO language called Procol [van den Bos & Laffra, 1989]. Its goal was to support the development of graphical user interfaces, 2D animation, and geographical information systems. It was immediately realized that the toolkit should be based on a "structured graphics" approach and support localized, efficient, and flicker-free drawing. Instead of needing to draw complex scenes, the user of the toolkit creates the appropriate components and simply tells them to move around, change color, or resize. The whole scene is redrawn automatically and incrementally. Having such a support structure in place, it is very easy to develop new graphical items, such as GUI widgets or easy-to-use layout managers.

Another complexity GUI developers may become involved with is the handling of enduser events. These events are typically created by pressing keys on the keyboard or by moving and pressing buttons of the mouse. The validity or target of these events is often limited to a given area on the screen. Unfortunately, most toolkits lose the connection between the event and the intended target. The software receives the event at a high level, and has to devote considerable attention to dispatching and handling these events. Most toolkits use an underlying window system to create many small windows, helping the software to locate the target of the event. Representing each widget by one or more actual windows comes at a price, though. Namely, each of the windows consumes some of the (often limited) window system resources. For complicated widgets, such as tables and spreadsheets, this strategy even breaks down, as the resulting widget simply is not efficient enough.

LTK does not use windows for any of its widgets. Rather, every widget occupies a symbolic area on the screen and is drawn inside another (real) window. Such lightweight widgets are commonly referred to as *gadgets*. In LTK, the widgets are added to a display list canvas, which also handles the events for the widget. A widget, like a software button, will normally register with its canvas for mouse button press events, but the canvas will only report them when they happen inside the button's own area. The button will give the canvas the name of a method to be called whenever the mouse press event occurs. Such a method is generally referred to as a callback method. Inside the body of the call-back method, the button would react by drawing a pressed down image of itself and by registering for both mouse motions and mouse button-up events. (See Figure 1.) This strategy allows the designer of the button widget to segment the logic of handling the events inside appropriate methods.

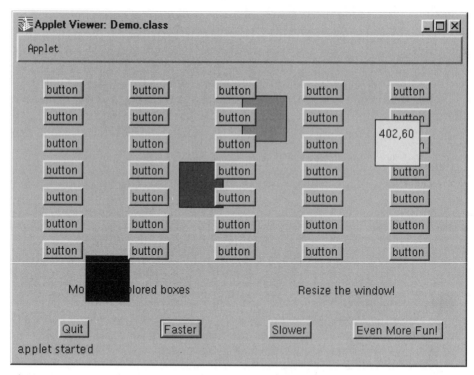

Figure 1. An LTK example, using buttons, labels, moving boxes, and tabbing.

Java does not support pointers and therefore does not support method pointers. A method pointer is a concept in C++ where the address of a method can be stored in a variable and used later to actually execute the method on an object directly. Section 16 in Chapter 1 contains a full description of implementing call-back methods in Java. The technique chosen in LTK uses interfaces and double dispatching to call objects when an event has occurred in which it has shown interest. The approach taken in AWT uses a special event handling method. Whenever a widget generates an event, the event handling method is called.

When a given event is not handled by the receiver, it is passed to its parent, until an ancestor is reached that is willing to handle it. The event-handling model in AWT has the implication that a user of AWT may have to define specialized classes. Their only function would be to serve as a container for a widget and translate the fixed protocol to one that makes more sense to the application. The alternative is the usage of one big if-then-else statement, determining which GUI element triggered a call to the event handler method. Using a design pattern (see [Gamma et. al., 1995]), such as the Command class pattern, may better structure the event handling process. However, it has the disadvantage of distributing the application logic over multiple units, possibly making it harder to maintain the event logic code.

Developing a GUI is difficult. Developing a good GUI *toolkit* is exponentially more difficult. In fact, it can be just as difficult as designing a multipurpose programming language, such as Java. Drawing a parallel with Smalltalk, the success of Java is not really based on the language as such. It is much more dependent on the functionality and ease of use of the supporting class libraries and development environment. The design of Java has been driven primarily by the requirement to use native widget sets. Adherence to the local look and feel was believed to be very important by one of the major partners of Javasoft. This, combined with an extreme time-pressure, lead to giving more priority to ensuring portability of AWT itself to multiple platforms such as UNIX/Motif, Win32, and MacOS. Low level commonalities, such as the java.awt.Graphics class, show up at a high level in the toolkit (in fact, in the Applet class). Some people on the Internet vocally observed that AWT must have been a haste job. There is some truth in that, considering the fact that the toolkit was put together in an amazingly short period of little more than two months (from October to December 1995). The AWT developers did a commendable job to develop a multiplatform toolkit that allows a person to write applications on one platform. When a Java application uses AWT, it virtually guarantees that it will run on all platforms directly supported by Java. If the AWT designers would have had the luxury of being able to develop a toolkit based on a different design, a more flexible product could have been the result. Perhaps AWT would have looked more like LTK, if Arthur van Hoff and Sami Shaio would have had the opportunity to develop their portable toolkit based on a lower level of window system abstraction.

The old Dutch saying, "De beste stuurlui staan aan wal" (literally "the best navigator is on the shore," or "being a Monday-morning quarterback") is often used to put the remarks of a critical spectator to a soccer game (the Dutch national pastime) into perspective. In the context of the ATW discussion, it translates into having a very easy job to comment on a toolkit that one was not involved with designing and implementing. I am aware of this, and I want to do a fair and impartial evaluation of AWT for this book. This book is not about AWT-bashing. Personally, I do believe that AWT will undoubtedly be replaced by another, more robust GUI toolkit. I do not expect it to be LTK in its current form. Instead, the LTK toolkit has been developed especially for this book as an educational instrument, and to prove that an alternative implementation may work just as well. In contrast to developing LTK as independent of AWT as possible, in my work with Morgan Stanley, we did some work on widgets that are real *extensions* to AWT. There we reused as much as possible of the existing AWT toolkit. For this book, I was able to take more academic freedom. Furthermore, the result may also be more interesting for the reader, as I assume the educational content to be of more interest. I hope that you will get somewhat of an insight into the complex task of GUI toolkit development, and also gain even more respect for Arthur and Sami.

2. The Design of AWT

AWT is based on native widgets (widgets available on the client's machine). Here we enter the religious realm. When developing a multiplatform toolkit, one is always given the choice between using native widgets or defining a platform-independent toolkit. AWT has chosen the first form, for instance, by using MS Windows buttons on Win32 and using Motif buttons on UNIX. (See Figure 2.)

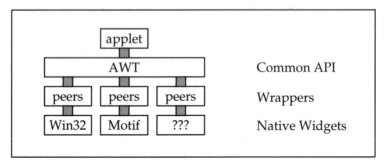

Figure 2. Design of the AWT toolkit.

In AWT, the widgets themselves are, therefore, part of the operating system hosting the java runtime system, and are not implemented and rendered in Java proper. The main reason for taking an approach such as this is the assumed inflexibility of the enduser to cope with a "hostile" GUI that an applet might otherwise have. There are a number of problems with the native widgets approach:

- Because the AWT toolkit is implemented using widgets that are available natively on multiple platforms, this automatically includes only those that are readily available on each of these platforms. This aspect is generally referred to as the "least common denominator" problem. Problems start when one wants to use a toolkit such as AWT for developing applications that require complex GUI layouts supported by notebooks, tabbed forms, 2D-graph drawings, or grid-based (spreadsheetlike) widgets. Developing an application then becomes tedious, as these "more advanced" widgets are not commonly available on all the different platforms. This is not really a problem for small applets such as the ones spicing up a WWW home page. However, it poses a direct limitation for "Java in the real world," such as a financial portfolio management system.

- In reality, the look and feel of toolkits is already converging. Windows 95 widgets and Motif widgets are very similar in appearance and behavior. In fact, the look and feel of Windows 95 is very different from Windows 3.1. However, not many people complain that they no longer know how to use the scrollbar when upgrading to Windows 95.

- A more serious problem is in the area of extensibility. When a user wants to develop a new widget, say a spreadsheet widget, a difficult problem arises. To which native platform/toolkit do we target this widget? AWT has no support for abstracting the look and feel of the native platform, therefore, the user has to develop a style that is in between all of the different targeted platforms. The result is that most of the applets that have been developed so far and those that implement new widgets do not share a common look and feel with each other. This seems to defeat the whole purpose of using native widget sets.

AWT does not provide abstractions for the support of native look and feel into their design. In contrast, LTK tries to separate policy from implementation, as proposed in the Design Patterns book [Gamma et. al., 1995]. Based on their extensive experience with building GUI toolkits and applications, the authors suggest the use of a WidgetFactory class to generate individual widgets, taking into account the toolkit that the user chooses. This makes it possible to change toolkits on the fly. LTK uses a similar approach, but does not actually use a WidgetFactory class to instantiate new widgets. Instead, widgets implicitly refer to the current GUIStyle instance being used. Examples could be MotifStyle, Win95Style, Win31Style, and others. The GUIStyle object can be used to delegate some responsibility, or to get style dependent information. For instance, the Button class in LTK uses the GUIStyle object to let it draw its background and to retrieve the appropriate color for its label. One GUIStyle implementation may draw a 3D look button, where others will simply draw a black rectangle. The button does not care. Now, when a developer creates a new widget with enhanced functionality (like a Table widget), a similar looking existing widget can be inspected, and its use of the GUIStyle can be copied and then modified.

Another argument for not using a WidgetFactory is that it is hard to extend existing widgets in the factory by subclassing. As the clients do not have direct access to the class definition of the individual widgets (they are simply returned an instance of a more abstract class), no subclass with modified behavior of it can be defined.

Separating out drawing policies is feasible to a large extent. However, separating out behavior is a lot less effective. For instance, in the case of the button class, there is one specific event that starts the selection: depressing a mouse button. From that moment on, two events can either activate (mouse button release) or cancel (mouse leaving the button area) the selection. When the selection is started, the button draws itself inverted as a visual feedback and when selected, it calls back the client to notify its activation. In any case, the button is then drawn in its normal state. Things get even more complicated when accelerators are being used. A button may be activated either by pressing the return key when it is highlighted or simply by pressing a certain key on the keyboard (like the character "y" for a button labeled "yes").

Therefore, LTK does abstract out the "look," but not the "feel" of widgets, because the required information exchange between individual widgets and the behavior manager would be defined by a complicated error-prone protocol. To capture the feel, a complete state-transition machine language would need to be designed and implemented—a task that has been tried out in previous research on which I have been involved but was quite unsuccessful at reaching an acceptable result. In practice, the behavior of "standard" widgets is almost the same on different platforms.

3. The Design of LTK

The LTK toolkit has been designed to be as simple as possible to use and understand. (See Figure 3.) The motto is: The fewer concepts the better. Actual drawing is avoided and abstracted as much as possible. Double buffering is naturally encapsulated within the toolkit, and the poor user is not left to worry about those kinds of basic things. The kind of complexity a novice user of Java/AWT is exposed to is unnecessary. AWT does not directly incorporate double buffering. Solutions for implementing double buffering are adhoc and not standardized, forming a hurdle when trying to reuse code between applets.

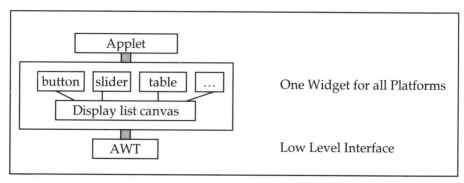

Figure 3. Design of the Little Toolkit

One of the most important aspects of object-oriented programming is finding the right abstractions for the right task. I personally feel that the designers of AWT did not choose the right abstractions in some cases, and in other cases unnecessarily closed the door for doing really interesting optimizations. This will probably always be the case for abstract window toolkits, and I am very much aware of the fact that a lot of people will not like the abstractions I have chosen for LTK. But, let's consider them for a while.

LTK is based on a layer of graphical objects, such as boxes, texts, and circles. Each graphical object communicates with a special display list manager. Unlike conventional graphical applications (and typical applets), there is no need to redraw the entire scene whenever one or more objects changes location or size. In general, redrawing such a scene can be quite difficult, especially when the scene gets complicated. In the case of LTK, when a graphical object moves, or resizes, it does not restore the whole scene by erasing the entire background and redraw all graphical components involved. Instead, it simply tells another object (a display list manager) that it moved to a new location. The display list manager will then erase only that part of the background that is damaged, and instruct only those graphicals that overlap with the damaged area to redraw themselves in the right order.

This setup makes it very easy to program animated scenes (such as complex objects moving around in an arbitrary complex screen). Note that these "animations" are quite different from the family of "waving Duke" and "bouncing heads" demos that come with the Java distribution. Those examples use bitmaps and produce an animated effect by drawing different bitmaps in a certain order. The problem there is that all possible scenes will have to be precomputed and stored in individual GIF files. Often, that is not possible. The approach used by LTK is more general and can be used to maintain any complicated 2D scene.

The display list behavior is encapsulated into two classes:

- The ltk.DisplayListCanvas class extends the canvas that is part of the Java AWT toolkit and adds the capabilities of a display list manager to it. It has methods for adding and removing graphicals to and from the scene. It also provides a method to react to the fact that a given graphical has moved. When that happens, the area involved will be repaired, using double buffering. Each graphical is told to draw itself in an off-screen graphics object, which is eventually copied to the canvas. Therefore, redrawing happens smoothly, without showing any flickering. The graphicals themselves are not even aware of this arrangement, and the canvas is free to either use double buffering or not. This separates this particular policy from the rest of the application, which is something software designers should always strive for.

- The ltk.Graphical class works in close symbiosis with the DisplayListCanvas. When a graphical is constructed, it adds itself to the display list, and when it is destroyed, it removes itself from the display list. When it moves, it notifies the display list, and it accepts orders to redraw itself at any given time. The Graphical class maintains an Area object that represents the area that the graphical occupies in the canvas, and the display list uses that object to determine whenever the graphical overlaps with a damaged area. The class Graphical is abstract, as it does not implement the "draw" method. Derived classes are supposed to implement this, as done by the Box, Label, and Button classes, for instance.

4. A Simple Example of Using LTK

The following class represents a rectangular object that knows how to draw itself, can be moved and resized, and will repair the rest of the screen when it changes size or position. The Box class is a subclass of Graphical. The constructor of the super class is passed the canvas and area to occupy initially. Each graphical object maintains a possible constraint on the way it can be moved and resized (more about this later). Furthermore, the Box class knows how to draw itself by filling a rectangle and drawing its outline.

```
public class Box extends Graphical {
    public Box(DisplayListCanvas canvas, int x, int y, int w, int h) {
        super(canvas, x, y, w, h);
        constraint = Constraint.None;
    }
    public void draw() {
        canvas.setColor(fill_color);
        canvas.fillRect(area.x, area.x, area.w, area.h);
        canvas.setColor(color);
        canvas.drawRect(area.x, area.x, area.w-1, area.h-1);
    }
};
```

Objects of type Box can be created and moved around to generate an animation, for instance. The users of Box objects will never have to do any drawing themselves. In fact, none of the LTK examples really do any drawing at all. They simply move graphical objects around. An example using this Box class is

```
Box box1 = new Box(canvas, 100, 75, 50, 50);
Box box2 = new Box(canvas, 200, 100, 50, 50);
while (true) {
    for (int x=0; x<300; x++) box2.move(x, box2.area.y);
    for (int x=300; x>0; x--) box2.move(x, box2.area.y);
}
```

This would create one box with another box bouncing from left to right on top of it. The scene is automatically redrawn by the underlying graphics system.

The rest of this chapter will investigate the different classes in the LTK toolkit and explain their design and implementation.

5. The LTK Classes

5.1 ltk.DisplayListCanvas

The DisplayListCanvas implements a display list of graphical elements. Graphicals can be added to a DisplayListCanvas, and whenever one of them moves, resizes, or is removed from the canvas, the DisplayListCanvas will notify the others to redraw themselves. The redrawing is optimized to redraw only the area that is damaged, and the drawing is done using double buffering, resulting in efficient and flicker-free redrawing.

The first statement that is contained in any LTK source file is the package statement, identifying the package that the classes in this file are a part of. Due to package scoping rules, the resulting compiled class file should also be contained in a directory called "ltk."

```
package ltk;
```

Second, the external packages accessed from this file are mentioned. As described in Section 4 in Chapter 1, it is not a good idea to use the "*" syntax for including multiple packages. It is better to explicitly name each class that is used from a particular package. This will make the code better to understand, as it is easier to determine exactly which external classes are being used by this class. While writing parts of LTK, including this code, I was too lazy though, and this style of importing slipped into the frozen version of LTK for this book.

```
import java.awt.*;
import java.applet.*;
import java.awt.image.*;
```

First of all, the DisplayListCanvas class is a subclass of java.awt.Canvas, allowing its instances to be added to applets and AWT frames.

```
public class DisplayListCanvas extends Canvas {
```

The LTK toolkit provides an LTKApplet class, a subclass of java.applet.Applet, which will automatically create a DisplayListCanvas instance, add the canvas to itself, and make the canvas available through an instance variable. The following constructor creates a display list canvas inside a java.applet.Applet class (or any of its subclasses), at the specified location relative in the parent, with specified dimension

```
public DisplayListCanvas(Applet applet, int w, int h) {
    frozen_level = 0;
    frozen_area = new Area();
```

The frozen area remembers the area that will need to be redrawn when the canvas eventually will be *unfrozen*. As long as the canvas is frozen, the variable `frozen_level` records the current nesting level of calls to methods `freeze()` and `unfreeze()`. Furthermore, while the canvas is frozen, and a certain graphical moves to a new location, the canvas is not repaired directly. Instead, the `frozen_area` is updated, to join with both the old and new area of the graphical. When, at some time, a call to `unfreeze` causes the canvas to be unfrozen (`frozen_level` becomes 0), the frozen area includes all the graphicals that were updated during the frozen state, and this area will now be repaired in the conventional manner.

As has been explained before, a graphical might be told to draw itself at any time. In that case its `draw()` method is called. For abstraction purposes (keeping the interfaces as lean as possible), the call is not passed to the area that is actually being repaired. In the case that the graphicals occupy a large area (as can be the case for ltk.Table), and the area being repaired is small, an optimization is possible. In that rare case, access to the repaired area is given by the display list canvas through the method `getRepairArea()`. The following variable is stored inside the canvas class, and a reference to it is returned, rather than creating a new temporary instance for each call that is made to `getRepairArea()`. Using an instance variable for this seems to be overkill, but we have to ensure that LTK is as lightweight as possible, as it is used by all applets and applications on top of it. Optimizations such as not generating any temporary objects may dramatically influence performance. Garbage collection is an ease of mind, but it does not come for free!

```
repair_area = new Area();
```

The following two variables cache the location and dimension of the canvas and provide an easy way to specify interest in events happening anywhere in the canvas, respectively

```
area = new Area(0, 0, w, h);
anywhere = new Area(-10000, -10000, 20000, 20000);
```

The event manager class does whatever its name suggests: It manages events and clients for the canvas object. Whenever a graphical registers itself with the canvas to receive certain events, the request is passed on to the event manager. When events arrive to the canvas, they are given to the event manager to dispatch to the appropriate graphical. The only reason for designing the event handling as such is to logically separate different behavior in the display list class. It enables us to encapsulate some interesting behavior (like motion compression) into the event manager class without bothering the canvas with it, and keep its design clean and simple.

```
event_manager = new EventManager();
```

The following statement sets the background color to light gray by calling a method defined in java.awt.Canvas (whose methods are automatically inherited)

```
setBackground(Color.lightGray);
```

Finally, there are the last few statements in the display list constructor. First, the identity of the applet to which this canvas belongs is stored for later use. In fact, currently, the only use is to be able to create a java.awt.Image off it, and we could have used the java.awt.Toolkit instead (by using something like getCurrentToolkit().getImage(…) defined in class java.awt.Component). Because the identity of the applet may come in handy later (when potentially subclassing the display list class), it is still remembered here, even though it causes a certain overhead. Planning for future inheritance is important also. Second, the canvas is repainted, by repairing its own area. Third and last, the focus is requested from AWT. This is where it gets a little hazy, as I still don't quite understand exactly the way focus handling works in AWT on all the different platforms. Just to be sure, the canvas class grabs the focus when it is created. This seems to work rather nicely on all X Windows servers, Windows 95, and Windows NT systems that I tested LTK on.

```
this.applet = applet;
    double_buffering = true;
    requestFocus();
}
```

An important role of the canvas object is to encapsulate and hide the existence of the java.awt.Graphics class altogether. As I argued before, the graphics class is an unnecessary complication, and it is amusing to pick up any introductory Java book and see what a hard time authors have trying to explain the concept of the Graphics class. At best, parallels with window systems such as the low level concept of the Device Context in MS Windows are given. Therefore, in LTK, only the display list canvas is aware of the existence of the Graphics class. We also abstract out the use of double buffering, and the following couple of statements take care of creating the required image and graphics instance. In current versions of AWT, the createImage call will return null, when the frame that contains the applet is not yet shown at the time of the call (which is the case when run as an application, using a main() routine. Every time the applet is redrawn, a check is made to see if an off-screen image and graphics already exist. Otherwise, they will be created. The following method initializes the buffer image and graphics to be used for double buffering

```
void initializeGraphics() {
    if (double_buffering) {
        if (buffer_graphics != null) return;
        buffer_image = applet.createImage(area.w, area.h);
        if (buffer_image == null) return;
        buffer_graphics = buffer_image.getGraphics();
    }
    else {
        buffer_graphics = getGraphics();
    }
```

The following two statements indicate some advanced use of double buffering. Namely, there are cases where a graphical represents a very complicated object, which takes a lot of time to draw (such as a complex 3D scene or a table with many cells). Ideally, the application would like to keep a carbon copy around of the generated drawing commands. Later, when the graphical needs to redraw itself, but the image has not changed at all due to the state of the underlying object that has not changed in the meantime, the graphical might use the carbon copy to efficiently copy it to the canvas. This is instead of actually redrawing the whole thing or even a portion of it again. See the ltk.Table class that utilizes this well-known (and here informally described) design pattern in its draw() method. Furthermore, see also methods setBufferImage(Image) and resetBufferImage() for usage of the following two variables

```
        original_buffer_image = buffer_image;
        original_buffer_graphics = buffer_graphics;
    }
```

After spending quite some time in the constructor of ltk.DisplayListCanvas, the first actual method we will look at is called by graphicals when they move, resize, or for any reason want to be repaired. An optimization is performed, after which the frozen area is updated, or a call is made to AWT to repaint the area indicated, whenever AWT thinks it is a good time.

```
public void repairArea(int x, int y, int w, int h)
{
    if (w<=0 || h<=0) return;
    if (frozen_level > 0)
        frozen_area.join(x, y, w, h);
    else
        repaint(x, y, w+2, h+2);        // update will be called
}
```

The next method in the display list canvas class is the most important one. It really forms the core of the ltk toolkit and certainly represents the gist of the toolkit. The `repaint()` method repaints the indicated area (retrieved from the clipping rectangle). When double buffering is used, everything is painted in an off-screen bitmap, after which that bitmap is copied to the requested Graphics. First of all, the area is erased. Then, the lowest graphical in the display list that overlaps with the area is told to draw itself, after which all other graphicals are inspected; finally, the top graphical is told to draw itself. Note that this algorithm is $O(n)$. Other algorithms are much more appropriate, such as the R-tree algorithm, a spatial data structure with $O(log\ n)$ performance.[1]

```
public synchronized void paint(Graphics graphics) {
    if (graphics == null) return;
    Rectangle rect = graphics.getClipRect();

    int x = rect.x, y = rect.y, w = rect.width, h = rect.height;
    if (!double_buffering) buffer_graphics = graphics;
    else initializeGraphics();

    buffer_graphics.setColor(getBackground());
    buffer_graphics.fillRect(x-2, y-2, w+4, h+4);    // erase

    repair_area.set(x, y, w, h);
    for (DisplayListElement e = first; e != null; e = e.next)
        if (e.graphical.visible &&
            !(x+w < e.graphical.area.x ||
              y+h < e.graphical.area.y ||
              x > e.graphical.area.x+e.graphical.area.w ||
              y > e.graphical.area.y+e.graphical.area.h))
            e.graphical.draw();
    if (double_buffering)
        graphics.drawImage(buffer_image, 0, 0, null); // copy
}
```

Comparing whether a graphical overlaps with the repaint area happens so often that the code doing the comparison is manually inlined here. Normally, we would call `e.graphical.area.overlaps(x,y,w,h)`. Declaring the

---

[1] One of the graduate students at Leiden University where I did a major part of my Ph.D., actually implemented such an algorithm in the Procol implementation of LTK. However, I never integrated that copy into my own source code, and his work got lost (as is the case with many graduate students' hard sweat). Sorry, Robert.

overlaps() method final and compiling the code with an optimization flag for the Java compiler, would do the same trick, in principle.

The update() method in a component always needs to be overridden, to disable the default behavior that erases the background of the window before paint() is called. The reason why repainting is so "complicated"—by adopting to the paint-repaint-update triad—is because it is convenient to have all drawing done by one single thread (the AWT callback thread). If threads would be allowed to do their own drawing, it is very difficult, if not impossible, to synchronize access to the display list and the screen. This is not really a limitation of Java, as we would have the same problem in every multithreaded graphics application. In fact, I have tried to make LTK work without calling repaint and allocating a graphics by calling getGraphics() on the canvas. The resulting graphics is remembered and all drawing is done inside it, right away, without ever involving the AWT repaint thread. This greatly enhances the effect for (more) real-time graphics, as drawing can happen on demand, and no unpredictable delay will be involved.

```
public void update(Graphics graphics)
{
    paint(graphics);
}
```

The following two methods are used for the "carbon copy" design pattern described previously (see also the ltk.Table class)

```
void setBufferImage(Image image) {
    if (image != null) {
        buffer_image = image;
        buffer_graphics = buffer_image.getGraphics();
    }
}
void resetBufferImage() {
    buffer_image = original_buffer_image;
    buffer_graphics = original_buffer_graphics;
}
```

Along with some utility functions to enable/disable the double buffering mode. Every time double buffering needs to be enabled, a new image is created in the current implementation. This is rather expensive since widgets constantly switch between enabling and disabling double buffering. In that case, an image has to be created (involving communication with the underlying window system), which is quickly disposed of. Such operations tend to be very expensive, and the canvas should really optimize such behavior, by keeping a reference to the image when the user disables double buffering. Therefore, when double buffering is enabled again, we can simply reuse a previously created image and graphics.

```
public void doubleBuffering(boolean do_double_buffering)
{
    if (double_buffering == do_double_buffering) return;
    double_buffering = do_double_buffering;
    if (buffer_graphics != null)
        buffer_graphics.dispose();
    buffer_graphics = null;
}
```

The following two utility functions create an image and form a shortcut for repairing a given area

```
public Image createImage(int w, int h) {
    return applet.createImage(w, h);
}
public void repairArea(Area area)
{
    repairArea(area.x, area.y, area.w, area.h);
}
```

The current implementation of the display list is a doubly linked list (quick traversal from bottom to top and quick removal of objects in the middle). Note that the implementation uses no optimization at all. In case we remove objects from the list or a given graphical needs to be moved to the bottom or top of the display list, using a hash function to find targets may result in a faster algorithm. An alternative to using a hash function is to keep a reference to the display list element inside each graphical. Now, with every function that used to require a search in the display list, the graphical has to provide the ID of its display list element, removing the need for any search at all (at the cost of one extra reference per graphical). Finally, considering the close cooperation between a graphical and its display list element, it would make sense to merge the two classes and move the instance variables and methods from the display list element into the graphical. Then, graphicals and display list elements would be one and the same object. We lose some flexibility, though. In conclusion, many design considerations are available for something as simple as a display list.

The "normal" use of the display list, during repainting of a given area will not benefit from any optimizations as discussed previously, such as merging class definitions or using a hash function. Namely, in order to determine if an object overlaps, we have to visit *each* object explicitly and inquire if it overlaps with the area or not. As explained before, a potentially more successful optimization for that kind of search would be to use a spatial data structure.

The following two methods serve to add and remove graphicals to or from the display list. When a graphical is added, it is added on top of all other already added graphicals. All edge conditions need to be taken care of: for instance, when the list is empty; a graphical is added; or an element is removed if it was the first or the last of the list, in addition to a reference to the first element. When an element is removed from the display list, a check is made to see if the object is in the list at all. In this case, we should really throw an exception. Furthermore, to enable the display list to quickly add a new graphical, a reference to the last element in the list is kept. Finally, when a graphical is removed from the display list, the area it currently occupies will be repaired.

```
public void addGraphical(Graphical graphical) {
    DisplayListElement element = new DisplayListElement();
    element.graphical = graphical;
    if (last != null) last.next = element
    element.next = null
    element.previous = last;
    last = element;
    if (first == null) first = element;
}
public void removeGraphical(Graphical graphical) {
    DisplayListElement e = findGraphical(graphical);
    if (e == null) return;
    if (e.previous == null) first = e.next;
    else e.previous.next = e.next;
    if (e.next == null) last = e.previous;
    else e.next.previous = e.previous;
    repairArea(e.graphical.area);
}
```

Two other display list element maintenance functions move a graphical to the top or the bottom of the display list. No methods are provided for moving graphicals up or down relative to their current location.

```
public void raiseGraphical(Graphical graphical) {
    DisplayListElement e = findGraphical(graphical);
    if (e == null) return;
    if (e.next == null) return;
    freeze();
    removeGraphical(e.graphical); // remove graphical from middle
```

```
        addGraphical(e.graphical);  // and add graphical on top
        unFreeze();
    }
    public void lowerGraphical(Graphical graphical) {
        DisplayListElement target = findGraphical(graphical);
        if (target.previous == null) return;
        target.previous.next = target.next;
        if (target.next != null) target.next.previous = target.previous;
        if (target == last) last = target.previous;
        target.previous = null;
        target.next = first;
        first = target;
    }
```

The following two methods freeze and unfreeze the display list. During the frozen state nothing is drawn. A call to `freeze()` freezes the canvas, until the matching call to `unfreeze()` is made. At that point, all pending draw calls will be made. Calls to `freeze()` and `unFreeze()` can be nested.

```
    public void freeze () {
        if (frozen_level == 0)
            frozen_area.set(0, 0, 0, 0); // initialize area
        frozen_level++;
    }
    public void unFreeze () {
        if (frozen_level == 0) return; // throw exception?
        frozen_level--;
        if (frozen_level == 0)
            repairArea(frozen_area); // repair area
    }
```

Below is a method that finds the corresponding display list element for a given graphical. This method could be enhanced with a hash function.

```
    private DisplayListElement findGraphical(Graphical graphical) {
        DisplayListElement e;
        for (e = first; e != null; e = e.next)
            if (e.graphical == graphical)
                break;
        return e; // if not found, throw exception?
    }
```

Whenever the applet or application is resized, the following method is called by the AWT toolkit. When double buffering is enabled, the corresponding off-screen image may no longer be large enough, in which case we create a new one. The current area is cached in a special instance variable, and finally, the reshape method of the superclass is called with the same parameters.

```
public void reshape(int x, int y, int width, int height) {
    if (double_buffering && (width > area.w || height > area.h)) {
        buffer_image = applet.createImage(width, height);
        if (buffer_image != null)
            buffer_graphics = buffer_image.getGraphics();
        original_buffer_image = buffer_image;
        original_buffer_graphics = buffer_graphics;
    }
    area.set(x, y, width, height);
    super.reshape(x, y, width, height);
}
```

In addition to encapsulating a display list, the display list canvas class also manages events for clients that are interested in events that occur in a certain area. The client has to implement the CallBackable interface, and identify the method number to be called when the event with the given type actually occurs in the supplied area. To simplify the design, the actual management of the clients is implemented in a separate class. This class also takes care of mapping a given event to its intended target.

```
public void addClient(CallBackable client, int callback_method,
                                  Area area, int type) {
    event_manager.addClient(client, callback_method, area, type);
}
public void removeClient(CallBackable client, int callback_method,
                                  Area area, int type) {
    event_manager.removeClient(client, callback_method, area, type);
}
public boolean handleEvent(Event e) {
    event_manager.dispatchEvent(e);
    return true;
}
public Event getLastEvent() {
    return event_manager.getLastEvent();
}
```

When graphicals are told to redraw themselves, they may be interested in knowing what area is currently being repaired by the canvas. This method returns the area that is currently being repaired.

```java
public Area getRepairArea() {
    return repair_area;
}
```

The following collection of methods provide an abstraction layer that hides the existence of the java.awt.Graphics class altogether.

```java
public void setFont(Font f) {
    buffer_graphics.setFont(f);
}
public void setColor(Color color) {
    buffer_graphics.setColor(color);
}
public void drawString(String s, int x, int y) {
    buffer_graphics.drawString(s, x, y);
}
public void drawLine(int x1, int y1, int x2, int y2) {
    buffer_graphics.drawLine(x1, y1, x2, y2);
}
public void drawRaisedRect(int x, int y, int width, int height) {
    buffer_graphics.draw3DRect(x, y, width, height, true);
}
public void drawSunkenRect(int x, int y, int width, int height) {
    buffer_graphics.draw3DRect(x, y, width, height, false);
}
public void fillRaisedRect(int x, int y, int width, int height) {
    buffer_graphics.fill3DRect(x, y, width, height, true);
}
public void fillSunkenRect(int x, int y, int width, int height) {
    buffer_graphics.fill3DRect(x, y, width, height, false);
}
public void fillRect(int x, int y, int width, int height) {
    buffer_graphics.fillRect(x, y, width, height);
}
public void drawRect(int x, int y, int width, int height) {
    buffer_graphics.drawRect(x, y, width, height);
}
```

```
    public void fillRoundRect(int x, int y, int width, int height,
                                    int arcWidth, int arcHeight) {
        buffer_graphics.fillRoundRect(x, y, width, height,
                                    arcWidth, arcHeight);
    }
    public void drawRoundRect(int x, int y, int width, int height,
                                    int arcWidth, int arcHeight) {
        buffer_graphics.drawRoundRect(x, y, width, height,
                                    arcWidth, arcHeight);
    }
    public void drawPolygon(.Polygon polygon) {
        buffer_graphics.drawPolygon(polygon);
    }
    public void fillPolygon(int xpoints[], int ypoints[], int npoints) {
        buffer_graphics.fillPolygon(xpoints, ypoints, npoints);
    }
    public void fillPolygon(Polygon polygon) {
        buffer_graphics.fillPolygon(polygon);
    }
    public void drawImage(Image image, int x, int y) {
        if (image != null)
            buffer_graphics.drawImage(image, x, y, null);
    }
    public void flush() {
        try { java.lang.Thread.sleep(40); }
        catch (InterruptedException e) { }
    }
```

Finally, there are some instance variables that are either part of the public or the protected interface

```
    public Area area;
    public Area anywhere;
    public Area repair_area;
    protected EventManager event_manager;
    protected DisplayListElement first, last;
    protected int frozen_level;
    protected Area frozen_area;
    protected Applet applet;
```

```
    protected Image buffer_image;
    protected Graphics buffer_graphics;
    protected Image original_buffer_image;
    protected Graphics original_buffer_graphics;
    protected boolean double_buffering;
};
```

In the same file, the following nonpublic class is declared, making it only visible to classes of the same package, and not to any class outside of LTK.

```
class DisplayListElement {
    Graphical graphical;
    DisplayListElement previous;
    DisplayListElement next;
};
```

5.2 Class ltk.Graphical

This class forms the most important class that communicates with the display list canvas class. Most of the useful classes in LTK are derived from this class, including all widgets and basic graphical components. Each graphical exports three instance variables, indicating the area that the graphical occupies in its canvas, whether it is visible or not, and what kind of resize constraints are relevant for this graphical.[2]

```
public class Graphical {
    public Area area;
    public boolean visible = true;
    public int constraint = Constraint.None;
```

The constructor is very basic. It adds the graphical to whatever canvas is passed, it initializes the area, and set its color and line width (two minimal attributes assumed common enough to be placed this high in the inheritance tree).

```
    public Graphical(DisplayListCanvas canvas,int x,int y,int w,int h) {
        this.canvas = canvas;
        area = new Area(x, y, w, h);
        color = Color.black;
        line_width = 0;
        canvas.addGraphical(this);
    }
```

---

[2] Admittedly, there is an inconsistency in the design here, as accessor functions should have been used. However, access to these variables happens so often that they are part of the public interface.

A graphical can be removed from its canvas. After the graphical is removed, the canvas will repair the area involved. When many objects are removed in succession, it makes sense to freeze the canvas first, and unfreeze it after all graphicals have been removed from the canvas. The method to remove the graphical follows.

```
public void remove() {
    canvas.removeGraphical(this);
    canvas = null;
}
```

The following method could have been declared fully abstract, as it does not have an implementation and pure instances of Graphical will never be created.

```
public void draw() { }
```

In JDK 1.0, there was no possibility to set the line width when drawing lines, polygons, arcs, and so on. Although all underlying window systems have provisions for supporting multiple line widths, it was found hard to implement consistently in a more abstract layer. Of course, the result is that the question "How do I draw thick lines in Java?" easily made it to the top of the Java frequently-asked questions lists; therefore, a lot of people resort to adhoc solutions, such as using filled polygons (see also the ltk.Line class).

```
public void setLineWidth(int line_width) {
    if (this.line_width != line_width) {
        this.line_width = line_width;
        update();
    }
}
public void setColor(Color color) {
    if (this.color != color) {
        this.color = color;
        update();
    }
}
```

Graphicals can be moved to the top or the bottom of the display list. Currently, there is not much freedom to move objects up or down the display list by smaller steps.

```
public void lower () {
    canvas.lowerGraphical(this);
}
public void raise () {
    canvas.raiseGraphical(this);
}
```

The following methods are available to move or resize a graphical. Moving is done either absolutely or incrementally. The latter form allows for a simple, animated behavior as is used in the "Towers of Hanoi" example that comes with LTK. One could imagine other forms of animated motion behavior, using tricks from animated cartoons (anticipation, overemphasized deformation of objects, and laws of physics, such as inertia).

```
public void move(int x, int y) {
    if (x != area.x || y != area.y) reset(x, y, area.w, area.h);
}
public void move(int x, int y, int increment) {
    int dx = (x > area.x) ? increment : (x < area.x) ? -increment : 0;
    int dy = (y > area.y) ? increment : (y < area.y) ? -increment : 0;
    for (;;) {
        if (dx > 0 && area.x + dx >= x) break;
        if (dy > 0 && area.y + dy >= y) break;
        if (dx < 0 && area.x + dx <= x) break;
        if (dy < 0 && area.y + dy <= y) break;
        move(area.x + dx, area.y + dy);
        canvas.flush();
    }
    move(x, y);
}
public void resize(int w, int h) {
    if (w != area.w || h != area.h) reset(area.x, area.y, w, h);
}
```

The reset method is the most important method in ltk.Graphical. It makes certain that the graphical will actually change size or position, synchronize with the canvas, and perform smart repairing of the graphical's old and new areas. When the old and new areas do not overlap, the old area is repaired first followed by the repair of the new area. This is to prevent a repaint of a large area in case the object moves far away. If the old and new areas do overlap, the areas are merged, and the joint area is redrawn. This is to prevent a graphical being drawn twice as a result of one single move or resize. In both cases, the area is reset, taking the current resize constraint into account. This method returns true when the object is actually resized or moved (depending on the constraint) and false otherwise.

```java
public boolean reset(int x, int y, int w, int h) {
    if (x == area.x && y == area.y && w == area.w && h == area.h)
        return false;                        // nothing changes?
    synchronized (canvas) {
        if (area.x + area.w < x || area.y + area.h < y ||
                        x + w < area.x || y + h < area.y) {
            int oldx = area.x;
            int oldy = area.y;
            int oldw = area.w;
            int oldh = area.h;
            setConstrainedArea(x, y, w, h, constraint);
            // return false when nothing changed
            if (!(x==area.x && y==area.y && w==area.w && h==area.h))
              return false;
            canvas.repairArea(oldx, oldy, oldw, oldh);
            canvas.repairArea(area.x, area.y, area.w, area.h);
        }
        else {
            int minx = (area.x < x) ? area.x : x;
            int miny = (area.y < y) ? area.y : y;
            int maxx = (area.x+area.w > x+w) ? area.x+area.w : x+w;
            int maxy = (area.y+area.h > y+h) ? area.y+area.h : y+h;
            setConstrainedArea(x, y, w, h, constraint);
            // return false when nothing changed
            if (!(x==area.x && y==area.y && w==area.w && h==area.h))
                return false;
            canvas.repairArea(minx, miny, maxx-minx+1, maxy-miny+1);
        }
    }
    return true;
}
```

The following (nonpublic) method is used to compute the new area for a graphical, using the given resize constraint. Resize constraints are used to influence the layout algorithm in the layout managers. See also the LTK layout example.

```
void setConstrainedArea(int x,int y, int w,int h, int constraint) {
    if (constraint != Constraint.None) {
        if ((constraint & Constraint.Left) != 0)
            w = area.w;
        if ((constraint & Constraint.Right) != 0) {
            x = x + w - area.w;
            w = area.w;
        }
        if ((constraint & Constraint.Top) != 0)
            h = area.h;
        if ((constraint & Constraint.Bottom) != 0) {
            y = y + h - area.h;
            h = area.h;
        }
        if ((constraint & Constraint.FixedWidth) != 0)
            w = area.w;
        if ((constraint & Constraint.FixedHeight) != 0)
            h = area.h;
        if ((constraint & Constraint.FixedSize) != 0) {
            x = x + (w - area.w)/2;
            y = y + (h - area.h)/2;
            w = area.w;
            h = area.h;
        }
        if ((constraint & Constraint.Centered) != 0) {
            x = x + (w - area.w)/2;
            y = y + (h - area.h)/2;
            w = area.w;
            h = area.h;
        }
    }
    area.set(x, y, w, h);
}
```

The following method simply redraws the graphical. Note that calling draw
directly will not work for two reasons. If double buffering is used, the graphical
may draw somewhere, but the drawing will never be actually copied to the
screen. Furthermore, if the graphical is partially obscured by other graphicals,
they will have to be redrawn also. There is no way for a graphical to find out

who obscures it, so the canvas needs to be involved. In retrospect, the name of this method may be a bad choice (as it is used in the Component class already). However, it is mainly used inside graphicals and their subclasses. There is normally no need for external classes to call update on a graphical. This makes it a candidate for making it `protected` instead of `public`.

```
public void update() {
    canvas.repairArea(area);
}
```

The following accessor functions set the constraint and visibility attributes of a graphical. When the visibility attribute is set to false, the object will not be drawn the next time the display list canvas repairs an area. Layout managers can set the visibility for all the children they manage, and that technique is made use of in the notebook widget. When the notebook switches to another page, all graphicals on the current page are made invisible, and all graphicals on the new page are made visible. Of course, the canvas is frozen before doing all this, and unfrozen when the notebook handles all graphicals.

```
public void setConstraint(int c) {
    constraint = c;
    update();
}
public void setVisibility(boolean mode) {
    visible = mode;
    update();
}

protected Color color;
protected int line_width;
protected DisplayListCanvas canvas;
};
```

5.3 Class ltk.Constraint

As described above, each graphical has its own resize constraint. The following class describes the kind of constraints that are appropriate

```
public class Constraint {

    public static final short None = 0;
    public static final short Left = 1;
    public static final short Right = 2;
    public static final short Top = 4;
    public static final short Bottom = 8;
```

```
    public static final short FixedWidth = 16;
    public static final short FixedHeight = 32;
    public static final short FixedSize = 48;
    public static final short Centered = 64;

public static Graphical setNone(Graphical g)
    { return set(g,None); }
    public static Graphical setLeft(Graphical g)
    { return set(g,Left); }
    public static Graphical setRight(Graphical g)
    { return set(g,Right); }
    public static Graphical setTop(Graphical g)
    { return set(g,Top); }
    public static Graphical setBottom(Graphical g)
    { return set(g,Bottom); }
    public static Graphical setFixedWidth(Graphical g)
    { return set(g,FixedWidth); }
    public static Graphical setFixedHeight(Graphical g)
    { return set(g,FixedHeight); }
    public static Graphical setFixedSize(Graphical g)
    { return set(g,FixedSize); }
    public static Graphical setCentered(Graphical g)
    { return set(g,Centered); }

    public static Graphical set(Graphical g, short constraint) {
        g.constraint = constraint; return g;
    }

};
```

The latter set of methods are actually utility functions which provide short-writes when graphicals are created and directly added to a layout. An example is given here

```
Label label1, label2;
new VerticalLayout(
    label1 = new Label(canvas, "left aligned"),
    label2 = new Label(canvas, "right aligned")
);
label1.setConstraint(Constraint.setLeft);
label2.setConstraint(Constraint.setRight);
```

which is functionally equivalent to, yet much more verbose than.

```
new VerticalLayout(
    Constraint.setLeft(new Label(canvas, "left aligned")),
    Constraint.setRight(new Label(canvas, "right aligned"))
);
```

5.4 Class ltk.Area

This class represents a rectangle area. Compatible to, yet simpler than, java.awt.Rectangle.

```java
public class Area {
    public int x, y, w, h;
    public Area(int x, int y, int w, int h) { set(x, y, w, h); }
    public Area(Area orig) { set(orig.x, orig.y, orig.w, orig.h); }
    public Area() { set(0, 0, 0, 0); }
    public void set(int x_,int y_,int w_,int h_){x=x_;y=y_;w=w_;h=h_;}
    public void set(Area a) { set(a.x, a.y, a.w, a.h); }
    public void join(int x, int y, int w, int h) {
        int x_min = Math.min(this.x, x);
        int y_min = Math.min(this.y, y);
        int x_max = Math.max(this.x+this.w, x+w);
        int y_max = Math.max(this.y+this.h, y+h);
        set(x_min, y_min, x_max-x_min, y_max-y_min);
    }
    public void join(Area a) { join(a.x, a.y, a.w, a.h); }
    public boolean inside(int px, int py) {
        return (px >= x && px <= x+w && py >= y && py <= y+h);
    }
    public static boolean inside(int px,int py,int x,int y,int w,int h){
        return (px >= x && px <= x+w && py >= y && py <= y+h);
    }
    public boolean outside(int px, int py) {
        return (px < x || px > x+w || py < y || py > y+h);
    }
    public boolean overlaps(int x, int y, int w, int h) {
        if (this.x > x+w) return false;
        if (this.x+this.w < x) return false;
        if (this.y > y+h) return false;
        if (this.y+this.h < y) return false;
        return true;
    }
};
```

5.5 Class ltk.Label

This class is one of the simplest graphicals provided with LTK. It implements a simple GUI component that displays a single-line label,[3] using the currently set GUI style.

```
public class Label extends Graphical {
```

There are three different ways of creating a new label object. The first form is typically used when the label is explicitly placed and sized inside a canvas and no layouts are used. The second form is similar but is useful for placing tags on a graph, for instance, when only the [x, y] coordinates are known. The third form is primarily for labels that are used in a layout, because it properly resizes and moves the label to the correct location.

```
    public Label(DisplayListCanvas canvas, int x, int y,
                                int w, int h, String label) {
        super(canvas, x, y, w, h);
        init(canvas, x, y, w, h, label);
    }
    public Label(DisplayListCanvas canvas, String label) {
        super(canvas, 0, 0, 0, 0);
        init(canvas, 0, 0, 0, 0, label);
        reset(10, 10, text_width, text_height);
    }
    public Label(DisplayListCanvas canvas, int x, int y, String label) {
        super(canvas, x, y, 0, 0);
        init(canvas, x, y, 0, 0, label);
        reset(x, y, text_width, text_height);
    }
```

Each of the three constructors uses the following initializer function. This function sets the label and initializes its color and font. The default GUI style is retrieved and cached locally. Notice that this method may suffer from the potential constructor behavior mentioned in Section 15 of Chapter 1. Namely, when a subclass of Label is defined that implements its own init method, the following init method will never be called. Instead, in the constructor mentioned above, the overridden version will be called. It is clear from the definition of the ltk.Label class that it was never the intention for an overridden init method to be called.

---

[3] Turning this widget into a multiline label is an exercise that is left to the reader.

```
public void init(String label) {
    this.label = new String(label);
    color = java.awt.Color.black;
    setStyle(GUIStyle.getDefaultStyle());
    setFont(gui_style.getLabelFont());
}
```

The following accessor functions set some attributes of the label, like its GUI style, the label text, and the font used to display the label

```
public void setStyle(GUIStyle style) {
    gui_style = style;
    setFont(gui_style.getLabelFont());
}
public void setLabel(String label) {
    this.label = new String(label);
    setFont(font);
    reset(area.x, area.y, text_width, text_height);
}
public void setFont(java.awt.Font font) {
    this.font = font;
    java.awt.FontMetrics fm = canvas.getFontMetrics(font);
    if (fm != null) {
        text_width = fm.stringWidth(label);
        text_height = fm.getAscent();
    }
    update();
}
```

Finally, the draw method is used to, you guessed it, draw the label. This method should only be called by the display list canvas, as the order and timing of drawing may be of importance. This method could be made protected (or local to the package) in class ltk.Graphical, but I was not sure if I would close the door for later extensions from outside of its subclasses, or even this package.

```
public void draw() {
    canvas.setColor(color);
    canvas.setFont(font);
    canvas.drawString(label, area.x + (area.w-text_width)/2 + 2,
            area.y + area.h - (area.h-text_height)/2 - 1);
}
```

```
    GUIStyle gui_style;
    String label;
    java.awt.Font font;
    int text_width, text_height;
};
```

5.6 Class ltk.EventManager

The event manager class abstracts the entire management of event handling for the display list canvas class. It allows for event clients to be added and removed, and dispatches events to the appropriate client, when they come in from the canvas. Basically, this class is nothing more than a glorified linked list (for managing the clients), enhanced with a big if-then-else statement (for dispatching the event). Putting this behavior in a separate class keeps the display list canvas class a lot simpler and localizes the logic. It allowed me to transparently implement *motion compression* (explained later), without the display list canvas ever being aware of this happening.

This class uses the java.awt.Event class, and initializes all event queues to null. Java initializes all object references to null, so these assignments are not really necessary, but they add to the readability of the constructor.

```
import java.awt.Event;
class EventManager {
    EventManager() {
        EnterNotifyQueue = null;
        LeaveNotifyQueue = null;
        KeyPressQueue = null;
        KeyReleaseQueue = null;
        ButtonPressQueue = null;
        ButtonReleaseQueue = null;
        MotionNotifyQueue = null;
        motion_compressor = new MotionCompressor();
    }
```

The following two methods either add an event client or remove it from this event manager. In the case of adding a new client, a node for it is created, and it is prepended to the appropriate event queue. For efficiency reasons, each type of event has its own queue, reducing the amount of time the event handler has to spend in locating a client when a certain event comes in. Because new clients are added to the front of the event queue, they become the primary target for events. Therefore, for instance, the last client that was added and who happens to solicit for key press events anywhere in the canvas, will in practice have a full grab of the keyboard.

```
synchronized void addClient(CallBackable client,
                                  int callback_method,
                                  Area area, int type) {
    EventClient e = new EventClient(client, callback_method, area);
    switch (type) {
        case Event.MOUSE_ENTER :
            e.next = EnterNotifyQueue; EnterNotifyQueue=e;
            break;
        case Event.MOUSE_EXIT :
            e.next = LeaveNotifyQueue; LeaveNotifyQueue=e;
            break;
        case Event.KEY_ACTION :
        case Event.KEY_PRESS :
            e.next = KeyPressQueue; KeyPressQueue=e;
            break;
        case Event.KEY_RELEASE :
        case Event.KEY_ACTION_RELEASE :
            e.next = KeyReleaseQueue; KeyReleaseQueue=e;
            break;
        case Event.MOUSE_DOWN :
            e.next = ButtonPressQueue; ButtonPressQueue=e;
            break;
        case Event.MOUSE_UP :
            e.next = ButtonReleaseQueue; ButtonReleaseQueue=e;
            break;
        case Event.MOUSE_DRAG :
        case Event.MOUSE_MOVE :
            e.next = MotionNotifyQueue; MotionNotifyQueue=e;
    }
}
synchronized void removeClient(CallBackable client,
                                  int callback_method,
                                  Area area, int type) {
    EventClient e;
    switch (type) {
        case Event.MOUSE_ENTER :
            e = EnterNotifyQueue;
            if (e == null) break;
```

```
    if (e.client == client && e.area == area) {
        EnterNotifyQueue = EnterNotifyQueue.next;
    }
    else {
        while (e!=null && e.next!=null) {
          if (e.next.client == client && e.next.area == area) {
            e.next = e.next.next;
            break;
          }
          e = e.next;
        }
    }
    break;
case Event.MOUSE_EXIT :
    e = LeaveNotifyQueue;
    if (e == null) break;
    if (e.client == client && e.area == area) {
        LeaveNotifyQueue = LeaveNotifyQueue.next;
    }
    else {
        while (e!=null && e.next!=null) {
          if (e.next.client == client && e.next.area == area) {
            e.next = e.next.next;
            break;
          }
          e = e.next;
        }
    }
    break;
case Event.KEY_ACTION :
case Event.KEY_PRESS :
    e = KeyPressQueue;
    if (e == null) break;
    if (e.client == client && e.area == area) {
        KeyPressQueue = KeyPressQueue.next;
    }
    else {
        while (e!=null && e.next!=null) {
```

```
             if (e.next.client == client && e.next.area == area) {
                e.next = e.next.next;
                break;
             }
             e = e.next;
          }
      }
      break;
   case Event.KEY_RELEASE :
   case Event.KEY_ACTION_RELEASE :
      e = KeyReleaseQueue;
      if (e == null) break;
      if (e.client == client && e.area == area) {
         KeyReleaseQueue = KeyReleaseQueue.next;
      }
      else {
         while (e!=null && e.next!=null) {
            if (e.next.client == client && e.next.area == area) {
               e.next = e.next.next;
               break;
            }
            e = e.next;
         }
      }
      break;
   case Event.MOUSE_DOWN :
      e = ButtonPressQueue;
      if (e == null) break;
      if (e.client == client && e.area == area) {
         ButtonPressQueue = ButtonPressQueue.next;
      }
      else {
         while (e!=null && e.next!=null) {
            if (e.next.client == client && e.next.area == area) {
               e.next = e.next.next;
               break;
            }
            e = e.next;
```

```
                }
            }
            break;
        case Event.MOUSE_UP :
            e = ButtonReleaseQueue;
            if (e == null) break;
            if (e.client == client && e.area == area) {
                ButtonReleaseQueue = ButtonReleaseQueue.next;
            }
            else {
                while (e!=null && e.next!=null) {
                    if (e.next.client == client && e.next.area == area) {
                        e.next = e.next.next;
                        break;
                    }
                    e = e.next;
                }
            }
            break;
        case Event.MOUSE_DRAG :
        case Event.MOUSE_MOVE :
            e = MotionNotifyQueue;
            if (e == null) break;
            if (e.client == client && e.area == area) {
                MotionNotifyQueue = MotionNotifyQueue.next;
            }
            else {
                while (e!=null && e.next!=null) {
                    if (e.next.client == client && e.next.area == area) {
                        e.next = e.next.next;
                        break;
                    }
                    e = e.next;
                }
            }
    }
}
```

The following method is called by the canvas whenever an event is dispatched to it (AWT calling its `handleEvent` method). Basically, the following method takes the event, determines the type of the event, finds the appropriate event queue (while handling a bug in AWT), and calls another function to do the actual dispatching. Because graphicals are implemented as gadgets and not as physical windows (e.g., subclass of java.awt.Component), there are no enter and leave events generated for them. Therefore, when a mouse motion event arrives, this method checks to see if it crossed the boundary of a given graphical, and if there is a client waiting to be notified of this event.

```
void dispatchEvent(Event event) {
    if (event == null || motion_compressor.needsCompression(event))
        return;
    EventClient target;
    last_event = event;
    if (event.id == Event.MOUSE_MOVE ||
            event.id == Event.MOUSE_DRAG ||
            event.id == Event.MOUSE_ENTER ||
                        event.id == Event.MOUSE_EXIT) {
        if (event.id == Event.MOUSE_ENTER) {
            oldx = -1000000;
            oldy = -1000000;
        }
        else if (event.id != Event.MOUSE_EXIT) {
            target = EnterNotifyQueue;
            while (target != null) {
                if ( ((Graphical)target.client).visible &&
                    target.area != null &&
                    target.area.outside(oldx, oldy) &&
                        target.area.inside(event.x, event.y)) {
                  if (target.client.activateCallback(target.method_nr))
                    break;
                }
                target = target.next;
            }
        }
        if (event.id == Event.MOUSE_EXIT) {
            oldx = -1000000;
            oldy = -1000000;
        }
```

```
if (event.id != Event.MOUSE_ENTER) {
    target = LeaveNotifyQueue;
    while (target != null) {
        if ( ((Graphical)target.client).visible &&
                            target.area != null &&
            target.area.inside(oldx, oldy) &&
                target.area.outside(event.x, event.y)) {
            if (target.client.activateCallback(target.method_nr))
                break;
        }
        target = target.next;
    }
}
oldx = event.x;
oldy = event.y;
}
target = null;
switch (event.id) {
    case Event.MOUSE_ENTER : target = EnterNotifyQueue; break;
    case Event.MOUSE_EXIT : target = LeaveNotifyQueue; break;
    case Event.KEY_ACTION :
    case Event.KEY_PRESS :
            if (last_keypress_time == event.when) {
             // handle bug in AWT implementation
             // that reports the same key twice
             // with the exact same time stamp.
             return;
            }
            last_keypress_time = event.when;
            last_keypress_key = event.key;
            target = KeyPressQueue; break;
    case Event.KEY_ACTION_RELEASE :
    case Event.KEY_RELEASE : target = KeyReleaseQueue; break;
    case Event.MOUSE_DOWN :target = ButtonPressQueue; break;
    case Event.MOUSE_UP : target = ButtonReleaseQueue; break;
    case Event.MOUSE_MOVE : target = MotionNotifyQueue; break;
    case Event.MOUSE_DRAG : target = MotionNotifyQueue; break;
    default :
```

```
            motion_compressor.endOfAction(event);
        return;
    }
    dispatch(target, event);
}
```

The actual event dispatching happens in the following method. Basically, it is passed to the head of a linked list of event clients, and the event as it was generated. Here, a linear search starts for the first client in the list that is willing to handle the event. A check is made to see if the graphical is visible and whether the event occurred inside the target's area. If the event is accepted by the client, the motion compressor is notified, so that it can record a time stamp of the last handled event (see below).

```
private void dispatch(EventClient target, Event event) {
    while (target != null) {
        if ( ((Graphical)target.client).visible &&
                        target.area.inside(event.x, event.y)) {
            if (target.client.activateCallback(target.method_nr)) {
                motion_compressor.endOfAction(event);
                return;
            }
        }
        target = target.next;
    }
}
```

This method can be used by clients to retrieve the event that resulted in their activation.

```
Event getLastEvent() {
    return last_event;
}


EventClient EnterNotifyQueue;
EventClient LeaveNotifyQueue;
EventClient KeyPressQueue;
EventClient KeyReleaseQueue;
EventClient ButtonPressQueue;
EventClient ButtonReleaseQueue;
EventClient MotionNotifyQueue;
int oldx, oldy;
```

```
    Event last_event = null;
    long last_keypress_time = 0;
    MotionCompressor motion_compressor;
};
```

The following class is used by the event handler to build up a linked list of event clients. Each event type has its own list of clients, so there is no type identifier necessary. A vector implementation could have been used, but vectors are quite expensive for such dynamic datastructures as this one.

```
class EventClient {
    EventClient(CallBackable client, int callback_method_nr, Area area)
{
        this.client = client;
        this.method_nr = callback_method_nr;
        this.area = area;
        this.next = next;
    }
    CallBackable client;        // the client
    int method_nr;              // the id of the method to be called
    Area area;                  // interested in this area
    EventClient next;           // next link in linked list
};
```

Motion compression is a window system optimization technique that tries to reduce the amount of drawing needed to be done when the user drags objects over the screen. When the objects, or the surrounding scenery gets too complicated, mouse events arrive faster than the system can draw the objects, and everything seems to drag behind. When the mouse is moved fast enough, it often takes a long time for the system to catch up. Normally, window systems give access to the event queue, so that interactive programs can "look ahead" to see if there are any other motion events pending in the queue. If that is the case, the current motion event is ignored, and the next one is taken. Another popular technique is not to use the motion events at all but actually query the *current* location of the mouse pointer. While the mouse button is being pressed, a loop is executed. Inside, the loop the mouse location is determined, and the screen is redrawn. Both techniques (motion compression and pointer querying), work acceptably, and make interactive systems look much more professional.

AWT does not give access to the event queue, and neither does it let users query the mouse pointer. Therefore, motion compression is hard to implement. The mechanism used here is a hack, which really uses "look back," instead of "look ahead," to see if the current motion event makes sense. It is based on a heuristic that motion events that arrive too quickly, also arrive close to one another (they have a time stamp that is only a short time apart). The motion compression technique is simple. If a motion comes in, and the previous motion happened less than 100 milliseconds ago, it probably arrives too quickly. A shortcoming is that drawings that take a lot longer than 100 milliseconds will still suffer from the effect we want to avoid here. The value 100 is based on heuristics and tuning on different platforms and operating modes. Another limitation of this approach is, that by definition, we always lose the *last* motion event. However, common usage of the mouse is that users move it slowly in the beginning, fast in the middle, and slow down again when the destination is reached. Therefore, events at the end tend to be longer apart in time but closer apart in geometrical distance. Overall, the compression technique works surprisingly well. Of course, we really would have liked to have access to the event queue.

```
class MotionCompressor {
    boolean needsCompression(Event event) {
        if (event.id==Event.MOUSE_MOVE || event.id==Event.MOUSE_DRAG) {
            if (System.currentTimeMillis() - last_motion_time < interval)
                return true;
        }
        return false;
    }
    void endOfAction(Event event) {
        if (event.id == Event.MOUSE_MOVE || event.id == Event.MOUSE_DRAG)
            last_motion_time = System.currentTimeMillis();
    }
    static final long interval = 100;
    private long last_motion_time = 0;
}
```

5.7 Class ltk.FilledGraphical
A FilledGraphical is a special kind of Graphical. In addition to having a line width, and color, it also has a fill color. The important aspect of this class is that it shows how easy it is to add behavior to an existing class in Java as is done here with filled graphicals and pass them to objects expecting regular graphicals. Note that this class is still an abstraction, as it does not do any drawing yet.

```
Import java.awt.Color;
public class FilledGraphical extends Graphical {
    FilledGraphical(DisplayListCanvas canvas,
                                 int x, int y, int w, int h) {
        super(canvas, x, y, w, h);
        fill_color = Color.white;
    }
    public void setFillColor(Color fill_color) {
        if (this.fill_color != fill_color) {
            this.fill_color = fill_color;
            update();
        }
    }
    Color fillColor() { return fill_color; }
    protected Color fill_color;
}
```

5.8 Class ltk.Moveable

This class is the first class to really add *behavior* to a graphical. It implements
drag-and-drop behavior by soliciting for mouse press, motion, and release
events inside its area. The canvas manages all events, and individual graphicals
can solicit for events with the canvas by calling the addClient method with
the appropriate parameters. In this case, we are initially interested in mouse
press events inside our area. The display list canvas will call us back whenever
the event occurs. In order to be able to call us back, it needs to be able to call a
certain function. That is why we implement CallBackable. Because the
mouse is not pressed when we start, we initialize the down variable to false

```
import java.awt.Event;
public class Moveable extends FilledGraphical implements CallBackable {
    Moveable(DisplayListCanvas canvas, int x, int y, int w, int h) {
        super(canvas, x, y, w, h);
        down = false;
        canvas.addClient(this, _mouseDown, area, Event.MOUSE_DOWN);
    }
```

When the user finally presses a mouse button inside our area, we can do what
we've been waiting for: ask for more events. In particular, as we want to *drag*
the graphical, we solicit for mouse drag and up events to happen anywhere
inside the canvas. (Due to the way most window systems work, the event will
also be passed when the mouse is dragged outside of the physical window. This

is to keep the mouse up event logically connected to its mouse down event.) We notice our state (useful for objects that want to draw a different picture depending on whether they are being dragged or are stationary). We compute our relative offset when the mouse was initially pressed (a standard interactive GUI trick), and we call method `moveToEvent` (a virtual method intended to be overwritten by subclasses, e.g., see the ltk.Box class).

```
public boolean mouseDown() {
    canvas.addClient(this, _mouseDrag,
                        canvas.anywhere, Event.MOUSE_DRAG);
    canvas.addClient(this, _mouseUp,
                        canvas.anywhere, Event.MOUSE_UP);
    down = true;
    Event e = canvas.getLastEvent();    // the event generated last
    dx = e.x - area.x;
    dy = e.y - area.y;
    moveToEvent(e.x, e.y);
    return true;
}
```

The following two callback methods are called by the canvas while the mouse is being dragged, and when it is released. All the callback methods return `true`, to indicate the event is handled by this object, and no other objects should be tried to see if they want to handle the event.

```
public boolean mouseDrag() {
    Event e = canvas.getLastEvent();
    moveToEvent(e.x, e.y);
    return true;
}
public boolean mouseUp() {
    canvas.removeClient(this, _mouseDrag,
                        canvas.anywhere, Event.MOUSE_DRAG);
    canvas.removeClient(this, _mouseUp,
                        canvas.anywhere, Event.MOUSE_UP);
    down = false;
    Event e = canvas.getLastEvent();
    moveToEvent(e.x, e.y);
    return true;
}
```

Inside each of the callback methods, the following method is executed, to be overridden by potential subclasses

```
public void moveToEvent(int x, int y) {
    move(x - dx, y - dy);
}
```

This method implements the `Callbackable` interface. It is called by the canvas only, and the method number passed while soliciting for mouse events will be used to index to the right callback method here.

```
public boolean activateCallback(int method_nr) {
    switch (method_nr) {
        case _mouseDown: return mouseDown();
        case _mouseUp: return mouseUp();
        case _mouseDrag: return mouseDrag();
    }
    return false;
}
static final int _mouseDown = 1;
static final int _mouseUp = 2;
static final int _mouseDrag = 3;
protected boolean down;
int dx, dy;
};
```

5.9 Class ltk.Box

This class represents the first graphical that has some useful behavior. It represents a colored rectangle that can be dragged around in a window. Figure 4 shows an example where four instances of this class are created.

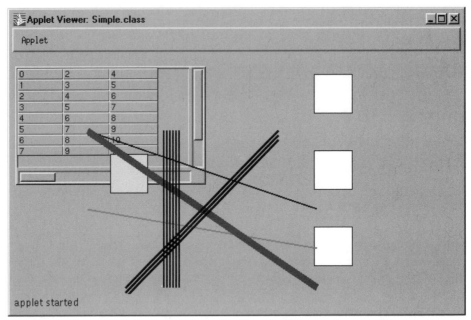

Figure 4. An example using four ltk.Box instances (one yellow and three white).

The Box class subclasses of `Moveable`, which in turn is a subclass of `FilledGraphical`, which is a subclass of `Graphical`. This class overrides its constructor (to satisfy a Java language rule), and sets the constraint for the Box to none, meaning that when the box is asked to resize itself, it will do so without using any constraints.

```
public class Box extends Moveable {
    public Box(DisplayListCanvas canvas, int x, int y, int w, int h) {
        super(canvas, x, y, w, h);
        constraint = Constraint.None;
        update();
    }
}
```

Furthermore, the class implements its own interpretation of what a colored box should look like.

```
public void draw() {
    canvas.setColor(fill_color);
    canvas.fillRect(area.x, area.y, area.w, area.h);
    canvas.setColor(color);
    canvas.drawRect(area.x, area.y, area.w-1, area.h-1);
}
};
```

Notice that the box is drawn with `area.w-1` and `area.h-1`. This is not a typo. As is common in window system drawing models, the fillRect method draws the *inside* of the area specified, whereas the specification for drawRect is as follows (ignoring the corner pixels being drawn multiple times)

```
void drawRect(int x, int y, int w, int h) {
    drawLine(x, y, x+w, y);
    drawLine(x, y+h, x+w, y+h);
    drawLine(x+w, y, x+w, y+h);
    drawLine(x, y, x, y+h);
}
```

The actual line segments are `w+1` and `h+1` pixels long. This is intentional and corresponds to the logical equivalent of drawing and filling polygon. If one would want to draw a rectangle using a polygon, the correction of `-1` would also have to be applied. Although it may initially not make much sense, the current drawing model is not a bug; it is an intentionally inherited behavior of the underlying window systems.

5.10 Class ltk.Line

The following class is more trivial than the Box class, as it does not have any dragging behavior attached. On the other hand, this class tries to compensate for the limitation in the AWT toolkit of JDK 1.0, which does not allow lines with multiple line widths. Therefore, this class will actually fill a polygon with the correct four corner points to simulate a thicker line width than the currently supported 1 pixel. Furthermore, as the line is defined by a begin point and an endpoint, these two points need to be remembered and stored inside the object (in addition to the already available `area` field). Notice that this makes the Line object rather heavyweight, a possible limitation for large-scale applications that use many line segments. See Figure 4 for an example that uses a couple of ltk.Line instances with variable color and line width attribute settings.

```
public class Line extends Graphical {
    public Line(DisplayListCanvas canvas, int x1,int y1,int x2,int
y2) {
        super(canvas, Math.min(x1,x2), Math.min(y1,y2),
                    Math.abs(x1-x2), Math.abs(y1-y2));
        this.x1 = x1; this.y1 = y1; this.x2 = x2; this.y2 = y2;
        update();
    }
    public boolean reset(int x1, int y1, int x2, int y2) {
        super.reset(Math.min(x1,x2), Math.min(y1,y2),
                    Math.abs(x1-x2), Math.abs(y1-y2));
        this.x1 = x1; this.y1 = y1; this.x2 = x2; this.y2 = y2;
        return true;
    }
    public void setLineWidth(int line_width) {
        super.setLineWidth(line_width);
        super.reset(Math.min(x1,x2)-line_width,
                    Math.min(y1,y2)-line_width,
                    Math.abs(x1-x2)+2*line_width,
                    Math.abs(y1-y2)+2*line_width);
    }
```

So, here comes my contribution for the "Most elegant hack of the month" contest. Basically, what happens is that in the simple case (line width equal to 1), the line is simply drawn using the standard line drawing method. If the line width is greater than one, we need to compose a polygon with the right coordinates. I won't explain the formula, as it only involves simple calculus.[4] As the draw method can be called many, many times, we do not want to create new points for each time we call it. Therefore, we cache the actual array objects in two instance variables. This will undoubtedly relieve the garbage collector and improve the performance of whatever applet is using this class. If we really want to optimize, we could make the array variables *static*, and only have two such variables, to be shared by all instances of the Line class. Of course, we need to take care that no two lines access these variables at the same time. We may need to synchronize access to these two variables (which comes again with a considerable runtime penalty). In this case, however, all calls to draw methods are already implicitly synchronized by the canvas, so it would be safe to make the arrays static. I am still not sure that there are no hidden side effects yet, though. Multiple threading and synchronization remain a nontrivial topic.

```
    public void draw() {
        canvas.setColor(color);
        if (line_width <= 1)
            canvas.drawLine(x1, y1, x2, y2);
```

---

[4] Actually, I had to consult my wife (who has a Master's in Mathematics) to help me with the formula :-).

```
        else {
            if (xpoints == null) {
                xpoints = new int[5];
                ypoints = new int[5];
            }
            int dx =
                (int) ((double)(y2-y1) *
                       (double)line_width /
                       ( 2 * Math.sqrt((x2-x1)*(x2-x1) +
                                       (y2-y1)*(y2-y1) ) ));
            int dy =
                (int) ((double)(x2-x1) *
                       (double)line_width /
                       ( 2 * Math.sqrt((x2-x1)*(x2-x1) +
                                       (y2-y1)*(y2-y1) ) ));

            if (dx == 0 && dy == 0)
                if (area.w > area.h)
                    dy = 1;
                else
                    dx = 1;

            xpoints[0] = x1 - dx;
            ypoints[0] = y1 + dy;
            xpoints[1] = x1 + dx;
            ypoints[1] = y1 - dy;

            xpoints[2] = x2 + dx;
            ypoints[2] = y2 - dy;
            xpoints[3] = x2 - dx;
            ypoints[3] = y2 + dy;

            xpoints[4] = xpoints[0];
            ypoints[4] = ypoints[0];
            canvas.fillPolygon(xpoints, ypoints, 5);
        }
    }
    public int x1, y1, x2, y2;
    int xpoints[], ypoints[];
}
```

A different implementation might use mathematical functions such as `sin`, `cos`, and `tan`. In any method, this calculation involves floating point arithmetic. Furthermore, we ignore the case where the line is either horizontal or vertical, in which case a filled rectangle with the right width can be used to simulate a line width greater than one. Rectangles are more efficient than polygons. Also ignored are special cases where slant lines of line width two appear to have holes in the middle, and we conveniently ignore what to do with the line caps (the ends where lines meet). However, all of this is really a quick hack, as future versions of AWT will better open up the interface to the underlying window system to allow more sophisticated drawings.

5.11 Class ltk.GUIStyle

The GUIStyle class tries to abstract the underlying window system and the GUI "look and feel." There is only one implementation for each of the basic GUI components, such as Button, Label, TextField, and so on. Instead of including platform dependencies into those objects (such as is done with AWT with the "peer" solution), LTK stores all platform dependencies into one single class: the GUIStyle class. For each GUI look and feel, a new subclass is defined that implements most of the functionality. The higher level widgets communicate with the currently selected GUIStyle, and ask it to do some drawing for it, or to return the appropriate foreground color for a certain operation. The result is a separation of implementation logic and behavior of widgets from the way they happen to appear on a given platform. The GUIStyle can be set and selected at runtime. (See Figure 5.) Therefore, it is very easy, for instance, to run an applet on a UNIX workstation, yet use the Windows 95 look and feel. An example of an applet that does this is supplied with the LTK toolkit.

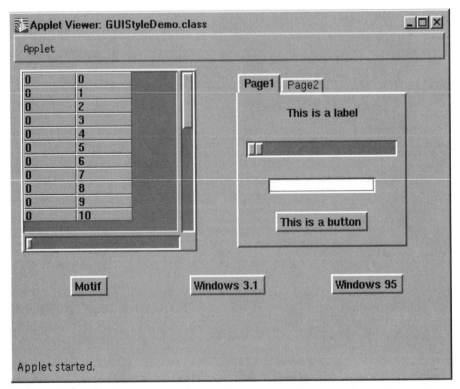

Figure 5. An example shows that the GUI style can be selected at runtime.

This class uses a couple of classes from the AWT toolkit. As discussed elsewhere, all classes are named explicitly, instead of importing `java.awt.*`. This enhances readability. I know exactly which classes are referenced when I inspect the first few lines of a Java file. A more dubious advantage is that it may positively influence compilation speeds. That however, depends a lot on the implementation model of the compiler and nature of the compiled Java code.

```
import java.awt.Color;
import java.awt.Graphics;
import java.awt.Font;
import java.awt.FontMetrics;
import java.lang.String;
```

The GUIStyle class is declared *abstract*, which means that some of its methods are mentioned here, but have no implementation yet. A recent change in the language rules forces developers to explicitly declare the class to be abstract. In earlier versions of the language, the class was implicitly declared abstract if one or more of its methods were declared abstract. Enforcing the new requirement results in better readable code, as it is clear in an instant what the status of the class is.

```
public abstract class GUIStyle {
```

The first category of methods provides GUI style independent drawing functions. Some GUI styles will implement them to actually draw 3D rectangles; others will draw a simple black rectangle, instead. See the ltk.MotifStyle, ltk.Win31Style, and ltk.Win95Style classes for different implementations of the following methods. The following methods are used in classes like ltk.Button, ltk.Slider, and ltk.Table

```
abstract public void drawSunkenRect(DisplayListCanvas canvas,
              int x, int y, int w, int h, int border_width);
abstract public void drawRaisedRect(DisplayListCanvas canvas,
              int x, int y, int w, int h, int border_width);
abstract public Color getSunkenColor();
abstract public Color getRaisedColor();
```

The following method is used in a class like ltk.Slider, and could be used for drawing a sash in a 3D look or a simple line in a 2D look

```
abstract public void drawLine(DisplayListCanvas canvas,
              int x1, int y1, int x2, int y2, int border_width);
```

Widgets can also inquire for the default background of a given GUIStyle (if it has any), the default border width (used in 3D looks), the padding (the room between labels and the edge on buttons, for instance), and the most appropriate font for text labels (used for buttons, labels, titles, table cells, etc.)

```
abstract public Color getBackground();
abstract public int getBorderWidth();
public int getPadding() { return 0; }
public Font getLabelFont() {
    if (label_font == null)
        label_font = new Font("Helvetica", Font.PLAIN, 12);
    return label_font;
}
```

Two methods follow that provide shortcuts for area-based drawing functions

```
public void drawSunkenRect(DisplayListCanvas canvas, Area area,
                                            int border_width) {
    drawSunkenRect(canvas, area.x, area.y,
                        area.w, area.h, border_width);
}
public void drawRaisedRect(DisplayListCanvas canvas, Area area,
                                            int border_width) {
    drawRaisedRect(canvas, area.x, area.y,
                        area.w, area.h, border_width);
}
```

The following functions allow the user to specify which GUI style to select and how to inquire for the currently selected GUI style

```
public static void selectStyle(short mode) {
    switch (mode) {
        case Motif: setDefaultStyle(new MotifStyle()); break;
        case Win31: setDefaultStyle(new Win31Style()); break;
        case Win95: setDefaultStyle(new Win95Style()); break;
    }
}
public final static short Motif = 1;
public final static short Win31 = 2;
public final static short Win95 = 3;
public static void setDefaultStyle(GUIStyle style) {
    defaultStyle = style;
}
public static GUIStyle getDefaultStyle() {
    if (defaultStyle == null) {
        String os_name = System.getProperty("os.name");
```

```
            if (os_name.equals("Windows NT") ||
                os_name.equals("Windows 95"))
                defaultStyle = new Win95Style();
            else
            if (os_name.equals("Solaris"))
                defaultStyle = new MotifStyle();
            else
            if (os_name.startsWith("Windows 3.1")) // ok?
                defaultStyle = new Win31Style();
            else
                defaultStyle = new Win95Style();
        }
        return defaultStyle;
    }
    static GUIStyle defaultStyle;
    Font label_font;
};
```

5.12 Class ltk.MotifStyle

To give you a flavor of what a specific GUI style implementation might look like, the implementation of the Motif GUI style class is given here. The Win31, and Win95 styles are similar in implementation yet interpret certain GUI style dependent aspects differently, of course. The given implementations are far from perfect. For instance, the Motif version does not use the Motif shadow color computation model, and the background for a sunken rectangle is incorrect. There was not enough time to carefully select the right implementation, and this is a mere proof of concept. It works rather well, though. Just try out the GUI style demo.

```
import java.awt.Color;
import java.awt.Font;
import java.awt.FontMetrics;
import java.lang.String;

public class MotifStyle extends GUIStyle {
    MotifStyle() {
        label_font = new Font("Helvetica", Font.BOLD, 12);
    }
    public void drawSunkenRect(DisplayListCanvas canvas,
            int x, int y, int w, int h, int border_width) {
```

```java
      canvas.setColor(background);
      canvas.fillRect(x, y, w, h);
      canvas.setColor(topShadow);
      for (int n=0; n<border_width; n++) {
         canvas.drawLine(x+n, y+h-n, x+w-n, y+h-n); // bottom shadow
         canvas.drawLine(x+w-n, y+n, x+w-n, y+h); // right shadow
      }
      canvas.setColor(bottomShadow);
      for (int n=0; n<border_width; n++) {
         canvas.drawLine(x+n, y+n, x+w-n, y+n); // top edge
         canvas.drawLine(x+n, y+n, x+n, y+h-n); // left edge
      }
      canvas.setColor(Color.black);
}
public Color getSunkenColor() {      return topShadow; }
public Color getBackground() {return foreground; }
public int getBorderWidth() { return 2; }
public int getPadding() {      return 3; }
public void drawLine(DisplayListCanvas canvas,
         int x1, int y1, int x2, int y2, int border_width) {
   if (x1 == x2) {
      canvas.setColor(bottomShadow);
      for (int n=0; n<border_width; n++)
         canvas.drawLine(x1-n, y1+n, x1-n, y2-n); // left part
      canvas.setColor(topShadow);
      for (int n=1; n<border_width; n++)
         canvas.drawLine(x1+n, y1+n, x1+n, y2-n); // right part
   }
   else if (y1 == y2) {
      canvas.setColor(bottomShadow);
      for (int n=0; n<border_width; n++)
         canvas.drawLine(x1+n, y1-n, x2-n, y1-n); // top part
      canvas.setColor(topShadow);
      for (int n=1; n<border_width; n++)
         canvas.drawLine(x1+n, y1+n, x2-n, y1+n); // bottom part
   }
   canvas.setColor(Color.white);
}
```

```
    public void drawRaisedRect(DisplayListCanvas canvas,
            int x, int y, int w, int h, int border_width) {
        canvas.setColor(foreground);
        canvas.fillRect(x, y, w, h);
        canvas.setColor(bottomShadow);
        for (int n=0; n<border_width; n++) {
            canvas.drawLine(x+n, y+h-n, x+w-n, y+h-n); // bottom shadow
            canvas.drawLine(x+w-n, y+n, x+w-n, y+h);// right shadow
        }
        canvas.setColor(topShadow);
        for (int n=0; n<border_width; n++) {
            canvas.drawLine(x+n, y+n, x+w-n, y+n); // top edge
            canvas.drawLine(x+n, y+n, x+n, y+h-n); // left edge
        }
        canvas.setColor(Color.black);
    }
    public Color getRaisedColor() {
        return Color.black;
    }
    public final Color foreground = Color.lightGray;
    public final Color bottomShadow = Color.lightGray.darker().darker();
    public final Color topShadow = Color.lightGray.brighter();
    public final Color background = Color.lightGray.darker();
};
```

5.13 Class *ltk.Button*

A software button is a component that displays a button image with a label, catches mouse events, and calls the appropriate application code whenever the button is activated. (See Figure 6.)

Figure 6. An example showing 4 buttons with one button having focus.

Buttons look different on different platforms, and often the implementation for a button is different for each platform (solved in AWT by using "peers"). LTK chooses a different solution, as there is only one single implementation of a button class, for all different platforms involved. The button uses a GUI style object to determine platform dependent GUI aspects, but the whole logic behind the button class is kept in one single place. (See Figure 7.)

Figure 7. A Button using Motif, Windows 3.1, and Windows 95 look and feel.

This allows us to guarantee the correct behavior of the button on all different platforms. The button class uses another class to implement the activation logic (class `ltk.Selectable`) and enhances that class to add a button image and call back a client

```
public class Button extends Selectable {
```

The button class has four different constructors, depending on whether the user wants to explicitly place the button or use layout managers instead. All mention the canvas this button is going to be added to, the client to be called back, and an identification of the method to be called when the button is activated

```
public Button(DisplayListCanvas canvas, CallBackable client,
              int method_nr,
              int x, int y, int w, int h, String title) {
    super(canvas, x, y, w, h);
    init(canvas, client, callback_method_nr, x, y, w, h, title);
    this.constraint = Constraint.Centered;
}
public Button(DisplayListCanvas canvas, CallBackable client,
              int method_nr, String title) {
    super(canvas, 0, 0, 0, 0);
    init(canvas, client, method_nr, 0, 0, 0, 0, title);
    reset(10, 10, text_width + 2*padding + 2*borderwidth,
              text_height + 2*padding + 2*borderwidth);
```

```
        this.constraint = Constraint.Centered;
    }
    public Button(DisplayListCanvas canvas, int constraint,
                    CallBackable client, int method_nr, String title) {
        super(canvas, 0, 0, 0, 0);
        init(canvas, client, method_nr, 0, 0, 0, 0, title);
        reset(10, 10, text_width + 2*padding + 2*borderwidth,
                    text_height + 2*padding + 2*borderwidth);
        this.constraint = constraint;
    }
    public Button(DisplayListCanvas canvas, CallBackable client,
                    int method_nr, int x, int y, String title) {
        super(canvas, x, y, 0, 0);
        init(canvas, client, method_nr, x, y, 0, 0, title);
        reset(x, y, text_width + 2*padding + 2*borderwidth,
                    text_height + 2*padding + 2*borderwidth);
        this.constraint = Constraint.Centered;
    }
```

The init method is called by all constructors (it is not part of the public interface). Notice that calling this method may fail when a future subclass of Button also implements the same method. Due to the behavior of Java's runtime system, the init method of the derived class will be called, and the following method will never be called at all

```
    void init(DisplayListCanvas canvas, CallBackable client,
                    int method_nr,
                    int x, int y, int w, int h, String title) {
        this.title            = new String(title);
        this.client           = client;
        this.callback_method_nr = method_nr;
        color = java.awt.Color.black;
        gui_style             = GUIStyle.getDefaultStyle();
        setFont(gui_style.getLabelFont());
        setPadding(gui_style.getPadding());
    }
```

The activation method is inherited from Selectable and is called whenever the button is activated (by means of mouse selection or keyboard accelerators). When called, the button will notify the client involved, and pass to it the callback method identification number passed to the button at construction time

```
public void activate() { // from class Selectable
    client.activateCallback(callback_method_nr);
}
```

If, for some reason, the user wants to change the GUI style used by this button to another one, the following method can be used. It receives the suggested GUI style, and retrieves a new value for the default font and padding (space between label and border; see the draw method)

```
public void setStyle(GUIStyle style) {
    gui_style = style;
    setFont(gui_style.getLabelFont());
    setPadding(gui_style.getPadding());
}
```

If the button uses a new font or changes its padding value, the button may need to resize to accommodate a larger label or padding space. Therefore, the current width and height are retrieved from a font metrics object. I found from experience that the string width returned could not be trusted in all cases. That is why a positive correction is made. Finally, a call is made to compute the current size of the button.

```
public void setFont(java.awt.Font font) {
    this.font = font;
    java.awt.FontMetrics fm = canvas.getFontMetrics(font);
    if (fm != null) {
        text_width = fm.stringWidth(title) + 1; // paranoid?
        text_height = fm.getAscent();
    }
    computeSizes();
}
public void setPadding(int padding) {
    this.padding = padding;
    computeSizes();
}
```

Resizing has to happen with some care, as the currently set resize constraint may limit the freedom with which the button can resize. For instance, a constraint of FixedHeight will ensure that the reset call will fail to resize the button vertically.

```
void computeSizes() {
    int old_constraint = constraint;
    constraint = Constraint.None;
    reset(area.x, area.y,
                text_width + 2*padding + 2*borderwidth,
                text_height + 2*padding + 2*borderwidth);
    constraint = old_constraint;
}
```

Then comes the magical part of the button, allowing it to behave like a
chameleon, looking different at all different platforms, yet really being the same
animal. The button has two states (pressed or not). The current state is inherited
from Selectable and is maintained in the variable down. If a pressed button
image is to be drawn, a sunken rectangle is drawn (however, delegating the
interpretation to the current GUI style). If the button has focus (also inherited by
the Selectable class), an extra rectangle is drawn around the buttons area.
Furthermore, the right color and font for the button label are set, and the label is
drawn. As all drawing happens inside this method, it is trivial to subclass this
class and turn it into an image button, displaying a bitmap, instead of a label.

```
public void draw() {
    int bw = (focus) ? borderwidth+1 : borderwidth;
    if (down) {
        gui_style.drawSunkenRect(canvas, area, bw);
        if (focus)
            canvas.drawRect(area.x, area.y, area.w, area.h);
        canvas.setColor(gui_style.getSunkenColor());
    }
    else {
        gui_style.drawRaisedRect(canvas, area, bw);
        if (focus)
            canvas.drawRect(area.x, area.y, area.w, area.h);
        canvas.setColor(gui_style.getRaisedColor());
    }
    canvas.setFont(font);
    canvas.drawString(title,
        area.x + padding + borderwidth +
                (area.w - text_width -
                            2*padding - 2*borderwidth)/2,
        area.y + area.h - padding - borderwidth -
                (area.h - text_height -
                            2*padding - 2*borderwidth)/2);
```

```
    }

String title;
    java.awt.Font     font;
    CallBackable      client;
    int    callback_method_nr;
    int    text_width;
    int    text_height;
    int    padding=2;
```

These two variables cause some problems. The GUI style should really not be public (as it should be set through a method call). Furthermore, the border width is GUI dependent, and should be retrieved from the current GUI style.

```
    public GUIStyle gui_style;
    static short borderwidth = 2; // gui style dependent?
};
```

5.14 Class ltk.Selectable

Abstraction is the key in designing complex systems. Therefore, even when implementing something as simple as a *button*, the actual logic that controls its activation is separated out of the ltk.Button class, and moved up the inheritance tree. Other widgets that have similar activation behavior (choice, switch, etc.), can benefit from this abstraction and simply override one single method for activation. By using inheritance, we take a conscious decision to fixate the behavior of ltk.Button. It is not possible to change the activation behavior of a button at runtime simply by plugging in another activation object. LTK does have that freedom for the *drawing* aspect (where different GUI styles can be used to change the appearance of widgets). It was deemed that *behavior* of widgets is something static and platform independent, whereas *appearance* is highly platform dependent.

The Selectable class abstracts the *activation* of devices, such as software buttons. Typically, such a component is activated using the mouse, or by using the keyboard (either by pressing the enter key when the widget has focus or by hitting an accelerator key). Because objects of this class receive events from the display list canvas, this class implements the CallBackable interface. Furthermore, in order to apply for focus handling support, this class implements the FocusClient interface

```
import java.awt.Event;
public abstract class Selectable extends Graphical implements
                                 CallBackable, FocusClient {
```

To initialize the class correctly, a canvas and an initial area to be passed to the constructor of class Graphical needs to be provided. After initializing the super class (which will create and properly initialize the `area` variable, the state for this class is initialized. Note that the assignments to `false` are, technically speaking, superfluous, but they add to the understanding of this class. The initial value of any important instance variable should be mentioned in the class's constructor even when their value results in the default value. Finally, we register with the canvas for any mouse press inside our area. If one happens in the future, our `activateCallback` method will be called, and the method identifier `_mouseDown` will be used by the canvas to let us know which method to invoke.

```
public Selectable(DisplayListCanvas canvas,
                              int x, int y, int w, int h) {
    super(canvas, x, y, w, h);
    down = false;
    focus = false;
    canvas.addClient(this, _mouseDown, area, Event.MOUSE_DOWN);
}
```

This method is to be implemented by any subclass. It is called whenever the widget is activated

```
public abstract void activate();
```

The following three methods are the event handlers for mouse events that happen inside our area. The event handling is based on object references, and no coordinates have been copied into the canvas. Therefore, when events do actually occur, each client that has registered for this kind of event is consulted to inspect if the event is inside the *area* object that it passed while registering for the event. The values of the object were not copied, but instead, a reference to the area object was stored. Therefore, objects are free to move without needing to notify their canvas. The event will still be dynamically forwarded to them.

When the mouse is pressed inside the Selectable's area, it registers for both mouse up and mouse leave events for the same area. The mouse up event will activate the widget, and the mouse leave event will cancel the selection.

```
public boolean mouseDown() {
    canvas.addClient(this, _mouseUp, area, Event.MOUSE_UP);
    canvas.addClient(this, _mouseLeave, area, Event.MOUSE_EXIT);
    down = true;
    canvas.repairArea(area);
    return true;
}
```

```
public boolean mouseLeave() {
    canvas.removeClient(this, _mouseUp, area, Event.MOUSE_UP);
    canvas.removeClient(this, _mouseLeave, area, Event.MOUSE_EXIT);
    down = false;
    canvas.repairArea(area);
    return true;
}
public boolean mouseUp() {
    canvas.removeClient(this, _mouseUp, area, Event.MOUSE_UP);
    canvas.removeClient(this, _mouseLeave, area, Event.MOUSE_EXIT);
    activate();
    down = false;
    canvas.repairArea(area);
    return true;
}
```

Activating widgets without needing a mouse is a critical requirement for a lot of users. It could be that the use of a mouse is too cumbersome (like on laptops), or that users are more familiar with using the keyboard. Hitting a certain sequence of the tab key, followed by a few numbers, and ended with a return, is often more efficient for fixed income traders at a trading desk who have to react to a changing market in minimal time, with no margin for errors.

Therefore, LTK provides a focus model that puts the current keyboard focus on a specifically selected widget, and allows the user to skip to the next widget using the tab key, and select the previous widget by using the shift-tab key. This "tabbing" is implemented by a FocusHandler class, in close cooperation with the focus clients involved. The FocusHandler class is independent of the canvas class. Its implementation is trivial. Basically, it is a linked list of focus clients with a reference to the client that currently has focus. Clients can be added and removed, and individual clients can request the focus or tab to the next or previous client in the list. The following two methods implement the FocusClient interface. The first serves to assign a focus handler to a focus client (typically called from the same code where the widget was created at, e.g., an applet's init method). The second method is called by the focus handler and serves to notify this client that it now has acquired the focus or lost it. If the focus was acquired, we register for keyboard events anywhere in the canvas (to capture a future tab event). If we lost the focus, we no longer have to listen to the tab key and unregister for key press events

```
public void setFocusHandler(FocusHandler handler)
    focus_handler = handler;
}
private FocusHandler focus_handler;
public void setFocus(boolean mode) {
    focus = mode;
    if (focus)
        canvas.addClient(this, _keyPress, canvas.anywhere,
                                    Event.KEY_PRESS);
    else
        canvas.removeClient(this, _keyPress, canvas.anywhere,
                                    Event.KEY_PRESS);
    update();
}
```

The following method can only be called if we have acquired the focus (see above). At this point, there are three events handled: pressing return, tab, or shift-tab. The return key will activate the widget (as we have the focus/selection). In the case of the tab and shift-tab key, we will notify the focus handler to move the focus to the next and previous focus client, respectively. If the event is not one we're interested in, and therefore do not handle, we return `false`. One special thing happens for handling the return key. We want to give a visual feedback during the handling of the activate method, and therefore redraw the button in its pressed form. However, if we're using double buffering, the effect does not work well. Therefore, we temporarily suspend double buffering, draw the button in pressed state, activate the widget, and redraw in unpressed state. In this case the activate method takes a short time; we insert a timer. With this model, the activation is very acceptable

```
public boolean keyPress() {
    Event event = canvas.getLastEvent();
    if (focus_handler != null && event.key == 9) { // the Tab key
        if (event.shiftDown())
            focus_handler.setFocusToPrevious(this);
        else
            focus_handler.setFocusToNext(this);
        return true;
    }
    else
    if (event.key == 10) {                     // the Return key
        down = true;
```

```
        canvas.doubleBuffering(false);
        draw();
        activate();
        try { Thread.sleep(100); } catch (InterruptedException e) { }
        down = false;
        draw();
        canvas.doubleBuffering(true);
        return true;
    }
    else
        return false;
}
```

When events happen inside our area, the following method is called by the canvas. This method may be used by subclasses, also. When they do so, and the event is not handled by the subclass, it is very important that this method is called. Therefore, subclasses of this class should not return false at the end of their activateCallback method but return super.activateCallback(method_nr) instead:

```
public boolean activateCallback(int method_nr) {
    switch (method_nr) {
        case _mouseDown: return mouseDown();
        case _mouseUp: return mouseUp();
        case _mouseLeave: return mouseLeave();
        case _keyPress: return keyPress();
    }
    return false;
}
static final int _mouseDown = 1;
static final int _mouseUp = 2;
static final int _mouseLeave = 3;
static final int _keyPress = 4;
```

The following variables can be used by a subclass to influence the way they draw themselves (e.g., see ltk.Button)

```
boolean down;    // mouse is pressed/dragged
boolean focus;   // focus is set to this widget
};
```

As mentioned before, the focus is handled by the focus handler between any number of focus clients. The focus handler is simply a manager, and its operational policy is implemented by all focus clients together. If one of the focus clients screws up and does not pass the focus on to the next, for instance, there is no way of repairing the situation. The way this democratic model is implemented is that the focus works like the remote control for the television set. Nothing is more annoying than being in the company of someone that keeps on zapping from channel to channel. All you can do is sit and wait for the person to put down the remote, so you can pick it up, and surf yourself. Which makes someone else wait for you to put down the remote control again, of course.

The function of the FocusHandler class is to remember how many focus clients there are, and who is next or was previous in the queue. The implementation uses a vector (not the fastest of implementations, but it will certainly do for the purpose). The implementation is trivial, if we do not forget to take care of the special cases (finding the "previous" of the first client, and finding the "next" of the last client). For some reason, I decided to cache the number of clients in a special variable, although it can be derived directly from the vector. Furthermore, I made the vector implementation visible for everyone. In general, a bad thing.

A disadvantage of the current implementation of focus handling is that it inherently is a *linear* approach, and not *hierarchical*. Focus is not nested, which makes it hard to do any sensible tabbing inside the notebook widget. A quick hack would be to attach a focus handler to each notebook page and add some additional behavior to these focus handlers, so that they can be enabled and disabled dynamically. It is better to look for a more general solution, based on a hierarchical model of nested focus handlers, perhaps based on layouts.

```
public class FocusHandler {
    public void add(FocusClient client) {
        clients.addElement(client);
        nclients++;
        client.setFocusHandler(this);
    }
    public void remove(FocusClient client) {
        clients.removeElement(client);
        nclients--;
        client.setFocusHandler(null);
    }
    public void setFocus(int client_nr) {
        for (int n=0; n<nclients; n++)
            ((FocusClient)clients.elementAt(n)).setFocus(false);
        ((FocusClient)clients.elementAt(client_nr)).setFocus(true);
```

```
    }
    public void setFocus(FocusClient client) {
        for (int n=0; n<nclients; n++)
            ((FocusClient)clients.elementAt(n)).setFocus(false);
        for (int n=0; n<nclients; n++)
            if (clients.elementAt(n) == client) {
                ((FocusClient)clients.elementAt(n)).setFocus(true);
                break;
            }
    }
    public void setFocusToNext(FocusClient client) {
        for (int n=0; n<nclients; n++)
            if (clients.elementAt(n) == client)
                setFocus((n+1) % nclients);
    }
    public void setFocusToPrevious(FocusClient client) {
        for (int n=0; n<nclients; n++)
            if (clients.elementAt(n) == client)
                setFocus((n-1+nclients) % nclients);
    }
    public java.util.Vector clients = new java.util.Vector();
    public int nclients;
};
```

The FocusClient interface has to be implemented by any object that wants to be
attached to a focus handler. Two functions need to be implemented

```
public interface FocusClient {
    public void setFocus(boolean mode);
    public void setFocusHandler(FocusHandler handler);
};
```

A typical implementation (as in ltk.Selectable) would be

```
    public void setFocusHandler(handler) { focus_handler = handler; }
    private FocusHandler focus_handler;
```

When the focus needs to be traversed, one of the following needs to be called

```
    focus_handler.setFocusToNext(this);
    focus_handler.setFocusToPrevious(this);
```

Typically, this is done when the tab key or the shift-tab key is received.

5.15 Class ltk.Layout

One of the more difficult aspects of developing a well-balanced graphical user interface (also referred to as a GUI), is how to place and resize individual GUI components inside the area that the application occupies. Embedding the placement logic inside the application by doing explicit moving and resizing of components is a tedious task and very often leads to disappointing and esthetically poor interfaces. A much better approach is to use specialized *layout* objects, whose only function is to lay out objects according to general user-interface design rules, or based on additional constraints that the GUI designer wants to apply. Once the layout objects have been set up appropriately, the application or applet can be resized, and the layout objects will then move and resize the individual components. The programmer is no longer bothered with this process and can concentrate on the more important process of implementing the application functionality.

Different toolkits have different strategies for layouts. AWT uses a versatile set of layout classes. Some of them are simple to use yet rather limited and inflexible for specialistic layouts. Therefore, a special layout class was designed in AWT that allows the programmer to attach special constraints to a component while adding it to the layout. These constraints may limit the relative width and height of the component, or influence the placement of the component. Adding this functionality to the layout complicates its interface and has made it hard for people to completely understand.

LTK also provides layout classes with constraints. To keep everything as simple as possible, only two layout classes are provided. Both classes lay out components added to them, either horizontally, or vertically. Individual resize or placement constraints are attached to the components, rather than specified in the layout's interface. Special constructors were designed, so that use of the layout objects is simplified as much as possible, rendering a very *declarative* form of layouts. An example is given here

```
new VerticalLayout(
    new HorizontalLayout(
        new Label(canvas, "Label 1"),
        new Label(canvas, "Label 2")
    ),
    new HorizontalLayout(
        new Label(canvas, "Label 3"),
        new Label(canvas, "Label 4")
    )
);
```

This specific piece of Java code will create a vertical layout object, containing two horizontal layout objects, each containing two labels. The vertical layout will occupy the whole area of the canvas (as it is the top-level layout), while the two horizontal layouts will each occupy one-half of the canvas's area.

In order to create some padding space between components in a layout, the following special class has been added to LTK

```
public class Space extends Graphical {
    Space(DisplayListCanvas canvas, int x, int y, int w, int h) {
        super(canvas, x, y, w, h);
        constraint = Constraint.FixedSize;
    }
};
```

Basically, it is a graphical that does not draw anything and cannot be resized after it is created. The mechanism used in LTK for implementing this behavior is the use of constraints. After creating a graphical, a given move/resize constraint can be attached to it at any point in time, thereby influencing the resizing and placement behavior of the widget inside its layout. An example is given here

```
Label label1 = new ltk.Label(canvas, "Label 1");
Label label2 = new ltk.Label(canvas, "Label 2");
new VerticalLayout(label1, label2);
label1.setConstraint(Constraint.FixedHeight);
label2.setConstraint(Constraint.FixedWidth);
```

Two labels are created; resize constraints are assigned, and the labels are added to a vertical layout. This code is functionally equivalent to the following more declarative code:

```
Label label1, label2;
new VerticalLayout(
    label1 = new ltk.Label(canvas, "Label 1"),
    label2 = new ltk.Label(canvas, "Label 2")
);
label1.setConstraint(Constraint.FixedHeight);
label2.setConstraint(Constraint.FixedWidth);
```

An even more compact version is

```
new VerticalLayout(
    Constraint.setFixedHeight(new ltk.Label(canvas, "Label 1")),
    Constraint.setFixedWidth(new ltk.Label(canvas, "Label 2"))
);
```

The last version does not need variables for the two labels and uses two utility functions provided in the ltk.Constraint class. The utility functions attach the specified constraint to the graphical passed to them and then return it. The constraint class provides a corresponding set function for each of the following resizing constraint types

`Constraint.None`	no resize or move constraint
`Constraint.Left`	stay to left, no resize horizontally
`Constraint.Right`	stay to right, no resize horizontally
`Constraint.Top`	attach to top, no resize vertically
`Constraint.Bottom`	attach to bottom, no resize vertically
`Constraint.FixedWidth`	no resize horizontally
`Constraint.FixedHeight`	no resize vertically
`Constraint.FixedSize`	no resize at all
`Constraint.Centered`	center, no resize at all

Any combination of the above constraints can be set for a given graphical. Once applied, the graphical will use the constraint to interpret future moves and resize requests. For instance, if a graphical has a `FixedWidth` constraint set, and the graphical is asked to resize itself to a new size, the value for the width will be ignored, and only the value for the height will be used to resize the graphical. Only combinations that make sense will result in predictable results. For instance, the following overconstrained situation, where both `Top` and `Bottom` constraints are applied to a graphical, will simply invalidate one of the two constraints, according to the current implementation of ltk.Graphical. From all different combinations of constraints, only the following combinations of constraints make sense

```
Constraint.Left    | Constraint.FixedHeight
Constraint.Right   | Constraint.FixedHeight
Constraint.Top     | Constraint.FixedWidth
Constraint.Bottom  | Constraint.FixedWidth
Constraint.Left    | Constraint.FixedSize
Constraint.Right   | Constraint.FixedSize
Constraint.Top     | Constraint.FixedSize
Constraint.Bottom  | Constraint.FixedSize
```

The class ltk.Graphical sets the resize constraint to None. The implemented subclasses of ltk.Graphical that do not have default resize behavior, have the following resize constraints:

class	resize constraint
ltk.Graphical	`Constraint.None`
ltk.Button	`Constraint.Centered`
ltk.Slider	`Constraint.Centered`
ltk.Space	`Constraint.FixedSize`

The two classes ltk.HorizontalLayout and ltk.VerticalLayout are just two abstractions of different kinds of layouts. In addition, they provide an easier construction by overloading their constructors to accept any (limited) number of graphicals

```
public class HorizontalLayout extends Layout {
    public HorizontalLayout(DisplayListCanvas canvas) {
        super(canvas);
        orientation = Layout.Horizontal;
    }
    public HorizontalLayout(Graphical g1) { ... }
    public HorizontalLayout(Graphical g1, Graphical g2) { ... }
    ...
};
public class VerticalLayout extends Layout {
    public VerticalLayout(DisplayListCanvas canvas) {
        super(canvas);
        orientation = Layout.Vertical;
    }
    ...
};
```

All functionality and layout behavior is encapsulated in their superclass, ltk.Layout

```
public class Layout extends Graphical {
    public Layout(DisplayListCanvas canvas) {
        super(canvas, 0, 0, 0, 0);
        parent = null;
    }
```

When a client is added to a layout, it is added to the current list of clients, and the layout increments the number of clients it manages. When the added client is an instance of ltk.Layout or one of its subclasses, the client layout will be notified that it should set its parent to this layout. Because layouts are graphicals, they will be redrawn whenever the canvas resizes. In that case, the top-most layout will ask the canvas its current size, and resize itself. This works best if the layout is the bottom-most in the display list. Therefore, the layout is lowered. Finally, the layout rearranges itself, to include the new client

```
    public void addClient(Graphical client) {
        clients.addElement(client);
        nclients++;
        if (client instanceof Layout)
            ((Layout)client).setParent(this);
        lower();
        rearrange();
    }
```

In the uncommon situation where a graphical needs to be removed from a layout, the following method removes the client from the client list (no check is made to see if the element was in the list). Then, the number of clients is decremented.

```
public void removeClient(Graphical client) {
    clients.removeElement(client);
    nclients--;
}
```

When a layout is moved or resized, the clients that it manages should be rearranged. The following method is inherited from ltk.Graphical and is overridden to return false when layout does not want to resize (a constraint may have been assigned to this layout), or when the call has no effect

```
public boolean reset(int x, int y, int w, int h) {
    if (!super.reset(x, y, w, h)) return false;
    if (!(x == area.x && y == area.y && w == area.w && h == area.h))
        return false;
    rearrange();
    return true;
}
```

Visibility is a property of graphicals that specify whether the graphical is visible (to be drawn) or not. In the case that the visibility of a layout is changed, all the clients that it manages are also made visible or invisible

```
public void setVisibility(boolean mode) {
    visible = mode;
    for (int n=0; n<nclients; n++)
        ((Graphical)clients.elementAt(n)).setVisibility(mode);
    rearrange();
}
```

Layouts can be nested, in which case the nested layouts will keep a reference to their parent (used when the layout rearranges itself)

```
public void setParent(Layout layout) {
    parent = layout;
    rearrange();
}
```

The following method determines the amount of space the layout can use to arrange its clients, and depending on the resize constraints of the individual clients, the amount of free space is computed. Then, each client is moved and resized (adhering to the client's resize constraints). If they allow it, clients are resized; otherwise, they are simply moved. All extra space is allotted to the non-constrained graphicals. The canvas is frozen before rearranging all graphicals and unfrozen afterwards. This to reduce the amount of drawing that is done. If the layout has no parent, it resizes itself to occupy the same space as the canvas

```java
public void rearrange() {
    if (nclients == 0)
        return;
    if (parent == null)
        resize(canvas.area.w, canvas.area.h);

    canvas.freeze();
    if (orientation == Horizontal) {
        int n_free_clients = nclients;
        int free_width = area.w - 2 * padding;
        for (int n=0; n<nclients; n++) {
            Graphical client = (Graphical)clients.elementAt(n);
            if ((client.constraint & Constraint.FixedWidth) != 0) {
                free_width -= client.area.w;
                n_free_clients--;
            }
        }
        int x = area.x + padding;
        for (int n=0; n<nclients; n++) {
            Graphical client = (Graphical)clients.elementAt(n);
            int w;
            if ((client.constraint & Constraint.FixedWidth) != 0)
                w = client.area.w;
            else
                w = free_width / n_free_clients - padding;
            client.reset(x, area.y + padding, w, area.h - 2*padding);
            x += w + padding;
        }
    }
    else {
        int n_free_clients = nclients;
        int free_height = area.h - 2 * padding;
        for (int n=0; n<nclients; n++) {
            Graphical client = (Graphical)clients.elementAt(n);
            if ((client.constraint & Constraint.FixedHeight) != 0) {
                free_height -= client.area.h;
                n_free_clients--;
            }
        }
        int y = area.y + padding;
        for (int n=0; n<nclients; n++) {
            Graphical client = (Graphical)clients.elementAt(n);
            int h;
            if ((client.constraint & Constraint.FixedHeight) != 0)
                h = client.area.h;
            else
                h = free_height / n_free_clients - padding;
            client.reset(area.x + padding, y, area.w - 2*padding, h);
```

```
            y += h + padding;
        }
    }
    canvas.unFreeze();
}
```

Because layouts have no visible representation, they need not draw anything. However, the fact that they are told by the canvas to draw themselves anyway is used as a trick to resize the layout to the size of the canvas in the case that the layout is the top-level canvas

```
public void draw() {
    if (parent==null &&
            (canvas.area.w!=area.w || canvas.area.h!=area.h) )
        rearrange();
}
```

The following utility methods create space objects that can be used as padding to create some space between two other graphicals in a layout. A typical usage could be

```
new VerticalLayout(
    new ltk.Label(canvas, "Label 1"),
    Layout.largeSpace(canvas),
    new ltk.Label(canvas, "Label 2")
);
```

which would create two labels, one above the other, separated by a large space. The following predefined and flexibly-sized space methods are provided

```
public static Graphical space(DisplayListCanvas canvas) {
    return space(canvas, 10, 10);
}
public static Graphical largeSpace(DisplayListCanvas canvas) {
    return space(canvas, 40, 40);
}
public static Graphical hugeSpace(DisplayListCanvas canvas) {
    return space(canvas, 100, 100);
}
public static Graphical space(DisplayListCanvas canvas,
                                        int w, int h) {
    return new Space(canvas, 0, 0, h, h);
}
```

The following instance variables influences the amount of padding that is added between two clients that are laid out in a layout

```
public short padding = 4;
```

Instance variables that follow are used in the class

```
    Layout parent;
    java.util.Vector clients = new java.util.Vector();
    int nclients;
    short orientation = Horizontal;
    static final short Horizontal = 1;
    static final short Vertical = 2;
};
```

5.16 Class ltk.EntryField

This widget is almost an applet on its own. It handles keyboard events, mouse events, does some (nontrivial) drawing, and even uses multiple threading to animate a blinking cursor. In order to create another thread to do the animation, we have to import the proper class[5]

```
import java.lang.Thread;
```

This widget is a subclass of Graphical (so we are attached to a canvas, have an area, a resize constraint, a foreground color, and a line width). Furthermore, this widget supports tabbing (FocusClient), event handling (CallBackable), and multiple threads (Runnable)

```
public class EntryField extends Graphical implements
                    FocusClient, CallBackable, Runnable {
```

In order to create an entry field, we need to pass it a canvas, a client to be called back when the user types in a new value, and an identifier to the method to be called when activation occurs. The location and size of the widget are optional (depending on whether we use the widget with or without layouts)

```
    public EntryField(DisplayListCanvas canvas, CallBackable client,
                int method_nr, int x, int y, int w, int h) {
        super(canvas, x, y, w, h);
        init(canvas, client, callback_method_nr, x, y, w, h);
        constraint = Constraint.Centered;
    }
    public EntryField(DisplayListCanvas canvas, CallBackable client,
                int method_nr) {
        super(canvas, 0, 0, 120, 16);
        init(canvas, client, method_nr, 0, 0, 0, 0);
        constraint = Constraint.Centered;
    }
```

---

[5] Because the java.lang package is automatically imported, we need not import this class here.

```
public EntryField(DisplayListCanvas canvas, CallBackable client,
                int method_nr, int x, int y) {
    super(canvas, x, y, 120, 16);
    init(canvas, client, method_nr, x, y, 0, 0);
    constraint = Constraint.Centered;
}
```

As is the case for many classes, the bodies of the constructors share a lot of code with each other. Therefore, the following method implements that common initialization logic. Being GUI style independent, the currently selected GUI style is retrieved, and the appropriate font for the value is also obtained. The widget registers as a client for mouse presses in its area. That enables the widget to grab the focus when it is selected. A new thread is created to animate a blinking cursor. It is started and suspended.

```
public void init(DisplayListCanvas canvas, CallBackable client,
                int method_nr, int x, int y, int w, int h) {
    this.value = new String();
    this.client = client;
    this.callback_method_nr = method_nr;
    color = java.awt.Color.black;
    gui_style = GUIStyle.getDefaultStyle();
    setFont(gui_style.getLabelFont());
    canvas.addClient(this, _selected, area,
                            java.awt.Event.MOUSE_DOWN);
    blinker = new Thread(this);
    blinker.start();
    blinker.suspend();
```

The following method needs to be overridden by subclasses that implement a special domain to which values can be entered. An example could be an integer entry field or a date entry field. The subclass would test in this method whether the current value of the entry field represents a value in the specific domain. In the default case, we do not care what the user enters, so we return true

```
public boolean validate() {
    return true;
}
```

If the user enters a printable character, we add it to the current value and redraw the widget. If the character is the backspace, we back up one character and redraw. If the character is the tab key, we notify the focus handler, and if the character is the return key, we call the client, but only when the input is validated. The validation model is very primitive, because it does not handle the case when the validation is negative. Some kind of feedback should be given to the user. The current implementation of the keyPress method may be too inflexible to implement the right kind of feedback. Because everything is contained in one big if-statement, there is no way of overriding a small part of the key press event handling logic. The subclass may have to override the complete implementation if it wants to change only a smaller part. Breaking this method up in smaller methods, will facilitate more flexible subclassing. Basically, whenever a situation like this arises, an experienced OO designer will automatically split up a method like this, without perhaps even being aware of why he or she is doing it.

```java
public boolean keyPress() {
    java.awt.Event e = canvas.getLastEvent();
    if (allowedChars.indexOf(e.key) != -1) {
        value += (char) e.key;
        update();
        return true;
    }
    else {
        switch (e.key) {
            case 8:                             // backspace
                int len = value.length();
                if (len > 0 )
                    value = value.substring(0, len-1);
                update();
                return true;
            case 9:                             // tab
                if (focus_handler != null) {
                    if (e.shiftDown())
                        focus_handler.setFocusToPrevious(this);
                    else
                        focus_handler.setFocusToNext(this);
                    return true;
                }
                return false;
            case 10:                            // return
                if (validate()) {
                    client.activateCallback(callback_method_nr);
                    return true;
                }
```

```
                return false;
            default:
                return false;
        }
    }
}
public boolean keyRelease() {
    return false;
}
```

The entry field can be initialized with a user-defined value, by using the following method. It will replace the current text with the new one and place the cursor at the end of the string. Currently, this widget does not handle arrow keys to move back and forth inside the text.

```
public void setText(String text) {
    value = text;
    update();
}
```

If the user does not like the default font that is selected by the GUI style, the following method will assign it and retrieve a font metrics object for the font. Then, the widget is redrawn

```
public void setFont(java.awt.Font font) {
    this.font = font;
    fm = canvas.getFontMetrics(font);
    update();
}
```

The following callback method is called by the canvas whenever the user clicks inside the entry field's area. If the widget is currently managed by a focus manager, we request the focus with this manager. It will take away the focus from whoever had it, and then give it to this widget. In that case, the setFocus method is called on this widget. If the widget is not managed by a focus handler, the widget calls the method itself

```
public boolean selected() {
    if (focus_handler != null)
        focus_handler.setFocus(this);
    else
        setFocus(true);
    return true;            // event handled
}
```

The following method is called by either a focus handler or the widget itself
(see the previous method). This method tells the widget to either grab the focus
or to release it (depending on the value of the set_focus parameter). If the
widget has to grab the focus, it adds itself as a client to the canvas to get all key
press and release events that happen anywhere inside the canvas. The blinker
thread is then resumed. It will now wake up twice a second and repaint the
widget with the cursor on or off. If the widget is told to release the focus, it
basically does the opposite of the process described before. The blink variable
is used inside the draw method to determine whether the cursor should be
drawn or not.

```java
public void setFocus(boolean set_focus) {  // from FocusClient
    if (set_focus) {
        canvas.addClient(this, _keyPress,
            canvas.anywhere, java.awt.Event.KEY_PRESS);
        canvas.addClient(this, _keyRelease,
            canvas.anywhere, java.awt.Event.KEY_RELEASE);
        blinker.resume();
        blink = true;
    } else {
        canvas.removeClient(this, _keyPress,
            canvas.anywhere, java.awt.Event.KEY_PRESS);
        canvas.removeClient(this, _keyRelease,
            canvas.anywhere, java.awt.Event.KEY_RELEASE);
        blinker.suspend();
        blink = false;
    }
    update();
}
```

Two methods that assign a new focus handler and a different GUI style follow

```java
public void setFocusHandler(FocusHandler handler) {
    focus_handler = handler;
}
public void setStyle(GUIStyle style) {
    gui_style = style;
    setFont(gui_style.getLabelFont());
}
```

The following method is the main body of the blinker thread. When active, it
wakes up twice a second and redraws the entire widget with the cursor visible

or invisible, depending on the value of the `blink` instance variable. The widget redraws itself entirely, which is not really necessary if it would use an *xor* drawing mode. In that case, if we draw a line, the line is not really drawn on the canvas, but rather, each pixel value that is currently on the screen gets inverted. The result is that when we, for instance, draw a line twice at the same location, the result is the original picture. Using *xor* is a standard technique for drawing cursors and for doing things that involve *rubber banding* (such as, the effect that will happen while moving or resizing a window). LTK, however does not use *xor* drawing anywhere (for simplicity reasons)

```
public void run() {
    while (true) {
        blink = !blink;
        update(); // will result in call to draw()
        try { Thread.sleep(500); } catch (InterruptedException e) { }
    }
}
public void draw() {
    gui_style.drawSunkenRect(canvas, area, borderwidth);
    canvas.setColor(java.awt.Color.white);
    canvas.fillRect(area.x+borderwidth, area.y+borderwidth,
            area.w-2*borderwidth, area.h-2*borderwidth);
    canvas.setColor(java.awt.Color.black);
    canvas.setFont(font);
    canvas.drawString(value, area.x + borderwidth + 2,
            area.y + area.h - borderwidth - 2);
    int x = borderwidth + fm.stringWidth(value);
    if (blink)
        canvas.drawLine(area.x + x + 2, area.y + borderwidth + 2,
            area.x + x + 2, area.y + area.h - borderwidth - 2);
}
```

The following method dispatches canvas events to the proper method. Subclasses that override this method should call it to ensure that this class gets a change to handle the event also

```
public boolean activateCallback(int method_nr) {
    switch (method_nr) {
        case _keyPress: return keyPress();
        case _keyRelease: return keyRelease();
        case _selected: return selected();
```

```
        }
        return false;
    }
    static final int _keyPress = 1;
    static final int _keyRelease = 2;
    static final int _selected = 3;
```

Finally, there are some instance variables. The first one contains the full list of allowed characters that this entry field is willing to accept from the keyboard. There should be an easier way to find out if a certain character is printable, of course.

```
    static String allowedChars =
        "abcdefghijklmnopqrstuvwxyz" +
        "ABCDEFGHIJKLMNOPQRSTUVWXYZ" +
        "0123456789" + " #$%^&*()_+-=[]{}\\|;:'\",<.>/?~`";
    public GUIStyle gui_style;
    String value;
    boolean blink;
    java.awt.Font font;
    CallBackable client;
    java.awt.FontMetrics fm;
    Thread blinker;
    int callback_method_nr;
    int text_width;
    int text_height;
    static short borderwidth = 2;
    private FocusHandler focus_handler;
};
```

5.17 Class ltk.ScrollBar

The scrollbar and slider classes both implement a widget that can be used to enter and display an integer value. A slider has a fixed size handle, and a scroll-bar has a handle that can display the "visible ratio." Because the slider and scrollbar class share a lot of logic in their implementation, it was decided to make the scrollbar class a specialization of the slider class. (See Figure 8.)

Figure 8. A slider using Motif, Windows 3.1, and Windows 95 look and feel.

The slider class implements the generic behavior and assigns the `fixed_handle_size` variable to true. The scrollbar class assigns it to false. A scrollbar can be created by giving it an explicit location and dimension (the first constructor), or by deferring decisions about the size and the dimension to a later stage, as is the case when the widget is used in a layout (the second constructor is available for that). The scrollbar widget records the identity of a client to call whenever the enduser manipulates the widget. The method number is used to determine the method to call. A scrollbar has a minimum value and a maximum value. Furthermore, the value increment is to be specified, telling the scrollbar at what intervals to report a change of value.

The following specification

```
Scrollbar sb = new Scrollbar(..., ..., ..., 100, 400, 50);
sb.setViewedRatio(0.5);
```

creates a scrollbar that reports the following values: 100, 150, 200, 250, 300, 350, and 400. Furthermore, the size of the handle is half the size of the scrollbar itself. When a scrollbar or slider is resized, it automatically switches between being horizontal or vertical (therefore, there are no separate classes for the two different manifestations). A text editor that currently display a file with 500 lines and that has a visible buffer of 50 lines would create a vertical scrollbar with the following specification

```
Scrollbar vsb = new Scrollbar(..., ..., ..., 1, 500, 1);
vsb.setViewedRatio(0.1);
vsb.reset(..., ..., ..., ...);
```

Here is the class declaration for ltk.Scrollbar:

```
public class Scrollbar extends Slider {
    public Scrollbar(DisplayListCanvas canvas,
            CallBackable client, int method_nr,
            int x, int y, int w, int h,
            int minimum_value, int maximum_value,
            int value_increment) {
        super(canvas, client, method_nr, x, y, w, h,
            minimum_value, maximum_value, value_increment);
        fixed_handle_size = false;
        update();
```

```
    }

    public Scrollbar(DisplayListCanvas canvas,
            CallBackable client, int method_nr, int orientation,
            int minimum_value, int maximum_value,
            int value_increment) {
        super(canvas, client, method_nr, orientation,
            minimum_value, maximum_value, value_increment);
        fixed_handle_size = false;
        update();
    }
};
```

The ltk.Slider class is the generic implementation for the slider and scrollbar widgets. The slider is a subclass of `Moveable`, which performs all event handling logic for capturing mouse events. Whenever the mouse is dragged inside the slider, the `moveToEvent` method is called (see below). When a slider is created with the width larger than its height, it will become a horizontal slider. Otherwise, it will be a vertical slider.

```
import java.lang.Math;              // not really necessary


public class Slider extends Moveable {
    public Slider(DisplayListCanvas canvas,
            CallBackable callback_client, int method_nr,
            int x, int y, int w, int h,
            int minimum_value, int maximum_value,
            int value_increment) {
        super(canvas, x, y, w, h);
        if ( w > h )
            orientation = Horizontal;
        else
            orientation = Vertical;
        setDefaultSizes();
        init(callback_client, method_nr, minimum_value, maximum_value,
            value_increment);
        constraint = Constraint.Centered;
    }
```

```
public Slider(DisplayListCanvas canvas,
        CallBackable callback_client, int method_nr,
        int orientation,
        int minimum_value, int maximum_value,
        int value_increment) {
    super(canvas, 0, 0, 0, 0);
    this.orientation = orientation;
    setDefaultSizes();
    int w, h;
    if (orientation == Horizontal) {
        w = 2 * GUIStyle.getDefaultStyle().getBorderWidth() +
            handle_size +
            (maximum_value - minimum_value) / value_increment;
        h = defaultSize;
    }
    else {
        w = defaultSize;
        h = 2 * GUIStyle.getDefaultStyle().getBorderWidth() +
            handle_size +
            (maximum_value - minimum_value) / value_increment;
    }
    init(callback_client, method_nr,
        minimum_value, maximum_value, value_increment);
    resize(w, h);
    this.orientation = orientation;
    constraint = Constraint.Centered;
}
```

The following method initializes GUI style to be used, the width of the border (i.e., the thickness of the shadow, if there is one), and determines the default size of a slider handle

```
private void setDefaultSizes() {
    style = GUIStyle.getDefaultStyle();
    border = style.getBorderWidth();
    handle_size = 8 * border;
}
```

If the programmer does not like the default GUI style obtained from the ltk library, a new one can be assigned using the following method

```
public void setStyle(GUIStyle style) {
    this.style = style;
    update();
}
```

The following method initializes instance variables for the slider/scrollbar and is called from the two different variations of the constructor. Note again that this method is vulnerable to the constructor bug in Java, mentioned in Section 15 of Chapter 1. An area object is created to represent the area that the handle occupies (see also the `draw` method)

```
private void init(CallBackable callback_client, int method_nr,
            int minimum_value, int maximum_value,
            int value_increment) {
    value_inc = value_increment;
    min_value = minimum_value;
    max_value = maximum_value;
    if ( orientation == Horizontal)
        handle = new Area(area.x + border, area.y + border,
                                handle_size, area.h-2*border);
    else
        handle = new Area(area.x + border, area.y + border,
                                area.w-2*border, handle_size);
    client = callback_client;
    callback_method_nr = method_nr;
}
```

This method is inherited from class Moveable and is called every time the mouse is dragged inside the slider/scrollbar. The handle is moved to the new coordinates (using appropriate constraints). Inside the moveHandleTo method, the variable value gets assigned a new value. Whenever it was different from the last reported value, the client is notified of a new event. This is the only place from which the client is called.

```
public boolean moveToEvent(int x, int y) {        // from class Moveable
    moveHandleTo(x, y);
    if (value != last_reported_value) {
        client.activateCallback(callback_method_nr);
        last_reported_value = value;
    }
    return true;
}
```

The following method is typically called by layout classes. In some special cases it is also called by other widgets (for instance when they contain a vertical and horizontal scrollbar, as is the case for the table widget). A new size for the handle is determined, based on the fact that widget is a slider or a scrollbar. The new handle size is the width or height of the widget times the viewed ratio (see the example calls above)

```
public boolean reset(int x, int y, int w, int h) {
    super.reset(x, y, w, h);
    if ( area.w > area.h ) {
        orientation = Horizontal;
        if (!fixed_handle_size)
            handle_size = border + (int)(viewed_ratio * area.w);
        size = area.w;
        handle.y = area.y + border;
        handle.h = area.h - 2*border;
        handle.set(handle.x, handle.y, handle_size, handle.h);
        moveHandleTo(area.x + valueToPixel(value), area.y);
    }
    else {
        orientation = Vertical;
        if (!fixed_handle_size)
            handle_size = border + (int) (viewed_ratio * area.h);
        size = area.h;
        handle.x = area.x + border;
        handle.w = area.w - 2*border;
        handle.set(handle.x, handle.y, handle.w, handle_size);
        moveHandleTo(area.x, area.y + valueToPixel(value));
    }
    return true;
}
```

The following method is called only from within the widget itself and tries to move the handle to a new location. The handle is constrained to stay inside the enclosing widget, of course. Therefore, either the *x*, or the *y* value is ignored, depending on the fact that the widget is vertically or horizontally oriented. Furthermore, the side-effect of the method is that a new value is computed (the user *did* move the handle)

```
void moveHandleTo(int x, int y) {
    int hx = handle.x;
    int hy = handle.y;
    if ( orientation == Horizontal ) {
        value = pixelToValue(x - area.x);
        hx = area.x + valueToPixel(value);
    }
    else {
        value = pixelToValue(y - area.y);
        hy = area.y + valueToPixel(value);
    }
    handle.set(hx, hy, handle.w, handle.h);
    update();
}
```

The following utility function translates a pixel value into a slider value, using the appropriate attributes of the widget. Let's again use the above mentioned sample values 100, 400, and 50, for the minimum value, maximum value, and value increment, respectively. In that case `pixelToValue` would always produce a value in the range of 100, 150, 200, 250, 300, 350, and 400

```
int pixelToValue(int dxy) {
    int value;
    if (fixed_handle_size)
        value = min_value + (dxy-border)*value_inc;
    else
        if (dxy >= size-handle_size-border)  // prevent roundoff
            value = max_value;
        else
            value = min_value + ((max_value-min_value)*dxy / size);
    return Math.min(max_value, Math.max(min_value, value));
}
```

The following method produces exactly the opposite from the previous one and is called whenever the program explicitly moves the slider to a new value. An example could be a text editor that moves the scrollbar to value 275, when the last page of a 300 page document is shown, and the editor displays 25 lines per page

```
int valueToPixel(int value) {
    int xy;
    if (fixed_handle_size)
        xy = border + (value-min_value) / value_inc;
    else
        xy = border + size * (value-min_value) /
                            (max_value-min_value);
    return Math.min(size-handle_size-border, Math.max(border, xy));
}
```

The following public methods move the slider or scrollbar to a new value and retrieve the current value

```
public void setValue(int new_value) {
    if (new_value == value)
        return;
    if (orientation == Horizontal)
        moveHandleTo(area.x + valueToPixel(new_value), area.y);
    else
        moveHandleTo(area.x, area.y + valueToPixel(new_value));
}
public int getValue() {
    return value;
}
```

The following method is only useful in the case that the widget is a scrollbar. It sets the ratio of viewable area, which directly corresponds with the size of the handle

```
public void setViewedRatio(double ratio) {
    viewed_ratio = ratio;
    update();
}
```

The following method is only called by the display list canvas, whenever it thinks the widget needs to be redrawn. The window containing the widget may have been exposed, or the widget may have moved to a new location

```
public void draw() {
    drawBackground();
    drawHandle();
}
```

The background for the slider and scrollbar are the same: a sunken rectangle. Some GUI styles will not draw a 3D look and simply display a rectangle. This widget does not care

```
void drawBackground() {
    style.drawSunkenRect(canvas, area, border);
}
```

The handle drawing logic is simple also. The GUI style is asked to draw a raised rectangle, and only when the widget is a slider (fixed_handle_size is true), an extra ornament is drawn on the handle

```
void drawHandle() {
    style.drawRaisedRect(canvas, handle, border);
    if (fixed_handle_size) {
        if (orientation == Horizontal)
            style.drawLine(canvas,
                handle.x + handle.w/2, handle.y,
                handle.x + handle.w/2, handle.y + handle.h,
                border);
        else
            style.drawLine(canvas,
                handle.x,           handle.y + handle.h/2,
                handle.x + handle.w, handle.y + handle.h/2,
                border);
    }
}
```

And, finally, some instance variables

```
CallBackable client;
GUIStyle style;
Area handle;
int orientation = Horizontal;
int callback_method_nr;
int border;
int handle_size;
int size;
int value;
int value_inc;
int min_value;
int max_value;
```

```
    double viewed_ratio = 1.0;
    int last_reported_value = -1;
    boolean fixed_handle_size = true;
    static final int defaultSize = 17;
    public static final int Horizontal = -1;
    public static final int Vertical = -2;
}
```

5.18 Class ltk.Table

The table widget implements a 2D grid based, spreadsheet-like widget. The table can consist of any number of columns and rows. Two scrollbars are used to scroll the currently visible cells. The widget uses a bitmap to save the last drawing (making it able to redraw the widget quickly when no changes have been made to its state).

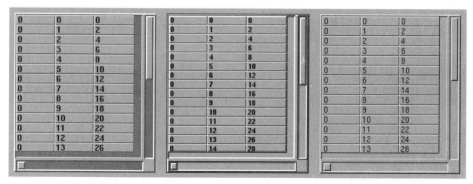

Figure 9. A table using Motif, Windows 3.1, and Windows 95 look and feel.

Furthermore, the actual contents of the widget is separated from its visual representation (not really model-view based, but it gets close to that). The following interface is defined to produce values for individual cells in the table widget

```
public interface TableProducer {
    public String getCellValue(int rowNumber, int columnNumber);
};
```

The table widget itself is a subclass of ltk.Graphical, and it implements the Callbackable interface (so it can receive keyboard events from the canvas) (See Figure 9.)

```
public class Table extends Graphical implements CallBackable {
```

Only one constructor exists for the table widget, specifying the canvas, the table cell value producer, and the number of rows and columns the table should manage

```
public Table(DisplayListCanvas canvas, TableProducer producer,
                              int rows, int columns) {
    super(canvas, 0, 0, 200, 200);
    setProducer(producer);
    init(rows, columns);
}
```

The following method lets the program assign a new producer for the table cell values. This allows a possible extension of the table to assign a new "model" to the widget

```
public void setProducer(TableProducer producer) {
    this.producer = producer;
}
```

The table widget uses a panel object as abstraction for the area covered by the cells plus two scrollbars. The vertical scrollbar will call the vscroll method, with minimum value 0 (for the first row), with the number of rows as maximum value, and 1 for the value increment. Both scrollbars are managed directly by the table widget and no layouts are used to manage them. Therefore, the default resize constraint is deactivated. The two scrollbars will be moved and sized whenever the table is moved or resized (see the reset method)

```
void init(int rows, int columns) {
    this.rows = rows;
    this.columns = columns;
    panel = new Area();
    vertical_scrollbar =
        new Scrollbar(canvas, this, _vscroll, 0,0,0,0, 0, rows, 1);
    vertical_scrollbar.constraint = Constraint.None;
    horizontal_scrollbar =
        new Scrollbar(canvas, this, _hscroll, 0,0,0,0, 0, columns, 1);
    horizontal_scrollbar.constraint = Constraint.None;
    setStyle(GUIStyle.getDefaultStyle());
    setFont(gui_style.getLabelFont());
    canvas.addClient(this, _key, canvas.anywhere,
                              java.awt.Event.KEY_PRESS);
    computeSizes();
}
```

Two callback methods below are called whenever the horizontal or vertical scrollbars change value

```
public boolean hscroll() {
    hscroll(horizontal_scrollbar.getValue());
    return true;
}
public boolean vscroll() {
    vscroll(vertical_scrollbar.getValue());
    return true;
}
```

The following two methods move the viewed area horizontally or vertically. After scrolling, the currently displayed image of the cells is no longer valid, so the image is invalidated. The next time a redraw happens (typically done as a result of update()), the widget will redraw all the visible cells

```
public void hscroll(int target_column) {
    first_column = java.lang.Math.max(0,
                   java.lang.Math.min(columns, target_column));
    horizontal_scrollbar.setValue(first_column);
    image_invalid = true;
    computeSizes();
    update();
}
public void vscroll(int target_row) {
    first_row =
        java.lang.Math.max(0, java.lang.Math.min(rows, target_row));
    vertical_scrollbar.setValue(first_row);
    image_invalid = true;
    computeSizes();
    update();
}
```

The following callback method is called whenever the widget has focus and the user hits a key. The widget can scroll left, right, up, or down, depending on which key is pressed

```
public boolean key() {
    java.awt.Event e = canvas.getLastEvent();
    switch (e.key) {
        case 'k' :
        case java.awt.Event.UP:
            vscroll(first_row-1);
            return true;
        case 'j' :
        case java.awt.Event.DOWN:
            vscroll(first_row+1);
            return true;
        case 'h' :
        case java.awt.Event.LEFT:
            hscroll(first_column-1);
            return true;
        case 'l' :
        case java.awt.Event.RIGHT:
            hscroll(first_column+1);
            return true;
    }
    return true;
}
```

Whenever the table widget draws itself, it does not draw itself directly on the canvas (as is the default behavior). Instead, it will draw itself in a private image and copy that one to the canvas. Now, when the widget is partly exposed, the widget does not have to redraw itself completely. It will use the "cached" image, and efficiently copy that to the canvas. Currently, the image is not used during scrolling (when most of the image could be translated, and only a portion of the widget needs to be redrawn). Rather, while scrolling, the widget redraws itself completely.

```
public void initializeImage() {
    background_image = canvas.createImage(panel.w, panel.h);
    image_invalid = true;
}
```

When the table widget is moved or resized, the panel will be recomputed, the scrollbars will be placed and resized, and a new image cache is created (when necessary)

```
public boolean reset(int x, int y, int w, int h) {
    int oldw = area.w;
    int oldh = area.h;
    canvas.freeze();
    super.reset(x, y, w, h);
    panel.set(area.x + borderwidth,
        area.y + borderwidth,
        area.w - 4*borderwidth - scrollbar_size,
        area.h - 4*borderwidth - scrollbar_size);

    computeSizes();

    if (area.w!=oldw || area.h!=oldh) {
        initializeImage();
        horizontal_scrollbar.setViewedRatio(
                (double)(last_column-first_column) / (double)columns);
        vertical_scrollbar.setViewedRatio(
                (double)(last_row-first_row) / (double)rows);
    }

    vertical_scrollbar.reset(area.x+area.w-scrollbar_size-borderwidth,
                    area.y + borderwidth,
                    scrollbar_size,
                    area.h - 4*borderwidth - scrollbar_size);
    horizontal_scrollbar.reset(area.x + 2*borderwidth,
                    area.y+area.h-scrollbar_size-borderwidth,
                    area.w - 4*borderwidth - scrollbar_size,
                    scrollbar_size);
    canvas.unFreeze();
    return true;
}
```

The following method computes how many columns and rows are visible for the current size of the table widget

```
void computeSizes() {
    int r, y = 2*borderwidth + rowHeight(first_row);
    for (r=first_row; r<rows && y < panel.h; r++)
        y += rowHeight(r)+1;
    last_row = r-1;
    int c, x = 2*borderwidth + columnWidth(first_column);
    for (c=first_column; c<columns && x < panel.w; c++)
        x += columnWidth(c) + 1;
    last_column = c-1;
}
```

Currently, the table widget has fixed sized columns. The following method always returns the same default value, independent of the actual value of the column. Future subclasses of the table widget may allow users to resize individual columns of the table and will also override the following method to return the appropriate value. Something similar is true for the height of a table row. Currently, each row is drawn with the same font, and

```
int columnWidth(int n) {
    return column_width;
}
int rowHeight(int n) {
    return text_height + 2 * borderwidth - 1;
}
```

Apart from separating the underlying model from its view, the program is able to asynchronously change individual cell values. This is, for instance, useful for programs that receive updates for values changing at real-time. When the selected cell is not visible, the method directly returns. Access to the canvas is synchronized, to make the widget thread-safe. A visual cue is presented to the user by drawing the new value in a number of different colors before drawing it in the default color. During drawing, double buffering is disabled

```
public void setValue(int row, int column, String value) {
    if (row < first_row || row >= last_row ||
            column < first_column || column >= last_column)
        return;
    int y = panel.y;
    for (int r=first_row; r<=row; r++)
        y += rowHeight(r) + 1;
    int x = panel.x;
    for (int c=first_column; c<=column; c++)
        x += columnWidth(c) + 1;
```

```
synchronized (canvas) {
    canvas.doubleBuffering(false);
    gui_style.drawRaisedRect(canvas, x+2, y+2,
                        columnWidth(column)-4, rowHeight(row)-3,
                        0);

    canvas.setFont(font);

    for (int n=0; n<cycleColors.length; n++) {
        canvas.setColor(cycleColors[n]);
        canvas.drawString(value,
            x + 4,
            y + rowHeight(row) - (rowHeight(row)-text_height)/2);
        try { Thread.sleep(CYCLE_TIME); }
        catch (InterruptedException e) { }
    }

    canvas.setColor(java.awt.Color.black);
    canvas.drawString(value,
        x + 4,
        y + rowHeight(row) - (rowHeight(row)-text_height)/2);

    canvas.doubleBuffering(true);
    }
}
```

When the table widget is drawn, a shadow is drawn for itself. When the image has been invalidated before (as a result of a full redraw, or scroll event), all the visible cells in the panel are drawn (hence the call to drawPanel). Then the contents of the bitmap is copied to the canvas.

```
public void draw() {
    computeSizes();
    gui_style.drawRaisedRect(canvas, area, borderwidth);
    if (background_image == null)
        initializeImage();
    if (image_invalid)
        drawPanel(canvas.getRepairArea());
    if (background_image != null)
        canvas.drawImage(background_image, panel.x, panel.y);
}
```

To draw all the visible cells as efficiently as possible, we want to minimize color changes and individual drawing calls. Therefore, all strings are first drawn. Then, all shadow lines are drawn

```
void drawPanel(Area repair_area) {
    canvas.setBufferImage(background_image);
    gui_style.drawSunkenRect(canvas,
                     0, 0, panel.w, panel.h, borderwidth);
    canvas.setFont(font);

    int x = panel.x - borderwidth;
    int y = panel.y - borderwidth;

    int minx=x, miny=y, maxx=minx+1, maxy=miny+1;
    int minc=100, minr=100, maxc=-100, maxr=-100;
```

First of all, the number of visible rows and columns are determined.

```
    for (int r=first_row; r<=last_row; r++) {
        int rh = rowHeight(r);
        x = panel.x + borderwidth;
        for (int c=first_column; c<=last_column; c++) {
            int cw = columnWidth(c);
            if (repair_area.overlaps(x, y, cw, rh)) {
                minx = java.lang.Math.min(minx, x);
                maxx = java.lang.Math.max(maxx, x + cw);
                minc = java.lang.Math.min(minc, c);
                maxc = java.lang.Math.max(maxc, c);

                miny = java.lang.Math.min(miny, y);
                maxy = java.lang.Math.max(maxy, y + rh);
                minr = java.lang.Math.min(minr, r);
                maxr = java.lang.Math.max(maxr, r);
            }
            x += cw + 1;
        }
        y += rh + 1;
    }

    minx -= panel.x - borderwidth;
    miny -= panel.y - borderwidth;
```

```
maxx -= panel.x - borderwidth;
maxy -= panel.y - borderwidth;

gui_style.drawRaisedRect(canvas,
                    minx, miny, maxx-minx, maxy-miny, 1);
```

Then, the strings for all the visible cells are drawn

```
y = miny;
for (int r=minr; r<=maxr; r++) {
    x = minx;
    for (int c=minc; c<=maxc; c++) {
    if (producer != null)
        canvas.drawString(producer.getCellValue(r, c),
            x + 4,
            y + rowHeight(r) - (rowHeight(r)-text_height)/2);
        x += columnWidth(c) + 1;
    }
    y += rowHeight(r) + 1;
}
```

Furthermore, all horizontal and vertical *bottom* shadow lines are drawn

```
canvas.setColor(java.awt.Color.darkGray);
y = miny;
    for (int r=minr; r<=maxr; r++) {
        canvas.drawLine(minx, y, maxx, y);
            y += rowHeight(r) + 1;
}
x = minx;
for (int c=minc; c<=maxc; c++) {
        canvas.drawLine(x, miny, x, maxy);
        x += columnWidth(c) + 1;
}
```

Finally, all horizontal and vertical *top* shadow lines are drawn

```
canvas.setColor(java.awt.Color.white);
y = miny+1;
    for (int r=minr; r<=maxr; r++) {
        canvas.drawLine(minx+1, y, maxx-1, y);
            y += rowHeight(r) + 1;
    }
x = minx+1;
for (int c=minc; c<=maxc; c++) {
        canvas.drawLine(x, miny+1, x, maxy-1);
        x += columnWidth(c) + 1;
    }
```

To finish off, the canvas is told to use its own bitmap again for double buffering (see the description of display list class at page 67). The image is no longer invalid, and can be used later to quickly copy it to canvas.

```
canvas.resetBufferImage();
image_invalid = false;
    }
```

When the program assigns a new GUI style to the table widget, the two scroll-bars need also to be communicated in the new style. Furthermore, the style is asked for the appropriate font to be used for drawing the table cells

```
public void setStyle(GUIStyle style) {
    gui_style = style;
    vertical_scrollbar.setStyle(style);
    horizontal_scrollbar.setStyle(style);
    setFont(gui_style.getLabelFont());
}
```

When a new font is selected for the table widget, a new metrics object is obtained, and the default text height (and therefore row height) is computed. After setting a new font, the image obviously needs to be redrawn

```
public void setFont(java.awt.Font font) {
    this.font = font;
    java.awt.FontMetrics fm = canvas.getFontMetrics(font);
    text_height = fm.getAscent();
    image_invalid = true;
    update();
}
```

When a table widget is made visible or invisible, the two scrollbars also need to be made visible or invisible. Widgets are typically made visible or invisible when they are part of a page in a notebook widget.

```
public void setVisibility(boolean mode) {
    super.setVisibility(mode);
    horizontal_scrollbar.setVisibility(mode);
    vertical_scrollbar.setVisibility(mode);
}
```

The following method is specified in the CallBackable interface. The method is either called by one of the two scrollbars or by the canvas when a key on the keyboard is pressed. This is the way callbacks are implemented in LTK (using double dispatching). See Section 16 in Chapter 1 for other techniques of implementing callbacks.

```
public boolean activateCallback(int method_nr) {
    switch (method_nr) {
        case _hscroll: return hscroll();
        case _vscroll: return vscroll();
        case _key: return key();
    }
    return false;
}
```

Finally, the widget uses the following instance variables

```
public GUIStyle gui_style;
java.awt.Font font;
static short borderwidth = 2;
static final int _vscroll = 11;
static final int _hscroll = 12;
static final int _key = 13;
int rows, columns;
TableProducer producer = null;
Area panel;
int text_height;
int first_column, last_column, first_row, last_row;
int column_width = 60;
Scrollbar vertical_scrollbar;
Scrollbar horizontal_scrollbar;
static int scrollbar_size = 15;
```

```
java.awt.Image background_image;
boolean image_invalid = true;
Area damaged_area;
public java.awt.Color cycleColors[] = {
    java.awt.Color.red, java.awt.Color.green, java.awt.Color.blue,
    java.awt.Color.white, java.awt.Color.orange, java.awt.Color.red
};
final static int CYCLE_TIME=100;
};
```

5.19 Class ltk.Notebook

This class implements a widget that is commonly referred to as a notebook widget or tabbed form. (See Figure 10.) It forms an interface to multiple pages, where each page may contain a complex set of GUI components. Only one page is visible at a time. Selecting another page with one of the tabs will hide the current page and will bring the other page forward.

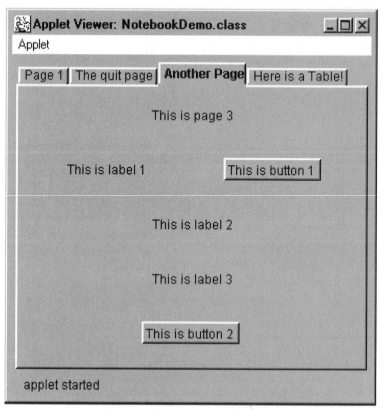

Figure 10. An example showing the use of the ltk.Notebook widget.

This widget is implemented as simple as possible, by making it a vertical layout to compose a tab container and the panel containing the pages. The tabs are in turn collected in a horizontal layout. The pages are collected using a specialized layout class. The current implementation of the complete widget is only 48 lines of Java. The two support classes to contain the pages and the tabs measure 10 and 48 lines, respectively. The tabs are subclasses of button, and its drawing code is overridden. The tabs themselves require as much code as the actual widget does.

In the constructor of the notebook widget, a container is created for the tabs; it is resized to be as wide as the widget and a certain number of pixels high. Next, the page container is created. Finally, the two layouts are added to the notebook widget

```
public class Notebook extends Layout implements CallBackable {
    public Notebook(DisplayListCanvas canvas) {
        super(canvas);
        orientation = Layout.Vertical;
        gui_style = GUIStyle.getDefaultStyle();

        tabs_container = new HorizontalLayout(canvas);
        tabs_container.resize(area.w, label_height);
        tabs_container.padding = 2;
        tabs_container.constraint =
                    Constraint.Left | Constraint.FixedHeight;
        panel = new NotebookPageLayout(canvas);

        addClient(tabs_container);
        addClient(panel);
    }
```

The following method will draw a border around the page container

```
    public void draw() {
        super.draw();
        gui_style.drawRaisedRect(canvas, panel.area, borderwidth);
    }
```

A page can be added to the notebook by calling the following method and passing it a title for the page (to be printed on the tab), and a widget is to be placed inside the notebook page. Typically, the kind of widgets added to a notebook are layouts themselves, containing any number of other layouts and widgets

```
public void addClient(String title, Graphical client) {
    int page_nr = panel.clients.size();
    tabs_container.addClient(new Tab(canvas, this, page_nr, title));
    panel.addClient(client);
}
```

The following method is called whenever one of the tabs is selected. The tab involved will call the method and passes its page number to the notebook. Subsequently, the right page will be selected by making the current page invisible and unselected. Finally, the specified page will be made visible and selected.

```
public boolean activateCallback(int client_nr) { // CallBackable
    selectPage(client_nr);
    return true;
}
public void selectPage(int page_nr) {
    canvas.freeze();
    int n = selected;
    ((Graphical)panel.clients.elementAt(n)).setVisibility(false);
    ((Tab)tabs_container.clients.elementAt(n)).setSelected(false);
    n = selected = page_nr;
    ((Graphical)panel.clients.elementAt(n)).setVisibility(true);
    ((Tab)tabs_container.clients.elementAt(n)).setSelected(true);
    canvas.unFreeze();
}
```

The following method resets the GUI style currently in use

```
public void setStyle(GUIStyle style) {
    gui_style = style;
}
int selected = 0;
public GUIStyle gui_style;
public static short label_height = 21;
final static short borderwidth = 2;
NotebookPageLayout panel;
Layout tabs_container;
};
```

The next (nonpublic) class is a container for the individual pages for the notebook widget. Because page switching is implemented by setting the visibility of the layout or widget representing the page, the individual pages are stacked on top of each other. By selectively making only one of them visible at a time, the illusion of page switching is created

```
class NotebookPageLayout extends Layout {
    public NotebookPageLayout(DisplayListCanvas canvas) {
        super(canvas);
    }
    public void rearrange() {
        for (int n=0; n<nclients; n++)
            ((Graphical)clients.elementAt(n)).reset(area.x, area.y,
                                            area.w, area.h);
    }
};
```

A tab is really a funny looking button. It has two kinds of representations: selected or not. After assigning an appropriate size, it is made fixed-sized

```
class Tab extends Button {
    Tab(DisplayListCanvas canvas, CallBackable client, int page_nr,
                                            String title) {
        super(canvas, client, page_nr, title);
        resize(area.w, Notebook.label_height);
        constraint = Constraint.FixedSize;
    }
```

The method below is called whenever the user switches between pages. It will either be called with *true* to select the page or with false to deselect the page. In both cases, the area that the tab occupies needs to be redrawn. Some extra space is added, because the tabs actually draw outside of their area (something graphicals shouldn't really do)

```
    void setSelected(boolean mode) {
        selected = mode;
        canvas.repairArea(area.x, area.y-5, area.w, area.h+10);
    }
```

To draw the tab, the GUI style is used to draw the tab's background and to get the canvas's background color. Depending on whether the tab is selected or not, a bold or a plain font is selected, and the label is drawn juxtaposed (see the use of dy)

```
public void draw() {
    int dy;
    if (selected) {
        gui_style.drawRaisedRect(canvas,
            area.x, area.y,
            area.w, area.h + borderwidth,
            borderwidth);
        canvas.setColor(gui_style.getBackground());
        canvas.fillRect(
            area.x + borderwidth - 2,
            area.y + area.h,
            area.w+1, borderwidth+1);
        dy = 0;
        canvas.setFont(boldFont);
    }
    else {
        gui_style.drawRaisedRect(canvas,
            area.x, area.y + borderwidth + 3,
            area.w, area.h - padding - borderwidth - 1,
            borderwidth);
        canvas.setColor(gui_style.getBackground());
        canvas.fillRect(
            area.x + borderwidth - 1,
            area.y + area.h + 3 - padding - borderwidth,
            area.w + 2 - 2*borderwidth, borderwidth);
        dy = 2;

        canvas.setFont(plainFont);
    }
    canvas.setColor(gui_style.getRaisedColor());
    canvas.drawString(title,
        area.x + (area.w-text_width)/2 + 2,
        area.y + dy + area.h - (area.h-text_height)/2 - 1);
}
```

The tab knows whether it has been selected or not, and two fonts are allocated, shared by all tabs

```
boolean selected = false;
static java.awt.Font plainFont =
    new java.awt.Font("Helvetica", java.awt.Font.PLAIN, 12);
static java.awt.Font boldFont =
    new java.awt.Font("Helvetica", java.awt.Font.BOLD, 12);
};
```

5.20 Class ltk.HTMLViewer

This class is about the simplest HTML interpreter I could write. It takes an HTML text (in the form of a Java String), and displays it inside its area. Basically, only the easiest and most used tags are supported (in fact, those that are context-insensitive and do not require more than a few minutes to implement). The whole parser is less than 200 lines now and can be used to view arbitrary HTML pages (see its use in the "home page notebook" example), but it could also be used to display text with multiple fonts and styles (e.g., in a "help" window). (See Figure 11.)

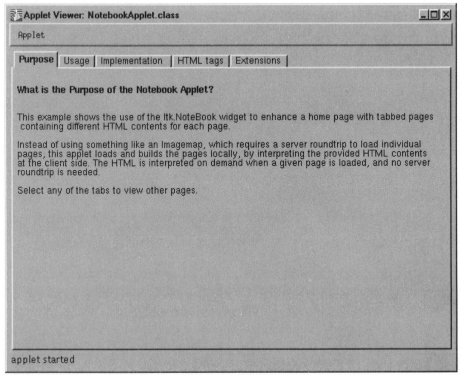

Figure 11. An HTMLViewer widget embedded in a notebook.

The currently recognized tags are

<p>	start of new paragraph
</p>	end of paragraph
 	end of line
<ul>	start of unordered list
</ul>	end of unordered list
<li>	new item
<b>	change font to bold
</b>	change font to normal
<i>	change font to italic
</i>	change font to normal
<tt>	change font to typewriter
</tt>	change font to normal
<h1>	start of section header
</h1>	end of section header
<h2>	start of section header
</h2>	end of section header
<hr>	draw a horizontal line
&quot;	the character "
&lt;	the character <
&gt;	the character >
&amp;	the character &

The limitations of this HTML parser are numerous. I can easily envision a large number of extensions, some of which are:

- The first extension would be images.

- The second extension would be hypertext links, telling the viewer to load another page and replacing the contents of the current page with another. This would not involve the browser, and the enclosing applet stays loaded where it is.

- On a similar topic, allow the contents of a page to be loaded from an URL, instead of out of a string.

- Another interesting option would be to implement the <form> tag, and use LTK widgets for the form elements. That option would be very nice. The HTML parser could also be made to work directly on top of AWT, using AWT widgets for the <form> tag elements.

- Some smart hacker would even be able to implement the <applet> tag, loading, and initializing the applet to be a child of the current notebook page. Should not be too difficult.

First of all, the class initializes and loads the fonts and font metrics that it needs to draw text in multiple fonts and to be able to determine how wide a certain string is

```
import java.util.*;
public class HTMLViewer extends Graphical {

    public HTMLViewer(DisplayListCanvas canvas, String contents) {
        super(canvas, 0,0,0,0);
        this.contents = contents;
        color = java.awt.Color.black;
        boldFont = new java.awt.Font("Helvetica",
                                        java.awt.Font.BOLD, FH);
        boldFm = canvas.getFontMetrics(boldFont);
        plainFont = new java.awt.Font("Helvetica",
                                        java.awt.Font.PLAIN, FH);
        plainFm = canvas.getFontMetrics(plainFont);
        italicFont= new java.awt.Font("Helvetica",
                                        java.awt.Font.ITALIC, FH);
        italicFm = canvas.getFontMetrics(boldFont);
        ttFont = new java.awt.Font("Courier",
                                        java.awt.Font.PLAIN, FH);
        ttFm = canvas.getFontMetrics(ttFont);
        fm = plainFm;
    }
```

The following method really implements the HTML interpreter. I do not bother to translate the text into an intermediate representation. Rather, the contents string gets interpreted as a string over and over. This will certainly prove to be problematic for larger contents. As the interpreter only does tags that are context-insensitive, the parser is basically one big if-statement. Adding a new tag would just be adding a new else-branch at the end of this method.

```
    public void draw() {
        if (contents == null) return;
        canvas.setColor(color);
        int startx = area.x;
        int x = startx;
```

```java
int y = area.y;
int w = area.w;

String line = "";
initWords();
String word;
canvas.setFont(plainFont);
while ((word=getWord())!=null) {
    if (word.equals("<p>") || word.equals("<br>") ||
            x + fm.stringWidth(line) +
                        fm.stringWidth(word) >= area.w) {
        canvas.drawString(line, x, y);
        line = "";
        y += FH;
        x = startx;
        if (word.equals("<p>")) {
            y += FH;
        }
    }
    else
        if (!word.equals("<br>"))
            line += word;
    }
    else if (word.equals(" ")) {
        if (!line.equals(""))
            line += " ";
    }
    else if (word.equals("<hr>")) {
        canvas.drawString(line, x, y);
        line = "";
        canvas.setColor(java.awt.Color.darkGray);
        canvas.drawLine(x, y-1, w, y-1);
        canvas.setColor(java.awt.Color.white);
        canvas.drawLine(x, y, w, y);
        y += FH;
        canvas.setColor(color);
    }
    else if (word.equals("<ul>")) {
        first_item = true;
```

```
        startx += fm.stringWidth(" ");
        x = startx;
    }
    else if (word.equals("<li>")) {
        canvas.drawString(line, x, y);
        line = "";
        if (!first_item) startx -= fm.stringWidth(" ");
        x = startx;
        y += FH;
        canvas.fillRect(x, y-FH/2, FH/2, FH/2);
        startx += fm.stringWidth(" ");
        x = startx;
        first_item = false;
    }
    else if (word.equals("</ul>")) {
        canvas.drawString(line, x, y);
        line = "";
        if (!first_item) startx -= fm.stringWidth(" ");
        startx -= fm.stringWidth(" ");
        if (startx < area.x) startx = area.x;
        x = startx;
    }
    else if (word.equals("<b>") ||
            word.equals("<h1>") || word.equals("<h2>")) {
        if (!word.equals("<b>")) { x = startx; y += FH; }
        canvas.drawString(line, x, y);
        x += fm.stringWidth(line);
        line = "";
        canvas.setFont(boldFont); fm = boldFm;
    }
    else if (word.equals("</b>") ||
            word.equals("</h1>") || word.equals("</h2>")) {
        canvas.setFont(boldFont);
        canvas.drawString(line, x, y);
        x += fm.stringWidth(line);
        if (!word.equals("</b>")) { x = startx; y += FH; }
        line = "";
        canvas.setFont(plainFont); fm = plainFm;
```

```
        }
        else if (word.equals("<i>")) {
            canvas.drawString(line, x, y);
            x += fm.stringWidth(line);
            line = "";
            canvas.setFont(italicFont); fm = italicFm;
        }
        else if (word.equals("</i>")) {
            canvas.setFont(italicFont);
            canvas.drawString(line, x, y);
            x += fm.stringWidth(line);
            line = "";
            canvas.setFont(plainFont); fm = plainFm;
        }
        else if (word.equals("<tt>")) {
            canvas.drawString(line, x, y);
            x += fm.stringWidth(line);
            line = "";
            canvas.setFont(ttFont); fm = ttFm;
        }
        else if (word.equals("</tt>")) {
            canvas.setFont(ttFont);
            canvas.drawString(line, x, y);
            x += fm.stringWidth(line);
            line = "";
            canvas.setFont(plainFont); fm = plainFm;
        }
        else if (word.startsWith("<") && word.length() > 1) {
        }
        else {
            char c = word.charAt(0);
            line += word;
        }
    }
    canvas.drawString(line, x, y);
}
```

The following method can be called to redraw the HTML viewer with new contents. This is useful for help windows that have a variable contents, for instance.

```
public void setContents(String contents) {
    this.contents = contents;
    update();
}
```

The utility functions that follow are used by this class to initialize the buffer, to skip spaces to the next word, and to read the next word from the current buffer

```
void initWords() {
    buffer = contents;
    bufp = 0;
}
boolean skipSpaces() {
    boolean spaceSeen = false;
    char c;
    try {
        c = buffer.charAt(bufp++);
        while (c==' '||c=='\r'||c=='\t'||c=='\n') {
            if (c==' '||c=='\t') spaceSeen = true;
            c = buffer.charAt(bufp++);
        }
    }
    catch (StringIndexOutOfBoundsException e) { }
    bufp--;
    return spaceSeen;
}
String getWord() {
    if (skipSpaces()) return " ";
    int start=bufp;
    char c;
    try {
        if (buffer.charAt(bufp)=='&') {
            do c = buffer.charAt(bufp++);
            while (c!=';');
            String special_char = buffer.substring(start+1,bufp);
            if (special_char.startsWith("lt")) return "<";
            if (special_char.startsWith("gt")) return ">";
```

```
        if (special_char.startsWith("quot")) return "\"";
        if (special_char.startsWith("amp")) return "&";
    } else if (buffer.charAt(bufp)=='<') {
        do c = buffer.charAt(bufp++);
        while (c!='>');
        bufp++;
    } else {
        do c = buffer.charAt(bufp++);
        while (c!=' '&&c!='\r'&&c!='\t'&&c!='\n'&&c!='<'&&c!='&');
    }
    bufp--;
    return buffer.substring(start,bufp);
    }
    catch (StringIndexOutOfBoundsException e) { return null; }
}
```

Finally, some instance variables used by this class are defined

```
java.awt.FontMetrics fm, plainFm, boldFm, italicFm, ttFm;
String contents;
int bufp;
java.awt.Font plainFont, boldFont, italicFont, ttFont;
String buffer;
static int FH=12;
boolean first_item = false;
};
```

5.21 Class ltk.LTKApplet

The ltk.LTKApplet class abstracts the use of java.awt.Applet and adds to it a canvas with the requested width and height. It is a little unfortunate that the designers of AWT took the design decision to do applet instantiation in a special *init* method, instead of using the constructor. Namely, it is critical that subclasses of LTKApplet call the init of their superclass, otherwise the applet does not get constructed properly. There is no way to enforce this. If initialization would occur in the default constructor, the default constructor for the superclass would automatically be called

```
public abstract class LTKApplet extends Applet {
    public void init() {
        setLayout(new BorderLayout());
        String width = getParameter("width");
        String height = getParameter("height");
        canvas = new ltk.DisplayListCanvas(this,
```

```
        (width == null) ? 10 : Integer.valueOf(width).intValue(),
        (height == null) ? 10 : Integer.valueOf(height).intValue());
    add("Center", canvas);
}
```

Unlike the case for `java.applet.Applet`, the following two inherited methods are made *abstract* here on purpose, so that subclasses cannot ignore them or confuse them with the init method

```
public abstract void start();
public abstract void stop();
```

If an applet provides a "main" method, it can be run as a Java application. Basically, what needs to be done is create a frame, create an instance of the applet, add it to the frame, resize and show the frame, and start the applet. Instead of seducing programmers to use the cut-and-paste approach, this complicated behavior is encapsulated inside the LTKApplet class, and a utility method is provided. Its usage is as shown in the following example

```
public class HelloWorld extends LTKApplet implements Runnable {
    ...
    public static void main(String args[]) {
        (new HelloWorld()).runAppletAsApplication("Hello World");
    }
};
```

The two versions of the utility method are given here (one using default sizes, and one allowing for user-specified width and height

```
public void runAppletAsApplication(String title) {
    runAppletAsApplication(title, 450, 350);
}
protected void runAppletAsApplication(String title, int w, int h) {
    frame = new Frame(title);
    running_as_applet = false;
    init();
    frame.add("Center", this);
    frame.resize(w, h-1);
    frame.show();
    start();        // call overridden method
    frame.resize(w, h);
}
```

When run as an application, any call to java.applet.Applet.getParameter will generate a null pointer exception. Therefore, this call is intercepted in case the applet does not run in applet mode. In that case, the method returns null, to indicate failure

```java
public String getParameter(String p) {
    return (running_as_applet) ? super.getParameter(p) : null;
}
```

Finally, some instance variables are declared

```java
public static Frame frame;
public DisplayListCanvas canvas;
public boolean running_as_applet = true;
}
```

6. LTK examples

This chapter shows some examples for LTK.

6.1 Widget Animation Demo

This demo show the usage of a large collection of buttons layed out efficiently using horizontal and vertical layouts. In addition to that, a yellow box will move inside the canvas, avoiding the other colored boxes it encounters. The yellow box will move either underneath all buttons or on top of them. (See Figure 12.)

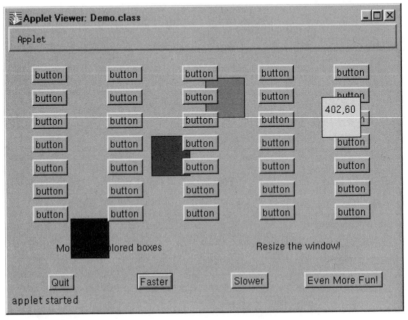

Figure 12. Example showing the use of the LTK display list canvas.

As the layouts are managers only, they do not occupy any area on the screen, and widgets can easily move outside their layout. An example is given when the "Even more fun" button is pressed. The yellow box will then avoid all buttons on its path by moving them aside. The buttons may overlap and even move off the screen. Although not directly visible, each row of buttons is managed by one horizontal layout, all of which are managed by one vertical layout. Buttons can easily move from the location computed by their horizontal layout and even out of the vertical layout. When the window is resized (possible when the appletviewer is used), the layouts are invalidated, and each layout is rearranged.

Physically, all graphical elements are a child of the same canvas (each LTKApplet instance has one canvas of the same size as itself). Because all graphicals share the same canvas, they also share the same display list, and objects can be easily made to hide or show, and to move up or down the display list hierarchy (making them appear behind or in front of others).

The animation is done by a separate thread, allowing for repaints and user events to be handled independently in another thread; this happens when one of the colored boxes is dragged with the mouse.

Here is the source of widget/animation demo (file demo.java)

```java
import ltk.*;
import java.awt.Color;

public class Demo extends LTKApplet implements CallBackable, Runnable {
    static String title = "A Sample LTK Applet";
    Box red_box, green_box, blue_box;
    XYBox yellow_box;
    Layout vlayout, hlayout;

    public boolean hello() {
        System.out.println("Hello");
        return true;
    }
    public boolean faster() {
        if (N < 128) N *= 2;
        return true;
    }
    public boolean slower() {
        if (N > 1) N /= 2;
        return true;
```

```
    }
    public boolean fun() {
        N = 4;
        avoid_buttons = true;
        return true;
    }
    public boolean quit() {
        System.exit(0);
        return true;
    }
    public void init() {                              // from LTKApplet
        super.init();
        N = 1;
        canvas.freeze();
        red_box = new Box(canvas, 30, 30, 50, 50);
        red_box.setFillColor(Color.red);
        green_box = new Box(canvas, 130, 30, 50, 50);
        green_box.setFillColor(Color.green);
        blue_box = new Box(canvas, 30, 130, 50, 50);
        blue_box.setFillColor(Color.blue);
        yellow_box = new XYBox(canvas, 170, 130, 50, 50);
        yellow_box.setFillColor(Color.yellow);
        vlayout = new VerticalLayout(Layout.space(canvas));
        vlayout.padding = 3;
        for (int y=0; y<NROWS; y++) {
            hlayout = new HorizontalLayout(canvas);
            hlayout.padding = 3;
            for (int x=0; x<NCOLUMNS; x++) {
                Button b = new ltk.Button(canvas, this, _hello, "button");
                hlayout.addClient(b);
            }
            vlayout.addClient(hlayout);
        }
        vlayout.addClient( Layout.space(canvas) );
        vlayout.addClient(
            new HorizontalLayout(
                new Label(canvas, "Move the colored boxes"),
                new Label(canvas, "Resize the window!")
```

```
            )
        );
        vlayout.addClient( Layout.space(canvas) );

        Button quit_button, fast_button, slow_button, fun_button;
        vlayout.addClient(
            new HorizontalLayout(
                quit_button = new Button(canvas, this, _quit, "Quit"),
                fast_button = new Button(canvas, this, _faster, "Faster"),
                slow_button = new Button(canvas, this, _slower, "Slower"),
                fun_button = new Button(canvas, this, _fun,
                                            "Even More Fun!")
            )
        );
        canvas.unFreeze();
        FocusHandler f = new FocusHandler();
        f.add(quit_button);
        f.add(fast_button);
        f.add(slow_button);
        f.add(fun_button);
        f.setFocus(fast_button);
        thread = new Thread(this);
        thread.start();
    }
    public void start() {                        // from LTKApplet
        thread.resume();
    }
    public void stop() {                         // from LTKApplet
        thread.suspend();
    }
    public void run() {
        int dx=-1, dy=-1;
        while (true) {
            yellow_box.move(yellow_box.area.x+dx*N,
                            yellow_box.area.y+dy*N);
            if (yellow_box.area.x > canvas.area.w - yellow_box.area.w)
                dx = -1;
            if (yellow_box.area.y > canvas.area.h - yellow_box.area.h)
                dy = -1;
```

```
        if (yellow_box.area.x < 1) dx = 1;
        if (yellow_box.area.y < 1) dy = 1;
        if (dx < 1) yellow_box.lower();
        else yellow_box.raise();

        avoid(red_box);
        avoid(green_box);
        avoid(blue_box);
        if (avoid_buttons) avoidButtons();
        try {
            Thread.sleep(100);         // make thread unselfish
        } catch (InterruptedException e) { }
    }
}
public void avoid(Graphical g) {
    int x = g.area.x;
    int y = g.area.y;
    //
    // detect overlap of two graphicals
    //
    if (yellow_box.area.inside(x, y))
        g.move(g.area.x, g.area.y + 3*N);
    else if (yellow_box.area.inside(x+g.area.w, y))
        g.move(g.area.x - 3*N, g.area.y);
    else if (yellow_box.area.inside(x, y+g.area.h))
        g.move(g.area.x, g.area.y - 3*N);
    else if (yellow_box.area.inside(x+g.area.w, y+g.area.h))
        g.move(g.area.x - 3*N, g.area.y - 3*N);
    //
    // keep the bounced graphical on the screen...
    //
    if (g.area.x < 0)
        g.move(0, g.area.y);
    else if (g.area.y < 0)
        g.move(g.area.x, 0);
    else if (g.area.x + g.area.w > canvas.area.w)
        g.move(canvas.area.w - g.area.w, g.area.y);
    else if (g.area.y + g.area.h > canvas.area.h)
        g.move(g.area.x, canvas.area.h - g.area.h);
```

```
    }
    public void avoidButtons() {
        for (int y=1; y<NROWS+1; y++) {
            Layout layout = (ltk.Layout)vlayout.clients.elementAt(y);
            for (int x=0; x<NCOLUMNS; x++)
                avoid((Graphical) layout.clients.elementAt(x));
        }
    }
    public static void main(String args[]) {
        LTKApplet applet = new Demo();
        applet.runAppletAsApplication(title);
    }
    public boolean activateCallback(int method_nr) { // CallBackable
        switch (method_nr) {
            case _hello: return hello();
            case _faster: return faster();
            case _slower: return slower();
            case _quit: return quit();
            case _fun: return fun();
        }
        return false;                        // event not processed
    }
    public String toString() {
        return "Demo[current speed=" + N + "]";
    }
    static final int NROWS = 7;
    static final int NCOLUMNS = 5;

    static final int _hello = 1;
    static final int _quit = 2;
    static final int _slower = 3;
    static final int _faster = 4;
    static final int _fun = 5;

    int N;

    boolean avoid_buttons = false;
    Thread thread;
}
```

```
class XYBox extends Box {
    public XYBox(DisplayListCanvas canvas, int x, int y, int w, int h) {
        super(canvas, x, y, w, h);
    }
    public synchronized void draw() {
        canvas.setColor(fill_color);
        canvas.fillRect(area.x, area.y, area.w, area.h);
        canvas.setColor(color);
        canvas.drawRect(area.x, area.y, area.w, area.h);
        canvas.drawString("" + area.x + "," + area.y,
                          area.x+5, area.y+20);
    }
    public String toString() {
        return ((down)?"a being dragged ":"") + "Box[" +
            area.toString() + "," +
            "fill color=" + fill_color.toString() +
            "]";
    }
};
```

6.2 Layout Demo

This example creates a vertical layout with five horizontal layouts, each acting as a row with two widgets (Labels, EntryFields, and Buttons). (See Figure 13.)

Figure 13. Nested layouts using resize constraints.

Widgets can be added to layouts at the construction time of the layout by passing the widgets to the constructor. Alternatively, widgets can be added or removed dynamically at a later stage. Using the constructor form yields a highly declarative form. The structure of the GUI can be read easily from the corresponding Java code. Constraints can be used to constrain widgets to the left, right, top, or bottom of a layout location (see the first two labels).

```
Layout layout = new VerticalLayout(
    new HorizontalLayout(
        Constraint.setLeft(new ltk.Label(canvas, "Press")),
        Constraint.setRight(new ltk.Label(canvas, "return"))
    ),
    new HorizontalLayout(
        new ltk.Label(canvas, "to"),
        new ltk.Label(canvas, "quit")
    ),
    new HorizontalLayout(
        new ltk.Label(canvas, "Name:"),
        e1 = new ltk.EntryField(canvas, this, _name)
    ),
    new HorizontalLayout(
        new ltk.Label(canvas, "Address:"),
        e2 = new ltk.EntryField(canvas, this, _name)
    ),
    new HorizontalLayout(
        new ltk.Button(canvas, this, _cancel, "Cancel"),
        button = new ltk.Button(canvas, this, _quit, "Quit")
    )
);
```

Most widgets in LTK, including Buttons and EntryFields, by default have their constraint set to `Constraint.Centered`. That means that when a button or entry field is resized to a larger size, it will not resize, yet will move to the center of the new area. After creation of a widget, its individual resize constraint can be changed at any time.

For this example, the initial constraint for the "quit" button is reset to `Constraint.None`. This means, in the future, this button will resize when told to by the layout it has been added to (best observed when using the appletviewer).

```
button.setConstraint(Constraint.None);      // allows resizing
```

The resize constraint is also set for the two entry fields, both constraining them to stay to the left of wherever they are moved to and to ignore request to resize their height. This means they will resize horizontally (occupying all requested space) but will only center themselves vertically in the requested space and not resize vertically.

```
e1.setConstraint(Constraint.Left | Constraint.FixedHeight);
e2.setConstraint(Constraint.Left | Constraint.FixedHeight);
```

Furthermore, the input focus is set to the quit button. The effect is that hitting the Enter key at any time quits the appletviewer by calling `System.exit(0);` something which is luckily ignored by browsers like Netscape. In that case, the event thread that handles the callback crashes, leaving the button in a funny state.

```
button.setHighlight(true);
```

The full source code (96 lines of Java) is given here

```java
import ltk.*;


public class LayoutDemo extends LTKApplet implements CallBackable {

    public void init() {                            // from LTKApplet
        super.init();
        Layout h1,h2;
        Layout layout = new VerticalLayout(
            new HorizontalLayout(
                Constraint.setLeft(new ltk.Label(canvas, "Press")),
                Constraint.setRight(new ltk.Label(canvas, "return"))
            ),
            new HorizontalLayout(
                new ltk.Label(canvas, "to"),
                new ltk.Label(canvas, "quit")
            ),
            h1 = new HorizontalLayout(
                new ltk.Label(canvas, "Name:"),
                e1 = new ltk.EntryField(canvas, this, _name)
            ),
            h2 = new HorizontalLayout(
                new ltk.Label(canvas, "Address:"),
                e2 = new ltk.EntryField(canvas, this, _address)
```

```
        ),
        new HorizontalLayout(
            cancel_button = new ltk.Button(canvas, this, _cancel, "Cancel"),
            quit_button = new ltk.Button(canvas, this, _quit, "Quit")
        )
    );
    h1.setConstraint(Constraint.FixedHeight);
    h2.setConstraint(Constraint.FixedHeight);

    e1.setConstraint(Constraint.Left | Constraint.FixedHeight);
    e2.setConstraint(Constraint.Left | Constraint.FixedHeight);

    quit_button.setConstraint(Constraint.None);   // allows resizing

    focus_handler = new FocusHandler();
    focus_handler.add(e1);
    focus_handler.add(e2);
    focus_handler.add(cancel_button);
    focus_handler.add(quit_button);
    focus_handler.setFocus(e1);

    // layout.rearrange();
}
public void start() { }                      // from LTKApplet
public void stop() { }                       // from LTKApplet

public static void main(String args[]) {
    (new LayoutDemo()).runAppletAsApplication("Layout test");
}

public boolean cancel() {
    System.out.println("Cancelled");
    e1.setText("");
    e2.setText("");
    focus_handler.setFocus(e1);
    return true;
}
```

```java
    public boolean name() {
        System.out.println("name changed, setting focus to address");
        focus_handler.setFocus(e2);
        return true;
    }

    public boolean address() {
        System.out.println("address changed, setting focus to button");
        System.out.println("could also have exited right away");
        focus_handler.setFocus(quit_button);
        return true;
    }

    public boolean quit() {
        System.exit(1);
        return true;
    }

    public boolean activateCallback(int method_nr) { // from CallBackable
        switch (method_nr) {
            case _cancel: return cancel();
            case _name: return name();
            case _address: return address();
            case _quit: return quit();
        }
        return false;                          // event not processed
    }

    public String toString() {
        return "ltk.LayoutDemo";
    }

    static final int _cancel = 1;
    static final int _quit = 2;
    static final int _name = 3;
    static final int _address = 4;
    private FocusHandler focus_handler;
    Button cancel_button, quit_button;
    EntryField e1, e2;
}
```

6.3 Notebook Demo

This example creates a notebook widget, after which each of the four pages is added. The notebook behaves as a layout; however, pages can not be added at construction time. Rather, pages are added explicitly by calling the "addClient" method, with the title of the page, and the widget that will occupy the page. For page one, we simply add one label. The second page contains more than one widget, which are, therefore, collected in a vertical layout. In fact, any combination of layouts can be added to a page, as is done on page three. Even something as complicated as a table can be added, done on page four. (See Figure 14.)

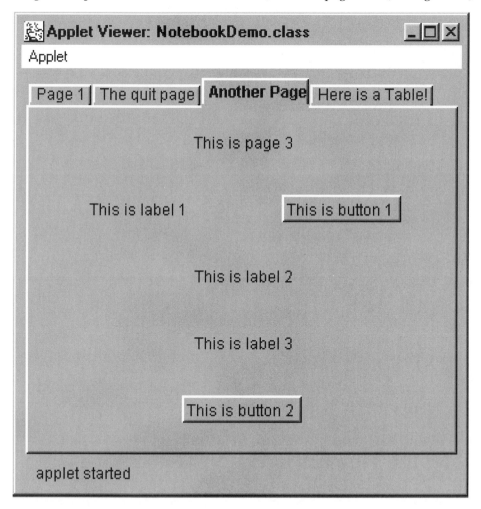

Figure 14. The notebook applet.

The notebook demo creates a table in one of the pages, and a corresponding table producer is declared at the end of the demo source. The full source of the notebook demo is given here

```
public class NotebookDemo extends LTKApplet implements CallBackable {
    public void init() {                              // from LTKApplet
        super.init();                                 // call LTKApplet
        canvas.freeze();
        GUIStyle.selectStyle(GUIStyle.Motif);
        GUIStyle.selectStyle(GUIStyle.Win95);
        notebook = new Notebook(canvas);
        notebook.addClient( "Page 1",
            new ltk.Label(canvas, "This is page 1")
        );
        notebook.addClient( "The quit page",
            new VerticalLayout(
                new ltk.Label(canvas, "This is page 2"),
                new ltk.Button(canvas, this, _exit, "Press here to Quit")
            )
        );
        notebook.addClient( "Another Page",
            new VerticalLayout(
                new ltk.Label(canvas, "This is page 3"),
                new HorizontalLayout(
                    new ltk.Label(canvas, "This is label 1"),
                    new ltk.Button(canvas, this, 0, "This is button 1")
                ),
                new ltk.Label(canvas, "This is label 2"),
                new ltk.Label(canvas, "This is label 3"),
                new ltk.Button(canvas, this, 0, "This is button 2")
            )
        );
        notebook.addClient( "Here is a Table!",
            new ltk.Table(canvas, new NotebookDemoTableProducer(), 30, 40)
        );
        notebook.selectPage(0);
        canvas.unFreeze();
    }
```

```
    public void start() { }                    // from LTKApplet
    public void stop() { }                      // from LTKApplet
    public boolean exit() {
        System.exit(0);
        return true;
    }
    public static void main(String args[]) {
        LTKApplet applet = new NotebookDemo();
        applet.runAppletAsApplication("Notebook test");
    }
    public boolean activateCallback(int method_nr) { // CallBackable
        switch (method_nr) {
            case _exit: return exit();
        }
        return false;                  // event not processed
    }
    static final int _exit = 1;
    Notebook notebook;
    Layout layout;
}
class NotebookDemoTableProducer implements ltk.TableProducer {
    public String getCellValue(int row, int column) {
        return "" + java.lang.Math.abs(row * column);
    }
};
```

6.4 Notebook/Homepage Demo

This demo uses a notebook widget, plus the HTMLViewer that come with LTK, to create a homepage applet. With this applet a home page can be enhanced with tabbed pages containing different HTML contents for each individual page. Instead of using something like an imagemap, which requires a server round-trip to load individual pages, this applet loads and builds the pages locally, by interpreting the provided HTML contents at the client side. The HTML is interpreted on demand when a given page is loaded, and no server round-trip is needed. The user can select any of the tabs to view other pages. (See Figure 15.)

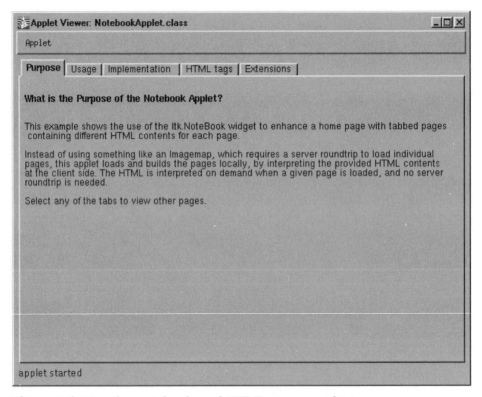

Figure 15. Use the notebook and HTML viewer widgets.

The following example of an HTML file shows how the homepage applet can be used. The pages themselves contain any HTML code. Special care needs to be taken, as the " character cannot be used, for it identifies the end of the string containing the page contents. Use & instead. For a similar reason, the & character cannot be used directly, because browsers like Netscape first scan the whole HTML page for special characters, including the contents of an applet parameter string. The & special character needs to escaped twice, therefore. In contrast, the Java appletviewer does not scan the parameters, so handling of parameter values is inconsistent here. Look at the source of the HTML document for the homepage demo, for inspiration.

```
<applet code=NotebookApplet.class width=600 height=400>
        <param name=title0 value="Title For the First Page">
        <param name=contents0 "
                ... any HTML code ...
        ">
        <param name=title1 value="Second Title">
        <param name=contents1 value="
                ... some more HTML code ...
        ">
</applet>
```

The notebook applet uses ltk.HTMLViewer, a very rudimentary HTML interpreter. The interpreter behaves as an LTK graphical. Therefore, it can be moved, resized, and embedded in any layout, including notebook pages (which are implemented as layouts). The resulting notebook applet is only 24 lines of Java. The core of the applet is the following piece of code

```
Notebook notebook=new Notebook(canvas);
for (int n=0; true; n++) {
    String title = getParameter("title" + n);
    if (title == null) break;
    String contents = getParameter("contents" + n);
    notebook.addClient(title,
        new VerticalLayout(
            Layout.space(canvas),
            new HTMLViewer(canvas, contents)
        )
    );
}
notebook.selectPage(0);
```

The applet dynamically loads each of the pages from the parameter values passed from the HTML pages. A new HTML viewer is created for each page and added to the notebook. Finally, the first page is selected. For the currently recognized set of tags, see the section on the HTMLViewer class.

6.5 *Towers of Hanoi Demo*

This applet is based on an old fable that reports (if my memory serves me well) that for some reason, a group of Buddhistic monks had to move a given number of golden disks from one peg to a second peg, using a third peg for temporary storage. The condition that made the effort more complicated was that a disk may only rest directly on a disk that is larger than itself. After all disks would have been moved to the target peg, something very bad would happen, or something very good (I forgot that little detail). Anyway, they are still working on it, my Artificial Intelligence professor at the Free University in Amsterdam claimed. (See Figure 16.)

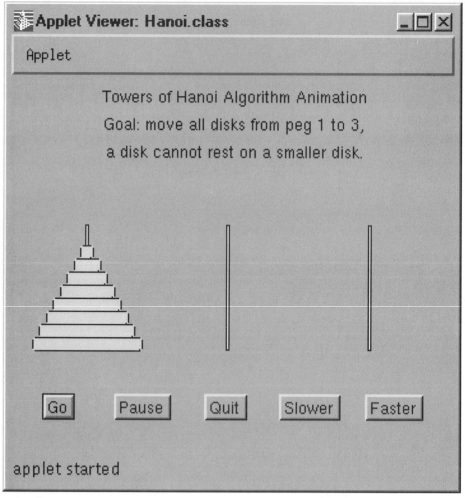

Figure 16. Towers of Hanoi demo, showing layouts and double buffering.

This demo is the most complete example of the little toolkit, and the best documented. The real algorithm is only a few lines of Java

```
public void hanoi(int ndisks, Peg from, Peg using, Peg to) {
    if (ndisks > 0) {
        hanoi(ndisks - 1, from, to, using);
        from.moveDisk(to);
        hanoi(ndisks - 1, using, from, to);
    }
}
```

The applet is loaded from an HTML page, as is done in the following example

```
<applet code=Hanoi.class align=center numberOfDisks=8
        width=350 height=290>
</applet>
```

Overall, the applet measures 350 lines, of which 200 are lines only containing comments. This applet demonstrates the use of:

- LTKApplet—how to run something as both an applet and a Java application.
- Smooth, double buffering animation using LTK.
- Nested Layouts (for the labels, the pegs, and the buttons).
- Easy callbacks (from the buttons).
- Recursion, see method hanoi().
- Using multiple threads, by using Runnable and Thread.

Needless to say, the applet does not directly do any drawing itself to perform the animation. Instead, it moves graphical elements from one location to another. The underlying canvas (with its display list management) will ensure that the scene is nicely repainted. Because of the use of layouts, the applet reacts nicely to resizing of the frame (when viewed in the appletviewer), even while the animation is running.

Here is the source of Towers of Hanoi (350 lines of Java)

```java
import ltk.*;
import java.awt.Color;          // Used in draw().
import java.util.Vector;        // Used by class Peg.


//
// This demo implements an animation of the Towers of Hanoi algorithm.
// It demonstrates the use of:
//
// - LTKApplet - how to run something as applet AND application
// - Smooth, double buffering animation using ltk.
// - Nested Layouts
// - Callbacks (from three buttons)
// - Recursion, see method hanoi().
// - Using multiple threads, by using Runnable and Thread.
//
// See variable Hanoi.numberOfDisks to set the number of disks to
// be moved.
// See variable Disk.speed usage in Disk.moveTo(Peg), Hanoi.slower(),
// and Hanoi.faster() for changing the speed of the animation.
//

public class Hanoi extends LTKApplet implements CallBackable, Runnable
{
    //
    // Callback for the "Go" button. See init() and use of variable _go.
    //
    public boolean go() {
        take_a_break = false;      // see pause(), and Disk.move()
        if (thread == null) {
            thread = new Thread(this);
            thread.start();          // will call run() ...
        }
        focus_handler.setFocus(pause_button);
        return true;
    }


    //
```

```
// Inherited from Runnable, implement main body of thread. See go().
//
public void run() {
    hanoi(numberOfDisks, peg1, peg2, peg3);
}


//
// The heart of this demo: the recursive Towers of Hanoi algorithm.
// Move <ndisks> disks from peg <from> to peg <to>, where <using>
// can be used to temporarily store disks.
//
// Example call:
//
//     hanoi(8, peg1, peg2, peg3) move 8 disks from 1 to 3
//     :=
//     hanoi(7, peg1, peg3, peg2) move 7 disks from 1 to 2
//     peg1.moveDisk(peg3)        move 1 disks from 1 to 3
//     hanoi(7, peg2, peg1, peg3) move 7 disks from 2 to 3
//
public void hanoi(int ndisks, Peg from, Peg using, Peg to) {
    if (ndisks > 0) {
        hanoi(ndisks - 1, from, to, using);
        from.moveDisk(to);
        hanoi(ndisks - 1, using, from, to);
    }
}


//
// Callback for the "Pause" button. See init() and use of
// variable _pause.
public boolean pause() {
    take_a_break = true;
    focus_handler.setFocus(go_button);
    return true;
}
```

```
//
// Callback for the "Quit" button. See init() and use of
// variable _quit.
public boolean quit() {
    System.exit(0);
    return true;
}


//
// Callback for the "Slower" button. See init() & use of
// variable _slower.
public boolean slower() {
    if (Disk.speed > 1) Disk.speed /= 2;
    return true;
}


//
// Callback for the "Faster" button. See init() & use of
// variable _faster.
public boolean faster() {
    Disk.speed *= 2;
    return true;
}


//
// Inherited from LTKApplet. Initialize the applet.
//
public void init() {
    super.init();                        // call LTKApplet.init

    String nDisks = getParameter("numberOfDisks");
    numberOfDisks = (nDisks==null) ? 5 :
                          Integer.valueOf(nDisks).intValue();

    canvas.freeze(); // do not draw in canvas until unFreeze() call.
```

```
//
// Create the three pegs.
//
// Create the three buttons. Pass the canvas to draw into, and
// get events from. Identify the owner (this) of the button,
// the method callback number (see activateCallback() method),
// and the label used by the button.
//

Button slow_button;
Button fast_button;

new VerticalLayout(
    new VerticalLayout(
       new ltk.Label(canvas, "Towers of Hanoi Algorithm Animation"),
       new ltk.Label(canvas, "Goal: move all disks from peg 1 to 3,"),
       new ltk.Label(canvas, "a disk cannot rest on a smaller
disk.")
    ),
    Layout.largeSpace(canvas),
    new HorizontalLayout(
      peg1 = new Peg(canvas, canvas.area.h/3, "1"),
      peg2 = new Peg(canvas, canvas.area.h/3, "2"),
      peg3 = new Peg(canvas, canvas.area.h/3, "3")
    ),
    Layout.space(canvas),
    new HorizontalLayout(
      go_button = new ltk.Button(canvas, this, _go, "Go"),
      pause_button = new ltk.Button(canvas, this, _pause, "Pause"),
      quit_button = new ltk.Button(canvas, this, _quit, "Quit"),
      slow_button = new ltk.Button(canvas, this, _slower, "Slower"),
      fast_button = new ltk.Button(canvas, this, _faster, "Faster")
    )
```

```
      );
      focus_handler = new FocusHandler();

      focus_handler.add(go_button);
      focus_handler.add(pause_button);
      focus_handler.add(quit_button);
      focus_handler.add(slow_button);
      focus_handler.add(fast_button);

      focus_handler.setFocus(go_button);

      //
      // Create <numberOfDisks> disks and place them on peg1
      //
      for (int n=numberOfDisks; n>0; n--)
          new Disk(canvas, peg1, (canvas.area.w/4) * n/numberOfDisks, // w
                          peg1.area.h / (numberOfDisks+1));       // h

      //
      // Finally, tell the canvas to activate all pending drawing calls.
      //
      canvas.unFreeze();
   }


//
// Inherited from LTKApplet, called when browser loads
// page with applet.
public void start() {
   if (thread != null) thread.resume();
}


//
// Inherited from LTKApplet, called when browser unloads
// page with applet.
public void stop() {
   if (thread != null) thread.suspend();
}
```

```
//
// Main routine, only used when executed as a Java application.
//
public static void main(String args[]) {
    LTKApplet applet = new Hanoi();
        applet.runAppletAsApplication("Towers of Hanoi Algorithm");
}


public boolean activateCallback(int method_nr) { // from CallBackable
    switch (method_nr) {
        case _go: return go();                  // "Go" button
        case _quit: return quit();              // "Quit" button
        case _slower: return slower();          // "Slower" button
        case _faster: return faster();          // "Faster" button
        case _pause: return pause();            // "Pause" button
    }
    return false;                               // event not processed
}


public String toString() {
    return "Hanoi[" +
        numberOfDisks + " disks, " +
        "3 pegs[" + peg1.nDisks + "," + peg2.nDisks + "," +
                                    peg3.nDisks + "]" +
        (take_a_break ? "pauze pressed, " : "") +
        "]";
}


Peg peg1, peg2, peg3;   // The three pegs
Thread thread;          // The separate thread to run the algoritm

Button go_button, quit_button, pause_button;

static boolean take_a_break;  // set to true when pause pressed

static int numberOfDisks = 5; // set this one in html...

FocusHandler focus_handler;
```

```
        static final int _go          = 1;  //
        static final int _quit         = 2;   //
        static final int _pause        = 3;   // used in activateCallback()
        static final int _faster       = 4;   //
        static final int _slower       = 5;  //
}


//
// Each instance of the Disk class represents one disk to be moved as
// part of the Hanoi algorithm.
// Each peg remembers all disks that are currently located on top of it,
// and each disk is aware on which peg it currently rests.
// Disks can be told to move to a new peg and will notify the old and
// new peg of this fact.
//
// Disks are Graphicals, and when moved redrawing is done automatically
// using double buffering.
//
class Disk extends Graphical {

    //
    // Create a disk on top of peg <peg>, <w> pixels wide, and <h> high.
    //
    Disk(DisplayListCanvas canvas, Peg peg, int w, int h) {
        super(canvas, peg.area.x + peg.area.w/2 - w/2,
                    peg.area.y + peg.area.h - (peg.nDisks+1)*h,
                    w, h);
        this.peg = peg;                // remember what peg we rest on
        peg.addDisk(this);  // add myself to the peg
        update();    // make sure we get drawn
    }


    //
    // Move this disk to a new peg.
    // Uses animated move method from Graphical to move disk smoothly.
    //
    void moveTo(Peg newPeg) {
        peg.removeDisk(this);      // remove from old peg
```

```
    // move up
    move(area.x, peg.area.y - area.h - 10, 2*speed);

    // move left/right
    peg = newPeg;
    move(peg.area.x + peg.area.w/2 - area.w/2, area.y, speed);

    // move down
    move(area.x, peg.area.y + peg.area.h - (peg.nDisks+1)*area.h, 2*speed);

    peg.addDisk(this);  // add to new peg
}


//
// Overridden from Graphical.
// Build in short delay for thread management.
// Stop here when "Pause" button has been pressed.
//
public void move(int x, int y, int increment) {
    super.move(x, y, increment);
    Thread.yield();                     // make thread unselfish
      while (Hanoi.take_a_break)
        try {
            Thread.sleep(1000);         // user pressed "pause" button
        } catch (InterruptedException e) {
          break;
        }
}


//
// Draw this disk.
// Called when moved (with methods above), or when the when is exposed,
// or when another graphical for some reason or another
// invalidated our appearance.
//
public synchronized void draw() {
        canvas.setColor(Color.yellow);
```

```
            canvas.fillRoundRect(area.x, area.y, area.w, area.h,
                                    area.h/4, area.h/4);
            canvas.setColor(Color.black);
            canvas.drawRoundRect(area.x, area.y, area.w, area.h,
                                    area.h/4, area.h/4);
        }


    public String toString() {
        return "Disk[" + "x=" + area.x + "," + "y=" + area.y + "," +
            "resting at peg " + peg.id + "]";
    }
    Peg peg;                    // the peg this disk rests on

    static int speed = 5;  // controls the speed of the animation
}


//
// A Peg is a simple container, capable of holding any number of disks.
// Its representation is inherited from Box.
//
class Peg extends Box {
    Peg(DisplayListCanvas canvas, int height, String an_id) {
        super(canvas, 0, 0, 3, height);
        constraint = Constraint.Centered;// inherited from Graphical
        disks = new Vector();
        nDisks = 0;
        id = an_id;
    }
    void addDisk(Disk disk) {
        disks.addElement(disk);
        nDisks++;
        arrangeDisks();                 // make sure disks are nicely stacked
    }
    // called by Layouts
    public boolean reset(int x, int y, int w, int h) {
        super.reset(x, y, w, h);
        arrangeDisks();
        return true;
```

```
    }
    void arrangeDisks() {
        canvas.freeze();
        for (int n=0; n<nDisks; n++) {
            Disk disk = (Disk)disks.elementAt(n);
            disk.move(area.x + area.w/2 - disk.area.w/2,
                        area.y + area.h - (n+1)*disk.area.h);
        }
        canvas.unFreeze();
    }
    void removeDisk(Disk disk) {
        disks.removeElement(disk);
        nDisks--;
    }
    void moveDisk(Peg other_peg) {
        if (nDisks > 0)
            ((Disk)disks.elementAt(nDisks-1)).moveTo(other_peg);
    }
    public String toString() {
        return "Peg " + id + "[number of disks=" + nDisks + "]";
    }
    Vector disks; // use java.awt.Vector
    int nDisks;       // is really redundant, available from Vector...
    String id;
}
```

6.6 Graph Layout

This demo is based on the graph layout algorithm that comes with Sun's standard Java distribution. The nodes can be dragged with the mouse. The algorithm has been extracted from its original context and enhanced with a new GUI. The major difference with the old version is the way the graph is drawn. The old version uses a technique that is very typical for animated scenes in the applets that initially appeared when Java came out. At each step in the animation, the scene is recomputed and drawn completely, even though some nodes may not have moved at all. It is too complicated for the programmer to keep track of which nodes have moved, and which haven't, and in general it is a lot easier to simply repaint the whole graph. (See Figure 17.)

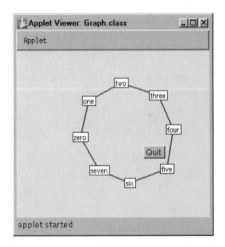 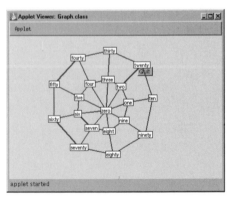

Figure 17. Graph layouts and a bouncing button.

In the new version, each node and edge is implemented as a graphical, and in effect, the applet no longer does any drawing at all! Instead, it can concentrate on doing what it is supposed to draw: to layout a graph. When individual nodes are layed out, they are moved to their new location, by simply calling the "move" method, implemented by all graphicals. When a node is moved, it will inform its canvas that it has moved. If the canvas is not frozen, the area occupied previously by the graphical and the new area are both redrawn. If the canvas is frozen (something the graph layout applet may do when it starts its layout algorithm), the canvas simply records both areas. When the canvas eventually is unfrozen, all pending redrawings are issued in the right order. All of this happens transparently to the graph layout applet, of course.

If a small portion of the graph gets invalidated, for instance, because the "quit" button moves underneath it, only those nodes and edges that overlap with the damaged area will be told to redraw. Never will the graph layout applet be told to redraw itself completely. It doesn't even implement a paint method.

Here is the source of the enhanced graph layout example, now using LTK for the GUI

```
import ltk.*;
import java.util.*;
import java.awt.*;
import java.applet.Applet;

public class Graph extends LTKApplet implements CallBackable, Runnable
{
    int nnodes;
```

```
Vector nodes;
int nedges;
Vector edges;
ltk.Button button;
Thread thread;

public boolean quit() {
    System.exit(0);
    return true;
}
Node findNode(String label) {
    for (int i = 0 ; i < nnodes ; i++) {
        if (((Node)nodes.elementAt(i)).label.equals(label)) {
            return ((Node)nodes.elementAt(i));
        }
    }
    return addNode(label);
}
Node addNode(String label) {
    double x = 10 + 380*Math.random();
    double y = 10 + 380*Math.random();
    Node n = new Node(this, canvas, (int)x, (int)y, 10, 10);
    n.setLabel(label);
    n.moveTo((int)x, (int)y);
    nodes.addElement(n);
    nnodes++;
    return n;
}
void addEdge(String from_label, String to_label, int len) {
    Node from = findNode(from_label);
    Node to = findNode(to_label);
    Edge e = new Edge(canvas, from.area.x, from.area.y,
                      to.area.x, to.area.y);
    e.from = from;
    e.to = to;
    e.len = len;
    e.setColor(Color.red);
    e.setLineWidth(3);
```

```
        edges.addElement(e);
        nedges++;
    }

public void arrange() {
    canvas.freeze();
    for (int max_tries=100; max_tries>0; max_tries--)
        if (relax() == false)
            break;
    canvas.unFreeze();
}

boolean relax() {
    for (int i = 0 ; i < nedges ; i++) {
        Edge e = (Edge)edges.elementAt(i);
        double vx = (double)(e.to.area.x - e.from.area.x);
        double vy = (double)(e.to.area.y - e.from.area.y);
        double len = Math.sqrt(vx * vx + vy * vy);
        double f = (((Edge)edges.elementAt(i)).len - len) / (len * 3) ;
        double dx = f * vx;
        double dy = f * vy;

        e.to.dx += dx;
        e.to.dy += dy;
        e.from.dx += -dx;
        e.from.dy += -dy;
    }

    for (int i = 0 ; i < nnodes ; i++) {
        Node n1 = ((Node)nodes.elementAt(i));
        double dx = 0;
        double dy = 0;

        for (int j = 0 ; j < nnodes ; j++) {
            if (i == j) {
                continue;
            }
            Node n2 = ((Node)nodes.elementAt(j));
```

```
      double vx = (double)(n1.area.x - n2.area.x);
      double vy = (double)(n1.area.y - n2.area.y);
      double len = vx * vx + vy * vy;
      if (len == 0) {
          dx += Math.random();
          dy += Math.random();
      } else if (len < 100*100) {
          dx += vx / len;
          dy += vy / len;
      }
  }
  double dlen = dx * dx + dy * dy;
  if (dlen > 0) {
    dlen = Math.sqrt(dlen) / 2;
    n1.dx += dx / dlen;
    n1.dy += dy / dlen;
  }
}


for (int i = 0 ; i < nnodes ; i++) {
   Node n = ((Node)nodes.elementAt(i));
   if (!n.fixed && !n.moving) {
     double x = (double)n.area.x + Math.max(-5,
                               Math.min(5, n.dx));
     double y = (double)n.area.y + Math.max(-5,
                               Math.min(5, n.dy));
     if (x < 0) {
        x = 0;
     } else if (x > canvas.area.w) {
        x = canvas.area.w;
     }
     if (y < 0) {
        y = 0;
     } else if (y > canvas.area.h) {
        y = canvas.area.h;
     }
     n.moveTo((int)x, (int)y);
   }
```

```
        n.dx /= 2;
        n.dy /= 2;
    }
    boolean changed = false;
    for (int i = 0 ; i < nedges ; i++)
        if (((Edge)edges.elementAt(i)).check())
            changed = true;
    return changed;
}

public void init() {                            // from LTKApplet
    super.init();

    nnodes = 0; nodes = new Vector();
    nedges = 0; edges = new Vector();

    canvas.setBackground(Color.yellow);

    canvas.freeze();
    String edges = getParameter("edges");
    for (StringTokenizer t = new StringTokenizer(edges, ",") ;
                            t.hasMoreTokens() ; ) {
        String str = t.nextToken();
        int i = str.indexOf('-');
        if (i > 0) {
            int len = 50;
            int j = str.indexOf('/');
            if (j > 0) {
                len = Integer.valueOf(str.substring(j+1)).intValue();
                str = str.substring(0, j);
            }
            addEdge(str.substring(0,i), str.substring(i+1), len);
        }
    }
    button = new ltk.Button(canvas, this, _quit, "Quit");
    button.lower();            // moves underneath everything else
```

```
        String center = getParameter("center");
        if (center != null){
            Node n = findNode(center);
            n.moveTo(canvas.area.w / 2, canvas.area.h / 2);
            n.fixed = true;
            n.setFillColor(Color.red);
            n.setColor(Color.white);
        }
        arrange();
        canvas.unFreeze();

        thread = new Thread(this);
        thread.start();
}
public void start() {                      // from LTKApplet
    thread.resume();
}
public void stop() {                       // from LTKApplet
    thread.suspend();
}


public void run() {                        // from Runnable
    int dx=1, dy=-1;

    //
    // try and hit it :-)
    //
    while (true) {
        button.move(button.area.x+dx*2, button.area.y+dy*2);
        if (button.area.x > canvas.area.w - button.area.w) dx = -1;
        if (button.area.x < 1)                 dx = 1;
        if (button.area.y > canvas.area.h - button.area.h) dy = -1;
        if (button.area.y < 1)                 dy = 1;
        try {
          Thread.sleep(50);                // make thread unselfish
        } catch (InterruptedException e) {
          break;
        }
    }
```

```
            }
        }

    public static void main(String args[]) {
        LTKApplet applet = new Graph();
        applet.runAppletAsApplication("Graph Layout Demo");
    }

    public boolean activateCallback(int method_nr) { // CallBackable
        switch (method_nr) {
            case _quit: return quit();
        }
        return false;                           // event not processed
    }

    public String toString() {
            return "a demo: ltk.Graph[]";
    }

    final int _quit = 1;
}

class Node extends Box {
    Node(Graph graph,DisplayListCanvas canvas,int x,int y,int w,int h) {
        super(canvas, x, y, w, h);
        this.graph = graph;
        font = new java.awt.Font("Helvetica", java.awt.Font.PLAIN, 10);
    }
    void setLabel(String label) {
        this.label = label;
            FontMetrics fm = canvas.getFontMetrics(font);
        reset(10,10,fm.stringWidth(label)+4, fm.getAscent()+4);
    }
    public void draw() {
            canvas.setColor(fill_color);
            canvas.fillRect(area.x, area.y, area.w, area.h);
            canvas.setColor(Color.black);
            canvas.drawRect(area.x, area.y, area.w, area.h);
```

```
            if (label != null) {
                    canvas.setColor(color);
                canvas.setFont(font);
                canvas.drawString(label, area.x+2, area.y+area.h-2);
            }
        }
        public void moveTo(int x, int y) {
            if (Math.abs(x - area.x) > 2 || Math.abs(y - area.y) > 2) {
                reset(x, y, area.w, area.h);
            }
        }
        public void move(int x, int y) {
                canvas.freeze();
                super.move(x, y);
            moving = true;
                graph.arrange();
            moving = false;
                canvas.unFreeze();
        }
        public String toString() {
            return "ltk.Node[" + label +
                (moving ? ",moving" : "") + (fixed ? ",fixed" : "") + "]";
        }
        double dx, dy;
        boolean fixed;
        boolean moving;
        String label;
        Graph graph;
        Font font;
}


class Edge extends Line {
    Node from, to;
    double len;
    public Edge(DisplayListCanvas canvas,int x1,int y1,int x2,int y2) {
        super(canvas, x1, y1, x2, y2);
        lower();
    }
```

```
boolean check() {
    int x1 = from.area.x + from.area.w/2;
    int y1 = from.area.y + from.area.h/2;
    int x2 = to.area.x + to.area.w/2;
    int y2 = to.area.y + to.area.h/2;
    if (this.x1 != x1 || this.y1 != y1 ||
                      this.x2 != x2 || this.y2 != y2) {
        reset(x1, y1, x2, y2);
        return true;
    }
    return false;
}
}
```

6.7 Slider Demo

This example highlights the use of Sliders, and how to react to callbacks generated by them. Two sliders are created, a horizontal and a vertical:

```
layout = new VerticalLayout(
    slider1 = new ltk.Slider(canvas,this,_slider1,Slider.Vertical,
                                      100, 400, 7),
    slider2 = new ltk.Slider(canvas,this,_slider2,Slider.Horizontal,
                                      100, 400, 2)
);
```

Each slider is given the same values for the minimum (100) and maximum (400) values, but is given a different value for the value increment (denoting how much "value" each pixel represents). Of course, a simple layout is used to place the two sliders. Both sliders are passed a symbolic reference to the callback to be activated when a user event has occurred. The applet implements CallBackable and implements the "activateCallback" method. When the callback is received, one of the two symbolic callbacks is dispatched to call the right callback method (this complication is due to the fact that Java has no method references, and that I did not want to use the "complicated" solutions proposed by some people on the Internet). The callback methods retrieve the current value from the slider that activated it, resize the box, and synchronize with the other slider. (See Figure 18.)

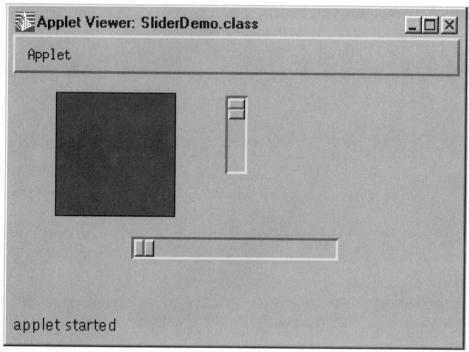

Figure 18. Two synchronized sliders and a moveable box

Here is the full source of the slider demo

```
import ltk.*;
public class SliderDemo extends LTKApplet implements CallBackable {

    public void init() {                          // from LTKApplet
        super.init();
        layout = new VerticalLayout(
            slider1=new ltk.Slider(canvas,this,_slider1,Slider.Vertical,
                                            100, 400, 7),
            slider2=new ltk.Slider(canvas,this,_slider2,Slider.Horizontal,
                                            100, 400, 2)
        );
        box = new ltk.Box(canvas, 10, 10, 100, 100);
        box.constraint = Constraint.None;
    }
    public void start() { }                        // from LTKApplet
    public void stop() { }                         // from LTKApplet
```

```
public static void main(String args[]) {
   LTKApplet applet = new SliderDemo();
   applet.runAppletAsApplication("Layout test");
   applet.move(300,300);
}
public boolean activateCallback(int method_nr) { // CallBackable
   switch (method_nr) {
      case _slider1: return slider1moved();
      case _slider2: return slider2moved();
   }
   return false;                          // event not processed
}
public boolean slider1moved() {
   box.setFillColor(java.awt.Color.red);
   setValue(slider1.getValue());
   return true;
}
public boolean slider2moved() {
   box.setFillColor(java.awt.Color.green);
   setValue(slider2.getValue());
   return true;
}
public void setValue(int value) {
   box.resize(value, value);
   slider1.setValue(value);
   slider2.setValue(value);
}
Layout layout;
Box box;
Slider slider1, slider2;
static final int _slider1 = 1;
static final int _slider2 = 2;
}
```

6.8 Widget Animation Demo

The example shows multiple graphicals and animation. Basically, it demonstrates the use of the underlying LTK display list structure. Yellow and white boxes are created that can be dragged with the mouse. The boxes are also managed with layouts, so resizing the appletviewer will rearrange them again. (See Figure 19.)

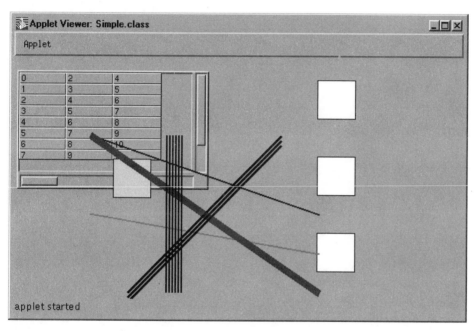

Figure 19. Moveable boxes, thick lines, and a bouncing table widget.

The applet also creates a couple of line objects that are placed explicitly without using layouts. This shows that the two placement models can easily be integrated. Also notice that the lines have multiple line widths, something not supported in the first versions of Java/AWT, and therefore, encapsulated inside the ltk.Line class.

```
import ltk.*;
import java.applet.*;
import java.lang.*;
import java.awt.*;


public class Simple extends LTKApplet implements Runnable {

    public void init() {                          // from LTKApplet
        super.init();
```

```
table = new ltk.Table(canvas, new SimpleTableProducer(), 10,10);
table.resize(250, 150);
table.constraint = Constraint.FixedSize;

new HorizontalLayout(
    table,
    new VerticalLayout(
      Constraint.setCentered(new ltk.Box(canvas,130,130,50,50)),
      Constraint.setCentered(new ltk.Box(canvas,130,130,50,50)),
      Constraint.setCentered(new ltk.Box(canvas,130,130,50,50))
    )
);
box = new ltk.Box(canvas, 130, 130, 50, 50);
box.setFillColor(Color.yellow);

line = new ltk.Line(canvas, 100, 100, 400, 200);
line.setLineWidth(2);
line.setColor(java.awt.Color.blue);

line = new ltk.Line(canvas, 100, 200, 400, 250);
line.setLineWidth(3);
line.setColor(java.awt.Color.green);

line = new ltk.Line(canvas, 400, 300, 100, 100);
line.setLineWidth(10);
line.setColor(java.awt.Color.red);

line = new ltk.Line(canvas, 200, 100, 200, 300);
line.setLineWidth(2);
line = new ltk.Line(canvas, 204, 100, 204, 300);
line.setLineWidth(2);
line = new ltk.Line(canvas, 208, 100, 208, 300);
line.setLineWidth(2);
line = new ltk.Line(canvas, 212, 100, 212, 300);
line.setLineWidth(2);
line = new ltk.Line(canvas, 216, 100, 216, 300);
line.setLineWidth(2);
line = new ltk.Line(canvas, 220, 100, 220, 300);
line.setLineWidth(2);
```

```
        line = new ltk.Line(canvas, 150, 300, 350, 100);
        line.setLineWidth(3);
        line = new ltk.Line(canvas, 150, 306, 350, 106);
        line.setLineWidth(3);
        line = new ltk.Line(canvas, 150, 312, 350, 112);
        line.setLineWidth(3);

        thread = new Thread(this);
        thread.start();
    }
    public void start() {                        // from LTKApplet
        thread.resume();
    }
    public void stop() {                         // from LTKApplet
        thread.suspend();
    }

    public void run() {
        int dx=1, dy=-1, N=7;

        try { Thread.sleep(10000); } catch (InterruptedException e) { }
        if (1==1)
        while (true) {
            table.move(table.area.x+dx*N, table.area.y+dy*N);
            if (table.area.x > canvas.area.w - table.area.w) dx = -1;
            if (table.area.x < 1)                dx = 1;
            if (table.area.y > canvas.area.h - table.area.h) dy = -1;
            if (table.area.y < 1)                dy = 1;
            try { Thread.sleep(100); } catch (InterruptedException e) { }
        }
    }

    public static void main(String args[]) {
        LTKApplet applet = new Simple();
        applet.runAppletAsApplication("ltk is Simple");
    }
    ltk.Box box;
    ltk.Line line;
    ltk.Table table;
    Thread thread;
```

```
}

class SimpleTableProducer implements ltk.TableProducer {
   public String getCellValue(int row, int column) {
      return "" + java.lang.Math.abs(row + 2 * column);
   }
};
```

6.9 GUI Style Abstraction Demo

This example shows how LTK tries to abstract out different GUI style dependencies, and how any given GUI style can be selected at run-time. Where possible, all GUI dependent drawing code is moved to one specific class implementing that drawing behavior to match a given GUI style as closely as possible. Therefore, the Button class does not draw its own background. Neither does it select its own color scheme. Instead, the current GUIStyle object is asked to draw a raised rectangle and also asked for a corresponding contrasting color to draw the label. In the case of Motif and Win95, the button will show up in 3D, whereas in the Windows3.1 style, the button shows up as just a black rectangle. The button itself is not aware of what kind of environment it is running. (See Figure 20.)

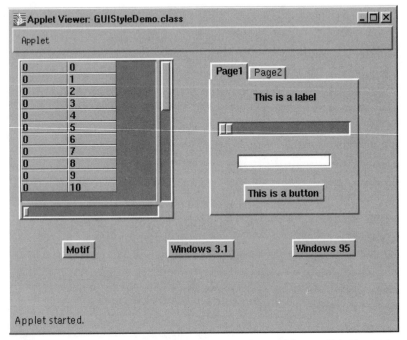

Figure 20. Example showing GUI style independence of LTK widgets.

I may not have chosen the right visual abstraction, but I did not have enough time to implement all different GUI styles, and this is just meant to highlight the principle. This the source of the GUI style abstraction demo

```
import ltk.*;
public class GUIStyleDemo extends LTKApplet implements CallBackable {
    public void resetStyles() {
        GUIStyle gui_style = GUIStyle.getDefaultStyle();
        field.setStyle(gui_style);
        notebook.setStyle(gui_style);
        slider.setStyle(gui_style);
        button.setStyle(gui_style);
        label.setStyle(gui_style);
        table.setStyle(gui_style);
        canvas.setBackground(gui_style.getBackground());
        canvas.repairArea(0, 0, canvas.area.w, canvas.area.h);
    }
    public boolean motif() {
        GUIStyle.selectStyle(GUIStyle.Motif);
        resetStyles();
        return true;
    }
    public boolean win31() {
        GUIStyle.selectStyle(GUIStyle.Win31);
        resetStyles();
        return true;
    }
    public boolean win95() {
        GUIStyle.selectStyle(GUIStyle.Win95);
        resetStyles();
        return true;
    }
    public boolean press() {
        return true;
    }

    public void init() {                        // from LTKApplet
        super.init();
        canvas.freeze();
```

```
        layout = new VerticalLayout(
           new HorizontalLayout(
              table = new Table(canvas, new GUITableProducer(), 30, 40),
              notebook = new Notebook(canvas)
           ),
           Layout.space(canvas),
           new HorizontalLayout(
              new Button(canvas, this, _motif, "Motif"),
              new Button(canvas, this, _win31, "Windows 3.1"),
              new Button(canvas, this, _win95, "Windows 95")
           )
        );

        notebook.addClient( "Page1",
           new VerticalLayout(
              label = new Label(canvas, "This is a label"),
              slider = new Slider(canvas, this, 0, Slider.Horizontal,
                                            100, 400, 2),
              field = new EntryField(canvas, this, 0),
              button = new Button(canvas, this, _press,
                                            "This is a button")
           )
        );
        notebook.addClient( "Page2",
              new Label(canvas, "This is a label")
        );
        notebook.selectPage(0);
        notebook.resize(200,200);
        notebook.setConstraint(Constraint.FixedSize);

        canvas.unFreeze();
        table.resize(200,200);
        table.setConstraint(Constraint.FixedSize);
        resize(500,450);
    }
    public void start() { }                    // from LTKApplet
    public void stop() { }                     // from LTKApplet
```

```
    public static void main(String args[]) {
        LTKApplet applet = new GUIStyleDemo();
        applet.runAppletAsApplication("Layout test");
    }


    public boolean activateCallback(int method_nr) { // CallBackable
        switch (method_nr) {
            case _press: return press();
            case _motif: return motif();
            case _win31: return win31();
            case _win95: return win95();
        }
        return false;                          // event not processed
    }


    static final int _press = 1;
    static final int _motif = 2;
    static final int _win31 = 3;
    static final int _win95 = 4;


    Layout layout;
    Button button;
    EntryField field;
    Slider slider;
    Label label;
    Table table;
    Notebook notebook;
}


class GUITableProducer implements ltk.TableProducer {
    public String getCellValue(int row, int column) {
        return "" + java.lang.Math.abs(row * column);
    }
};
```

6.10 Table Demo

The table widget is probably the most complicated widget in LTK. Still, its implementation is just a little less than 350 lines. The table widget separates the underlying data and its display by using a Table Producer. No data is copied from the application into the table, and the data is kept in one place only (making the table as lightweight as possible). In our example, the table producer is trivial, but in practice, it could read its values from a relational database, or retrieve the data from parameters given from the browser. In both cases a less trivial subclass of the TableProducer class would do the trick. A label is added, and a vertical layout is used to place both widgets. Finally, this demo shows how the table contents could be updated at run-time, for instance, when new market data arrives. (See Figure 21.)

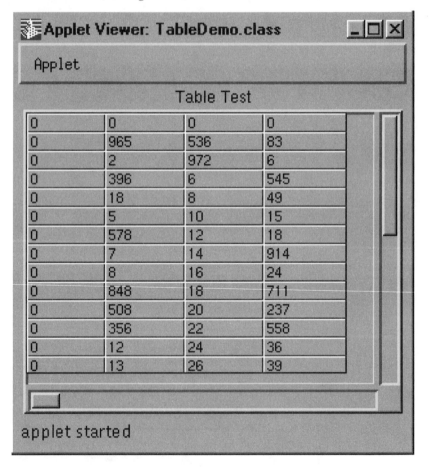

Figure 21. An example of a multicolumn table widget with real-time updates.

Here is the source of the table demo

```
import ltk.*;
public class TableDemo extends LTKApplet implements Runnable {
    public void init() {                              // from LTKApplet
        super.init();
        canvas.freeze();
        new VerticalLayout(
            Constraint.setFixedHeight(new ltk.Label(canvas,
                                                "Table Test")),
            table = new ltk.Table(canvas, new MyTableProducer(), 30, 40)
        );
        canvas.unFreeze();
        thread = new Thread(this);
        thread.start();
    }
    public void start() {                             // from LTKApplet
        thread.resume();
    }
    public void stop() {                              // from LTKApplet
        thread.suspend();
    }
    public void run() {
        int row, column;
        String value;
        try { Thread.sleep(5000); } catch (InterruptedException e) { }
        while (true) {
            row = (int)Math.abs(Math.random() * 1000 % 13 - 1);
            column = (int)Math.abs(Math.random() * 1000 % 5 - 1);
            value = "" + (int)(Math.random() * 1000);
            table.setValue(row, column, value);
            try {
                Thread.sleep(500); // make thread unselfish
              } catch (InterruptedException e) { }
        }
    }
    public static void main(String args[]) {
        LTKApplet applet = new TableDemo();
        applet.runAppletAsApplication("Table test");
    }
```

```
    Table table;
    Thread thread;
}
class MyTableProducer implements ltk.TableProducer {
    public String getCellValue(int row, int column) {
        return "" + java.lang.Math.abs(row * column);
    }
};
```

6.11 Thread Tester

This applet tries to create as many threads as it can, until finally your browser or your computer melts down. Click on "Start" only when you are ready to kill your browser, or to reboot your machine. My Windows NT machine got as far as 1600 threads until the machine did not do anything anymore, and the power switch was the only resort. It crashed different versions of Netscape on Unix when more than 90 threads had been created, and it crashed Windows 95 a couple of times.

The source code of the example

```
import ltk.*;
import java.applet.*;
import java.lang.*;
import java.awt.*;
public class ThreadTest extends LTKApplet implements
                                        CallBackable, Runnable {
    public void init() {                         // from LTKApplet
        super.init();
        new VerticalLayout(
            new ltk.Label(canvas, "Creating As Many Threads As I Can"),
            new HorizontalLayout(
                new ltk.Button(canvas, this, _go, "Start"),
                new ltk.Button(canvas, this, _quit, "Stop")
            ),
            label = new ltk.Label(canvas, "Thread Tester Main Thread")
        );
        label.setConstraint(Constraint.Left);
    }
    public void start() { }                      // from LTKApplet
    public void stop() { }                       // from LTKApplet
    public void run() {
        if (first_one) {
```

```
            first_one = false;
            for (int n=0; n<5000; n++) {
                (new Thread(this, "Thread " + n)).start();
                try { Thread.sleep(10); } catch (InterruptedException e) { }
            }
        }
        else {
            label.setLabel("" + Thread.currentThread());
            try { Thread.sleep(50000); }
            catch (InterruptedException e) { }
        }
    }
    public boolean go() {
        tester = new Thread(this, "Thread Tester Main Thread");
        tester.start();
        return true;
    }
    public boolean quit() {
        if (tester!=null) tester.suspend();
        System.exit(0);
        return true;
    }
    public boolean activateCallback(int method_nr) { // CallBackable
        switch (method_nr) {
            case _go: return go();
            case _quit: return quit();
        }
        return false;
    }
    public static void main(String args[]) {
        LTKApplet applet = new ThreadTest();
        applet.runAppletAsApplication("Thread Tester");
    }
    ltk.Label label;
    static boolean first_one = true;
    final static int _go = 1;
    final static int _quit = 2;
    Thread tester;
}
```

CHAPTER
3

- Java Debugging Techniques
- Using Visualization for Java Debugging
- Using Instrumentation
- Hacking the Java VM
- How to Write Your Own Visual Debugger

Java
Debugging
Techniques

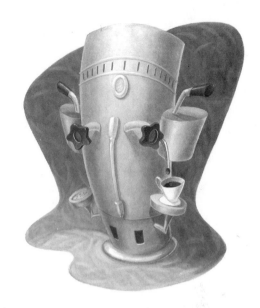

1. Java Debugging Techniques

Debugging software is the process of determining a wrong behavior in the software, followed by the understanding of why this behavior occurs, identifying the code that causes the bug, repairing the problem, and finally, making sure the bug actually has been corrected. Instrumental for debugging is understanding the internal behavior of the program: Does this statement get executed? Is this object actually created? Why is my applet so slow?

Two popular debugging techniques are

- Inserting special "debugging statements." At certain crucial locations in the code, special statements are inserted, typically print statements. These statements are not part of the program's functionality as such, but rather serve primarily to tell the programmer that a certain method is actually executed and what the value of a particular instance variable was at that time. In Java, `System.out.println()` statements are a popular technique (some can still be found in the awt toolkit, yet now commented out). More "advanced" debugging statements are typically enclosed in a conditional statement testing the state of a boolean flag.[1] Some systems even use different debugging levels to print out different levels of detail depending on the amount of information the programmer wants to see at this stage. A major problem with the print-statement approach is that debugging statements clutter the code, and because they distract from the real functionality of the code, they make the code harder to read and maintain. Furthermore, when the programmer thinks the code is fully debugged, all print statements are removed, potentially resulting in new bugs. From personal experience, I have often found a new bug just after

---

[1] Typically, Java compilers optimize out if-statements involving a test on a final static boolean variable. Therefore, the test `if(debug)` will cause no overhead if `debug` is known to be false at compile time..

removing all my debugging statements, forcing me to go through the whole process again. Moreover, no real programmer likes to hand over code to others when the code is lingered with debugging statements everywhere; a clear indication of the instability of the code. This entire process is expensive, as it requires a lot of unnecessary programming, yet it can renders a microscopic understanding of the execution of the program. The programmer can often very well understand the bigger picture by looking at the carefully constructed debugging statements.

- Using an off-the-shelf debugger, like *jdb*, the java debugger shipped with the Java jdk. In general, a debugger is a special program that is able to execute another program step by step, showing the method invocation stack, displaying the value of any variable or expression, and stopping at certain locations (referred to as "breakpoints"). A debugger can be useful for microscopic inspections of the program. Once a certain problem is detected, the programmer might expect the program to execute a certain statement, and consequently he or she sets breakpoints at that location. Then the program is executed until that breakpoint is reached. As a result, the program is suspended and variables can be inspected; additional breakpoints can be defined and execution could resume.

The latter process does not require a recompilation of code nor a link phase. All the information that is needed by the debugger is generated by the compiler and is readily available at run-time. This debugging technique is very useful when the programmer already has a certain feeling for where the problem might be, as it is impractical to insert breakpoints everywhere. Stepping through a multithreaded application is not something trivial, though. Furthermore, this technique does not address "hidden" problems, such as creating too many objects, creating objects that are never used, inefficiencies, and synchronization problems when using multiple threads.

1.1 Using Visualization to Understand and Debug Java Programs

Key to debugging any program is to find out what is going on inside the program when it executes. Print statements or breakpoints can be used, but visual techniques are much more powerful. Visualizations are less obtrusive and give a lot more "passive" information that can be assimilated better, simply because it arrives to us in the form of pictures.

Now, just suppose we could visualize all the objects in our Java program, showing whenever one object is calling another, and perhaps even how the various threads are executed and influence each other during the execution of the program.

The result would be an in-depth understanding of the internal behavior of a particular application. Program visualization has been used extensively to demonstrate specific algorithms, such as sorting algorithms and graph algorithms (see the examples that come with Java).

The problem with program visualization is that it can be enlightening but typically requires a considerable specific programming investment. Furthermore, coming up with the right visualizations is not trivial, and often the effort required for making the visualization outweighs the work it needs to implement the original algorithm.

What we need is a multipurpose visualization of the objects that requires minimal or no effort from the programmer. This visualization would provide, at minimal cost, a high level understanding of what happens inside the program and allows for more detailed inspections when wanted. The approach taken in two systems developed at the IBM T.J. Watson Research Center were quite successful at fulfilling that goal.

The Ovation system [De Pauw et.al., 1993; De Pauw et.al., 1994] approached the problem by initially showing object interaction at class level using intriguing constraint-based graph visualizations, showing the relationships between classes (such as a very nice class-cluster algorithm). When a broad understanding of the program has been gained, the system can be investigated into more individual detail, including the amount of time spent inside specific methods and objects. The Ovation system is independent of the actual language used. Current languages that are supported are C++ and Smalltalk. The Hotwire debugger [Laffra & Malhotra, 1993] concentrates more directly on individual object instances. Each instance is represented by an image that shows method invocations on this particular object. Each instance can be selected, after which its instance variables are shown with their values changing in real-time. A unique feature is a special script language that allows the user to define customized visualizations for specific object classes. Ideas from both systems ended up in the commercial version of VisualAge, the IBM Smalltalk system.

The debugger that is supplied with this book is inspired by techniques displayed by both these debugging/monitoring tools and shows all object instances in a grid sorted by class. I had the first version of the debugger up and running in a few hours, and directly identified an inefficiency in the LTK toolkit that I was not aware of before. Whenever a graphical object in LTK is moved or resized, it tells the display list canvas to repair a certain area. A temporary object was created each time a graphical was moved. Of course, the Java runtime system does have garbage collection, and these objects do not culminate in memory leaks, as in C++. However, garbage collection comes at a cost. In certain occasions, it makes a lot of sense to minimize the number of short-lived temporary objects, especially when they can be easily replaced by temporary variables of a basic type.

It was very instrumental to play with an example applet and simply see the result in the debugger window. After some observations, the cause of the problem was quickly determined, and the allocation of the temporary object was replaced by a reference to a static object. Less objects are created, less memory is used, and less burden is placed on the garbage collector.

Key to the visualizations used in the LTK debugger is that they run in real-time, that is, in parallel with the executing program. Typically, an applet is run, and the debugging windows are inspected only sparsely. They behave like indicator controls on a dashboard. As long as the fuel-level is OK, we can keep our eye on the road. As soon as we reach a critical situation, a red light may come up, begging for our attention. The LTK debugger operates on the same premises. It shows what is going on inside the program, but we are free to ignore it. Occasionally, we will glance at the debugging window, and we may see something out of the ordinary. Too many objects may be created for a certain operation, or object communication happens in a less than optimal manner. Until this stage, the debugger behaves more like a monitor (such as the ones that display CPU and disk usage). Once we identified a lurking problem, or bug, we can investigate it into deeper detail.

Individual objects are shown as little rectangles in the main window. Each time a method is called an instance, its representation is altered to indicate activity. When a given instance is selected (by clicking on it with the mouse), all the methods executed by it are listed in a separate scrolling window. The instance is also represented in a different color in the main window, to indicate that it now has an open method browser. In the current stage the debugger's functionality is very limited, on purpose, to minimize its complexity. No variable inspection is provided, nor breakpoints, nor step-by-step execution.

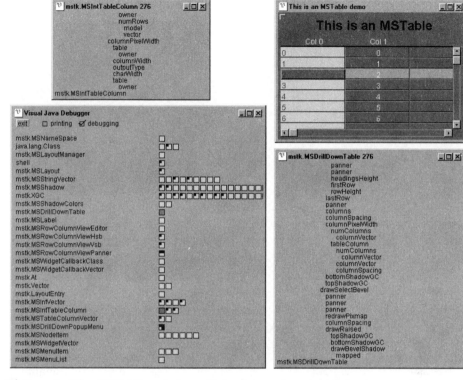

Figure 1. The LTK Visual Java Debugger, showing 2 instances being traced

Each instance in the visual debugger is represented by a little rectangle (see Figure 1). Whenever a method is executed by this instance, something has to be done to its representation to indicate this fact. Simply drawing the rectangle in another color, and then redrawing it in the original color does not work, because the "flashing" may happen too quickly to be noticed. What we need is a representation that has a concrete "delta" between the representation *before* and *after* the method has been executed. The representation currently implemented in this version of the debugger uses a rectangle with five phases: Completely yellow, the top left quadrant black, the top half black, three-quarters black, and entirely black. The representation is cyclical, so after five method calls, we're back to the original representation. Therefore, there is *no* meaning behind how "full" a rectangle is. This is a difficult point, because the very first question everyone asks is: "What does it mean when this one is more black than that one?" I have searched for a better representation for a long time and finally settled for this one.

In addition to a visualization of the program's state, the debugger also can simply dump all method calls made by any object instance in the program. When the user selects the "printing" option, all method-calls will be printed to standard output.

1.2 Possible Extensions in the User Interface

Basically, it does not really matter what kind of representation we choose for instances in the main window, as long as there is a noticeable difference between two subsequent method calls. Namely, this will alert the users of what is happening inside their applications: how many objects are created, which ones are active, what happens when I do this, and what happens when I do that, compare scenarios, and minimize creation of temporary objects to reduce garbage collection impact. Future versions of the debugger could enable the user to set a breakpoint for all methods in a class, for a given method in a class, or even on a given method for one particular object instance (a unique feature, not found in traditional debuggers). The emphasis in this debugger is on *object instances*, and their tracing drives the design. In the Hotwire debugger [Laffra & Malhotra, 1993], instance variables were also displayed in real-time while the program was executing. For example, when dragging an object over the screen, all the methods that are executed on it are displayed, as well as the instance variables, while they are updated.

The interface also had a method recorder, which recorded methods in a graphical fashion (similar to recording sound, and its representation as a frequency wave). After making a recording, the user could play it back in time, zoom in on a particular spot, and locate individual or all instances of a class in the recording. A call-graph animation was laid over the visualization shown above, so that the user could see which object called which other object. Most of these visualizations are now also included in the IBM Visual Age for Smalltalk product and render extremely interesting views of the execution of an object-oriented program. Hotwire went even one step further, by adding a script language that enabled users to customize the visualization of instances of a given class. Therefore, a linked-list data structure, representing a sorted list of objects, could be easily visualized as a bar-graph, requiring only a very small script. The script language was sort-of weird, so a visual front-end was built to generate the scripts in a point-and-click interface.

Another extension would be support for multiple threads in the GUI. Right now, all threads asynchronously enter the debugger and may interfere with each other. In addition to showing method invocations, the call stack for a given thread might be shown, and thread-unsafe object interactions might be detected.

1.3 How to Know Which Methods Are Executed?

There are three basic techniques of acquiring the information needed to make the visual debugger work:

- Use the *Java debugger API*. The Java virtual machine has debugging functionality built in, and provides a gateway to it through a special debugging API. A debugger that uses this API does not directly talk to the Java VM, yet talks to the Sun debugger, which really talks to the Java API. Access to an object instance is through a special proxy, a remote agent to the real instance, which is kept in memory somewhere in the Java VM. A debugger like *jdb* connects to the Java VM through the special debugger API. The remote debugger can actually execute on a different processor, thereby debugging an applet or application over the Internet. The design of the API is such that it is intrinsically oriented towards *conventional* debuggers. It is easy to set a breakpoint in a method, to load a new class, to get the instance variables of an instance, to step through an application, to inspect the call stack, and to see how many threads there are. However, the API is less suited to monitor the execution of all methods of a particular class. A breakpoint would have to be defined for each method, which is doable. Then, when the breakpoint is reached, we know a certain method has been entered, and execution could be resumed. However, activating a breakpoint means stopping the execution of an applet. For that, all active threads are suspended, the remote debugger is notified, which now can resume execution, or set new breakpoints, or inspect some variables. The problem is that the overhead incurred in this setup is prohibitive for the kind of visualizations we are looking for. Furthermore, at the time of the implementation of this visual debugger, the Sun Java debugger API was very unstable (stepping through code simply hung the virtual machine). Regardless of this bug in early versions of the debugger API, a different solution is required. Namely, to allow efficient method tracing and visualization in real-time, the debugger *has* to run inside the same address space as the Java VM. This lesson was already learned for Hotwire, where literally months were spent in optimizing the performance of the visualizations, thereby allowing the debugger to run in parallel with the execution of the program being debugged, yet not causing that much overhead that the debugger became useless. A solution where the process and the debugger run in separate address spaces was simply not acceptable.

- Use *instrumentation*. Instead of using `javac` to compile a Java source file, it is given to a special Java compiler that inspects the code and adds special statements at the beginning and end of each method body. Then, the instrumented code is handed over to the real Java compiler. For example, the following method in class ltk.Button

```
public void draw() {
    if (selected) {
        drawSelected();
        return;
    }
    drawNormal();
}
```

could be translated into:

```
public void draw() {
    ltk.Tracer.Tracer.enter("ltk.Button","draw",this);
    if (selected) {
        drawSelected();
        {
            ltk.Tracer.Tracer.leave("ltk.Button","draw",this);
            return;
        }
    }
    drawNormal();
    ltk.Tracer.Tracer.leave("ltk.Button","draw",this);
}
```

Special care needs to be given to return statements and exception handling clauses. Namely, the thread of control can easily leave the method through a return statement or because of a raised exception. In the case that the method does not catch an expression, but simply propagates it up the method call stack, the proposal sketched here fails. Therefore, an implementation based on *instrumentation* cannot be fully trusted.

- Connect directly to the *Java Virtual Machine*. The C++ version of Hotwire relied on instrumentation, as there is no available run-time information to detect method invocation. However, the GNU Smalltalk version of Hotwire simply connected to a patched version of the virtual machine. Every time the virtual machine invoked a method or executed a return statement, Hotwire was notified of this fact. In fact, the code for Hotwire was compiled and linked into the executable of the GNU Smalltalk VM interpreter. A similar approach is possible for Java. When one has access to the source code of the Java VM, it can be patched, and special hooks could be implemented to call a run-time system to notify the visual debugger. The advantage is that no instrumentation needs to be performed, and existing or third-party Java classes can be visualized, as well as newly written classes. No access to the original Java source code is necessary. Furthermore, this approach is guaranteed to catch all method calls and all return statements.

The following sections will describe the latter two techniques in more detail.

1.4 Instrumentation of Java Source Code

In order to take an existing Java source file, and instrument each method declaration with special instrumentation, two different approaches could be taken:

- A special parser can be written to read Java code and produce some other Java code that has to be compiled with a real Java-to-bytecode compiler. This preprocessor can be written in any language (C, C++, Java, Yacc/Lex, etc.). Basically, the parser needs to be able to read the entire Java syntax, simply copy whatever it reads, know when a method declaration starts to insert some extra code, and when return statements are being executed. One such parser, based on Yacc and Lex (two compiler tools), has been written by Scott Hudson, GVU Center, Georgia Tech. Information on this parser can be found at the following URL

  ```
  http://www.cc.gatech.edu/gvu/people/Faculty/Scott.E.Hudson.html
  ```

  In his documentation, Scott mentions problems he faced in developing the production rules, mainly caused by ambiguous syntax for casts and the "." operator. Letting him spend a lot of time on solving those issues, it was trivial for me to extend his parser and to insert the few statements I needed. The way the parser is enhanced is that it reads the original Java file and copies the contents to standard output, while inserting the required extra statements. Because public classes have to reside in a Java file with the same name, a small problem arises. Both the original file and the resulting file need to have the same name. If we generate the temporary file in the same directory as the original, it would overwrite our original. This is not going to make the user happy. Therefore, the output of the parser is written to a special *debug* subdirectory, and the original package name is updated accordingly to include the extra subpackage name. For example, java.awt would become java.awt.debug. After translating all files in a package, the special debug package is compiled and run the same way as we would with the original package. A slight complication is the fact that javac tends to compile more Java files than it is told to. When the file being compiled is depending on another file, which is also out-of-date, javac will compile the other file first. Therefore, if we change three files, run make on a project, the Makefile should be smart enough to first collect all out-of-date Java files, and process and copy them to the debug directory and run javac on them. This complication makes this approach hard to maintain, if no good support from the right set of makefiles, or a smart IDE exists.

- A much better approach would be to directly incorporate the above instrumentation inside the javac compiler, and expose the new capability with a flag compatible to -g. Basically, this approach would enhance the binary distribution from Javasoft, and licensing requirements limit the freedom with which third party vendors, even nonprofit providers, could redistribute this new tool. Of course Sun could add this capability to their compiler. Alternatively, other vendors of Java compilers could add it to their tools, to entice people into using their products.

The strong limitation of using instrumentation is that it may be hard to write a reliable preprocessor. If a Java compiler would be enhanced, there is considerable overhead incurred. The advantage of the instrumentation approach is that instrumented applet can be debugged, regardless of where it is actually running. The debugger really becomes part of the applet, and will travel with it wherever the applet moves. If we don't care for this mobility and want to be able to debug third-party or non-preprocessed applet code, the ideal and simplest solution is to enhance the virtual machine.

1.5 Enhancing the Java Virtual Machine

When you have access to the Java source code release and you are able to recompile the Java virtual machine, you are basically capable of enhancing the Java virtual machine with any behavior you want. Examples could be better support for meta-programming, or an extension of the language to implement *persistence*. I did not do any of those two (although they are intriguing topics), but instead I located the place in the virtual machine where methods are executed, and where methods return. This code is included in a file called `interpreter.c`, located somewhere in the shared (i.e., platform independent) implementation. I inserted something like 45 lines of C code at the right spots. Furthermore, I enhanced the `main` routine to pass it another flag, so that I can toggle debugging at run-time. I recompiled the virtual machine and produced a new `java.exe` and `javai.dll` (I compiled everything on Windows NT). Inside the special code I inserted, I made dynamic Java method calls (similar to calls from native C code), to `ltk.Tracer.Tracer.enter` and `ltk.Tracer.Tracer.leave`. The following code (enhanced from its version in interpreter.c) detects when a method is entered, or left (the highlighted lines are special hooks, added by me)

```
bool_t ExecuteJava(unsigned char *initial_pc, ExecEnv *ee)
{
    ...
    while (1) {
        ...
        switch (opcode) {
        ...
        case opc_invokevirtualobject_quick:
            ...
            goto callmethod;
        case opc_invokevirtual_quick:
```

```
          . . .
    callmethod:
        ...
        enter_method(ee, mb, args_size, o);
        ...
    case finish_return:
        ...
        leave_method(ee, frame->current_method, args_size, o);
        ...


      }
    }
  }
```

The visual debugger, itself, is really a set of Java classes, and it is notified by making dynamic method calls to the Java code from the C code that was added to the interpreter. To be able to access the debugger class, it first needs to be loaded. The following variable is added to provide a reference to the class.

```
static ClassClass *tracerClassClass = NULL;    // threadsafe??
```

The enhanced interpreter (the big 1600 lines of C switch statement with 164 case labels) is now enhanced to call two extra C functions. One of them is the following function, which is executed at the beginning of each method call

```
void static enter_method(struct execenv* ee, struct methodblock* mb,
                                     int args_size, HObject *obj)
{
    char *cn = classname(fieldclass(&mb->fb));
    char *mn = fieldname(&mb->fb);
    JavaFrame *frame;
    int depth = 0;
    int n;
    if (obj==NULL) return;
    for (frame = ee->current_frame;          // determine stack depth
         frame != NULL;
         frame = frame->prev)
       if (frame->current_method != 0) depth++;

    //
    // Infinite loops can easily happen (the interpreter calling the
    // debugger, the debugger invoking a method, the interpreter
    // handling the method, the interpreter calling the debugger,
    // etc. Therefore, we need to perform some kind of filtering.
    // We only trace objects that are either part of the ltk package,
    // or that are not part of a package at all (the typical applet).
    // We do fast compares, and avoid the use of "strcmp".
    //
    for (n=0; cn[n] && cn[n]!='/'; n++) ;
```

```
      if (cn[0]=='l' && !strncmp(cn,"ltk/Tracer/Tracer",17)) return;
      if (cn[n]=='\0' || (cn[0]=='l' &&         // fast compare
              cn[1]=='t' && cn[2]=='k' && cn[3]=='/')) {
          //
          // find the class representation for the Tracer
          //
          if (tracerClassClass == NULL) {
              fprintf(stderr, "find class ltk/Tracer/Tracer\n");
              tracerClassClass =
                      FindClass(ee, "ltk/Tracer/Tracer", TRUE);
              if (tracerClassClass == NULL) {
                  fprintf(stderr,
                          "Can't find class ltk/Tracer/Tracer\n");
                  exit(1);
              }
              fprintf(stderr, "loaded class ltk/Tracer/Tracer\n");
          }
          execute_java_static_method(
              ee, tracerClassClass,
              "enter",
              "(Ljava/lang/String;Ljava/lang/String;\
                              Ljava/lang/Object;II)V",
              makeJavaString(cn, strlen(cn)),
              makeJavaString(mn, strlen(mn)),
              obj,
              (long)obj,
              depth);
      }
  }
```

A similar function is executed for leaving a method. The end result is that the enhanced virtual machine dynamically loads the debugging GUI (written in Java), and calls two static methods declared inside the GUI to notify it whenever methods are entered and left. For explanation purposes, the GUI is written in Java (using plain AWT for the visualization). In order to limit the recursive problems caused when the debugger executes methods itself and activates the virtual machine, we could opt to write the GUI entirely in C or C++ code. It would be a little bit more difficult to write a portable GUI, though. The gain in performance would be minimal with the currently supported visualizations. Most time is spent in talking with the hardware, drawing individual pixels on the screen (and that code is mostly already written in C and/or C++).

1.6 Writing a Visual Debugger GUI in Java

First of all, any substantial set of classes should be put inside its own package. For one, it puts all the classes in their own name space, to limit possible name collisions. Furthermore, the classes will have to be placed in their own subdirectory. This allows for easier experimentation with different versions of a package, simply by resetting the CLASSPATH environment variable.

```
package ltk.Tracer;
```

The main class in the Tracer package displays all instances, sorted by class name (see Figure 2).

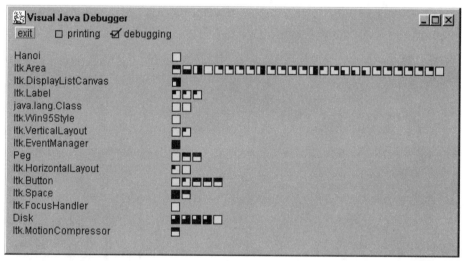

Figure 2. The main window of the LTK visual Java debugger.

Two public methods are available for an enhanced Java VM or instrumented Java code to call. First of all, a frame is created to draw everything in. Furthermore, a vector is created to contain a list of class representations. Vectors are much more expensive to access than arrays, and especially a debugger like this should use an array (considering the fact that the vector will be accessed twice for every method being executed).

```
public class Tracer implements TracerFrameOwner {
    Tracer() {
        frame = new TracerFrame("Visual Java Debugger", this);
        classes = new java.util.Vector();
    }
```

When a method is entered, the following method will be called. If the printing mode has been selected, a string representation for the method call is printed to the standard output. If the debugging mode has been selected, a check is made to see if the method starts with the character '<'. That is the case when a call is made to one of the object's constructors. Then, the object is located in the main window, or created when this is the first method call on it. If the object is found, its representation is altered. Note that this algorithm ignores class methods (methods declared *static*). When those methods are executed, the object variable equals null. This information is now lost, but could be visualized. Furthermore, the `finalize` method call is also ignored, which will result in instances never being removed from the visualization.

```java
public static void enter(String class_name, String method_name,
                         Object object, int objectID, int depth) {
    if (printing) {
        for (int n=0; n<depth; n++) System.out.print(" ");
        System.out.println(class_name+"."+method_name+"(...)
{");
    }
    if (!debugging) return;
    if (method_name.charAt(0)=='<') return;
    TracerObject obj =
        findOrCreateObject(object, class_name, objectID);
    if (obj != null) obj.enter(method_name, object, depth);
}
```

The `leave` method is similar to the previous one, but it only does something in the case that the printing mode has been selected. In that case it prints a closing bracket (again using the expensive "+" operator for the String class). The variable `depth` refers to the depth of the call stack of this thread when the method was executed. This depth is exact when the information is obtained through an enhanced Java VM, but less exact when obtained from instrumented code (as we could miss some calls to the `leave` method due to raised exceptions):

```java
public static void leave(String class_name, String method_name,
                         Object object, int objectID, int depth) {
    if (printing) {
        for (int n=0; n<depth; n++) System.out.print(" ");
        System.out.println("} " + class_name + "." +
                                            method_name);
    }
}
```

The following two methods are shorthand for use in instrumented Java code

```java
public static void enter(String method_name, Object object) {
    int id = (object == null) ? 0 : object.hashCode();
    enter(object.getClass().getName(), method_name,
        object, id, globalDepth++);
}
public static void leave(String method_name, Object object) {
    int id = (object == null) ? 0 : object.hashCode();
    leave(object.getClass().getName(), method_name,
        object, id, --globalDepth);
}
```

When the main frame needs to be redrawn, an exit button and two checkboxes are drawn, as shown in Figure 2. No AWT components (like `Button` and `Choice`) are used to reduce the intrusiveness of the debugger. The more we interact with AWT, the harder it gets to make any sensible observations from a visualization. Finally, each class representation is told to draw itself and all its instances

```
public void repaint(java.awt.Graphics graphics) {

    graphics.clearRect(0, 0, frame.width, start_y);

    graphics.setColor(java.awt.Color.lightGray);
    graphics.fill3DRect(5, 1, 25, 14, true);
    graphics.setColor(java.awt.Color.black);
    graphics.drawString("exit", 8, 13);

    graphics.drawRect(55, 5, 8, 8);
    graphics.drawString("printing", 70, 13);
    if (printing) {
        graphics.drawLine(53, 9, 58, 11);
        graphics.drawLine(53, 8, 58, 10);
        graphics.drawLine(58, 11, 66, 3);
        graphics.drawLine(58, 10, 66, 2);
    }

    graphics.drawRect(125, 5, 8, 8);
    graphics.drawString("debugging", 140, 13);
    if (debugging) {
        graphics.drawLine(123, 9, 128, 11);
        graphics.drawLine(123, 8, 128, 10);
        graphics.drawLine(128, 11, 136, 3);
        graphics.drawLine(128, 10, 136, 2);
    }

    for (int n=0; n<classes.size(); n++)
        ((TracerClass)classes.elementAt(n)).repaint(graphics);
}
```

There are a couple of items that can be selected in the main window. First of all, the exit button can be selected (the use of hard-coded coordinates in the following method is incredibly ugly and is unacceptable. Never copy this style of coding). Furthermore, one of the two selection boxes could be selected. Finally, one of the object instance representations may be clicked on to open up a method browser on to it. First, we inspect the object instance cache, to see if one of the most active objects has been selected. Otherwise, we search through all classes and all instances to see if one of them was selected.

```
public boolean mouseDown(java.awt.Event e, int x, int y) {
    if (x > 5 && y > 3 && x < 40 && y < 15) {
        System.exit(0);
        return true;
    }
    if (x > 55 && y > 0 && x < 120 && y < 15) {
        printing = !printing;
        repaint(frame.getGraphics());
        return true;
    }
    if (x > 125 && y > 0 && x < 210 && y < 15) {
        debugging = !debugging;
        repaint(frame.getGraphics());
        return true;
    }
    if (classes == null)
        return true;

    for (int n=0; n<cache_size; n++) {
        TracerObject obj = cache[n];
        if (cache[n] != null) {
            if (x>obj.x && y>obj.y &&
                        x<obj.x+obj.w && y<obj.y+obj.h) {
                obj.selected();
                return true;
            }
        }
    }

    for (int n=0; n<classes.size(); n++) {
        TracerClass class_rep = (TracerClass)classes.elementAt(n);
        for (int m=0; m<class_rep.objects.size(); m++) {
            TracerObject obj =
                (TracerObject)class_rep.objects.elementAt(m);
            if (x>obj.x && y>obj.y &&
                        x<obj.x+obj.w && y<obj.y+obj.h) {
                obj.selected();
                return true;
            }
        }
    }
    return true;
}
```

This method is used to find an object back that has been accessed before, or to create a representation for it, when this is the first time that the object turns up in the debugger. Here it shows that we ignore constructors, otherwise we would have *known* the object to be here, of course. If the method call is on a static method, it is currently ignored, therefore, this search method directly returns `null`. If an object in the cache with the same id can be found, its representation is returned.

```
public static TracerObject findOrCreateObject(Object object,
                   String class_name,
                   int oid) {
    if (object == null) return null;

    for (int n=0; n<cache_size; n++)
        if (cache[n] != null && cache[n].oid == oid)
            return cache[n];
```

If the object is not in the cache, its class representation is located. If no class representation exists yet, one is created now.

```
    TracerClass class_rep = null;
    for (int n=0; n<classes.size(); n++) {
        class_rep = (TracerClass)classes.elementAt(n);
        if (class_rep.name.equals(class_name)) break;
        class_rep = null;
    }
    if (class_rep == null) {
        class_rep = new TracerClass(frame, class_name,
                        start_y + (line_inc * classes.size())));
        classes.addElement(class_rep);
    }
```

At this stage, a class representation is available. Next, the object is located in its class representation's list of object instance representations. If the object is found, its representation is returned. If not found, a new representation is created and returned subsequently:

```
    TracerObject obj;
    for (int n=0; n<class_rep.objects.size(); n++) {
        obj = (TracerObject)class_rep.objects.elementAt(n);
        if (obj.oid == oid) return obj;
    }
    obj = new TracerObject(frame, oid, class_rep);
    class_rep.objects.addElement(obj);
    cache[cache_last] = obj;
    cache_last = (cache_last + 1) % cache_size;
    return obj;
}
```

The following variables are used. An expensive vector to hold the class representations, a cache of 64 most recently accessed objects, some hard-coded coordinates for drawing the object instances, boolean variables for the different modes the debugger could be in, and a single instance of the debugger (created whenever the class is first loaded)

```
static java.util.Vector classes = null;
static TracerFrame frame;
static final int cache_size = 64;
static int cache_last = 0;
static TracerObject cache[] = new TracerObject[cache_size];
static int start_x = 275;
static int start_y = 40;
static int box_inc = 13;
static int line_inc = 15;
static int box_size = 10;
static int globalDepth = 0;
static boolean debugging = false;
static boolean printing = false;
static Tracer singleton = new Tracer();
};
```

The class representation class is simply a place-holder for object instance representations. Each class representation has a name, a reference to the frame it is attached to, a "line number," represented by the parameter y, and a vector of object instance representations (need I repeat this is not the most efficient storage?)

```
class TracerClass {
    TracerClass(TracerFrame frame, String class_name, int y) {
        name = class_name;
        this.frame = frame;
        objects = new java.util.Vector();
        this.y = y;
        repaint(frame.getGraphics());
    }
    void repaint(java.awt.Graphics graphics) {
        graphics.drawString(name, 4, y);
        for (int n=0; n<objects.size(); n++)
            ((TracerObject)objects.elementAt(n)).repaint(graphics);
    }
    java.lang.String name;
    java.util.Vector objects;
    TracerFrame frame;
    int y;
};
```

The following class represents an object instance in the visual debugger. First, its location and dimensions are computed. Some attributes are stored, and three different Graphics objects are obtained from the frame, in order to draw the instance in one of its three colors. Basically, this particular use of AWT, obtaining Graphics objects from a component, is not properly documented. Some people go as far as warning me that this behavior is not supported, and the fact that it works, is sheer luck from my side. Namely, after obtaining the Graphics object, a lot of things may happen to the original component. It may be resized, or the window system could run out of resources forcing it to invalidate some or all of the Graphics objects. After obtaining a Graphics object, it may become useless at any stage is the reasoning. I find that a little strange. Why, in the first place, is there a method to obtain a Graphics object, if we cannot use it? And furthermore, it seems to work fine in all situations that I tested this approach on. In fact, the particular use here creates three Graphics objects *per* object instance being debugged, easily running into hundreds of Graphics objects. In retrospect, I should have created these instances as class variables, of course, so that they could be *shared* by all instances. However, leaving it the way it is, results in a nice stress test. Anyway, be warned of possible incompatibilities when copying this style of caching Graphics objects. Finally, the constructor checks to see if the newly created object still fits inside the current frame. If that is not the case, the frame will have to be resized.

```java
class TracerObject {
    TracerObject(TracerFrame frame, int oid, TracerClass a_class) {
        my_class = a_class;
        x = Tracer.start_x +
                Tracer.box_inc * a_class.objects.size();
        y = a_class.y - Tracer.box_inc;
        w = Tracer.box_size;
        h = Tracer.box_size;
        this.oid = oid;
        this.frame = frame;

        yellow_graphics = frame.getGraphics();
        yellow_graphics.setColor(java.awt.Color.yellow);
        black_graphics = frame.getGraphics();
        black_graphics.setColor(java.awt.Color.black);
        green_graphics = frame.getGraphics();
        green_graphics.setColor(java.awt.Color.green);

        black_graphics.drawRect(x, y, w, h);
        yellow_graphics.fillRect(x+1, y+1, w-1, h-1);

        frame.checkSize(x, y);
    }
```

Once an instance representation is drawn in the main window, method calls on it can be visualized. If the object instance has not been selected, its representation is updated to reflect the interaction upon it. If the instance *was* selected, a special method printer object would be available to scroll the methods calls. In that case, the method name and call stack depth is passed to it

```
void enter(String method_name, Object obj, int depth) {
  n_invocations++;
  if (method_printer == null)
   switch (n_invocations % 5) {
   case 0: black_graphics.fillRect(x, y, w/2,h/2); break;
   case 1: black_graphics.fillRect(x+h/2,y, w/2,h/2); break;
   case 2: black_graphics.fillRect(x+w/2,y+h/2,w/2,h/2); break;
   case 3: black_graphics.fillRect(x, y+h/2,w/2,h/2); break;
   case 4: yellow_graphics.fillRect(x+1, y+1, w-1,h-1); break;
   }
  else
   method_printer.enter(method_name, depth);
}
```

When leaving a method, the object instance representation is not animated. However, when a method printer is open, it is passed the method name, plus the current object, and the depth of the call stack.

```
void leave(String method_name, Object object, int depth) {
  if (method_printer != null)
    method_printer.leave(method_name, object, depth);
}
```

The following method draws the instance representation, either as a yellow box or as a green box (when the instance has been selected in the past)

```
void repaint(java.awt.Graphics graphics) {
  black_graphics.drawRect(x, y, w, h);
  if (method_printer == null)
    yellow_graphics.fillRect(x+1, y+1, w-1, h-1);
  else
    green_graphics.fillRect(x+1, y+1, w-1, h-1);
}
```

When the object instance is selected, a method trace printer is created or disposed of, depending on whether one was open already or not

```
void selected() {
  if (method_printer == null) {
    method_printer = new TracerMethodPrinter(this);
    green_graphics.fillRect(x+1, y+1, w-1, h-1);
  }
  else {
    method_printer.dispose();
    method_printer = null;
    yellow_graphics.fillRect(x+1, y+1, w-1, h-1);
  }
  black_graphics.drawRect(x, y, w, h);
}
```

Furthermore, a couple of instance variables are used by the object instance representation class

```
TracerClass my_class;
int oid, n_invocations, x, y, w, h;
TracerFrame frame;
TracerMethodPrinter method_printer;
java.awt.Graphics black_graphics;      // should be static
java.awt.Graphics yellow_graphics;     // should be static
java.awt.Graphics green_graphics;      // should be static
};
```

A method printer is a very simple object. It is a window that scrolls up every time a string is added to it. Initially, I used the java.awtTextArea class, but the performance of it was simply unacceptable, after writing a certain number of method calls to the window.

```
class TracerMethodPrinter extends java.awt.Canvas {
    public TracerMethodPrinter(TracerObject aTracerObject) {
        tracerObject = aTracerObject;
        frame = new java.awt.Frame(tracerObject.my_class.name +
                    " " + (tracerObject.x+1));
        frame.add("Center", this);
        frame.resize(width, height);
        frame.move(100, 400);
        frame.show();
        graphics = getGraphics();
    }
```

For performance reasons, a local Graphics object is cached, and whatever Graphics is passed is ignored. Because no history is kept, no list of methods called in the past is drawn, when the paint method is called.

```
    public void paint(java.awt.Graphics g) {
        java.awt.Dimension size = size();
        width = size.width;
        height = size.height;
        nlines = height/line_height;
        graphics.drawString(tracerObject.my_class.name,
                            0, height-2);
    }
```

When a method is entered or left, the current contents of the window is copied up one line, the lower portion is erased, and a string is printed at the bottom of the window. Doing this succession renders an animated effect.

```
public void enter(String method_name, int depth) {
    graphics.copyArea(0,0, width,height-line_height,
                          0,-line_height);
    graphics.clearRect(0, height-2*line_height,
                          width,line_height);
    graphics.drawString(method_name,
                          depth*10,height-line_height-2);
}
public void leave(String method_name, Object obj, int depth) {
    graphics.copyArea(0,0, width,height-line_height,
                          0,-line_height);
    graphics.clearRect(0, height-2*line_height,
                          width, 2*line_height);
    graphics.drawString("}", depth*10, height-line_height-2);
    graphics.drawString(tracerObject.my_class.name,
                          0, height-2);
}
```

The following method closes the method printer.

```
public void dispose() {
    frame.dispose();
}
```

Some variables

```
java.awt.Graphics graphics;
TracerObject tracerObject;
java.awt.Frame frame;
int width = 300;
int height = 100;
int line_height = 12;
int nlines;
};
```

A tracer frame creates a frame, can check to see if the frame is still large enough to hold all instance representations, and can receive mouse down events (which are passed to its owner)

```
class TracerFrame extends java.awt.Canvas {
    public TracerFrame(String name, TracerFrameOwner owner) {
        super();
        this.owner = owner;
        frame = new java.awt.Frame(name);
        frame.add("Center", this);
        frame.resize(400, 300);
        frame.move(100, 400);
        frame.show();
    }
```

```
    public void paint(java.awt.Graphics graphics) {
        java.awt.Dimension size = size();
        width = size.width;
        height = size.height;
        owner.repaint(graphics);
    }
    public boolean checkSize(int x, int y) {
        if (x + margin > width || y + margin > height) {
            frame.resize(width + Tracer.box_inc*10,
                         height + Tracer.line_inc*6);
            frame.move(100, 400);
        }
        return true;
    }
    public boolean mouseDown(java.awt.Event evt, int x, int y) {
        owner.mouseDown(evt, x, y);
        return false;
    }
    java.awt.Frame frame;
    TracerFrameOwner owner;
    int width;
    int height;
    static final int margin = 15;
    static final int menuBarHeight = 30;
};
```

The interface that follows is used in the visual debugger as a modeling concept. It declares two methods `repaint`, and `mouseDown`. Both of them are called by a tracer frame owned by the object implementing the interface

```
interface TracerFrameOwner {
    void repaint (java.awt.Graphics graphics);
    boolean mouseDown(java.awt.Event evt, int x, int y);
};
```

It may be obvious that the current implementation of the visual debugger is the most minimal one could imagine. It could form the basis for a nice tool, if certain optimizations would be applied. In its current stage, it provides amazing visualizations already, even for its limited scope and elegance. In my own code, I have detected more than one "pseudo memory leak," where the luxurious creation of temporary objects can easily be replaced by a static object, shared by many instances, or accessed many, many times (for instance, inside drawing code in an animation).

CHAPTER
4

- To Port or Not to Port—That's Not the Question

- C++ Features Covered by C2J

- Features Not Covered by C2J

- C2J in Action

- How C2J Works

Translating
C++ to Java

1. To Port or Not to Port—That's Not the Question

There seems to be an assumption in Java land that people will translate all their software from existing implementations into Java. That implies that a lot of "legacy" systems need to be translated from C and C++ into Java. Some people claim that all these old C and C++ systems are hard to maintain, difficult to configure, and expensive to modify. It is said that companies like Sun are reimplementing all their existing (C and C++) software into Java right now. Existing systems, like payroll, 401K, and medical insurance information systems will soon be available as Java programs. Therefore, other companies may consider following Sun's example, and also translate all their software. Regardless of whether you share this vision or not, the fact is that translating existing C++ software into the equivalent applet code is *not* trivial. Although C++ and Java are very similar on the surface, there are a lot of subtle differences between the two languages, and many, many small changes may need to be made to the original C++ code to get it successfully through the Java compiler.

This chapter will investigate one solution to reducing the amount of manual work involved in porting existing C++ code into Java. During the development of a pilot project at Morgan Stanley, I wrote a C++ to Java translator that takes a C++ header file (.H) and a source code file (.C) and produces one single Java file. The translator takes care of the most annoying and most error-prone tasks such as collecting all methods and inlining them into the class definition. In addition, incompatible basic types are automatically translated, such as converting the basic type unsigned into int. The parser was written in C++, because a previous version of it (used for analysis of C++ code) was written at the time Java was still called Oak. The parser *could* be reimplemented easily in Java (especially after using the translator on itself). The parser has been donated to the public domain, so perhaps someone will find the time to do this. I just did not find a free weekend to do it yet.

C2J translates roughly about 90 percent of the code correctly. It can save someone who is porting C++ code to Java a lot of manual editing time (such as, inlining all methods, consistently translating basic types, removing & and * operators in declarations, changing -> into ., etc. The success of C2J depends on the "cleanness" of the C++ programming style used. If the C++ code does not do any weird pointer arithmetic and passes variables mostly by reference, the entire design and architecture of the system can often be easily preserved. Of course, the mileage will vary for each different user and each different programming style.

2. C++ Features Covered by C2J

Although it is very hard to create a complete C++ to Java translator, C2J gets amazingly far. A number of different problems are tackled by this parser:

· In C++, a class is normally defined in a header file (typically a .H or .hpp file) containing the class declaration; at the same time, the implementation of the member functions is given in one or more other files (typically .C or .cpp files). In Java, there is only one file, containing the class declaration and all the methods "inlined." A C++ to Java translation needs to collect the class declaration and locate and merge in the individual member functions. This is a very error-prone job. It often is hard to locate a method. It may be inlined in the class definition or be specified somewhere else in the header file. Alternatively, it may be defined in a separate .C file. Furthermore, overloaded methods complicate matters, as for each overloaded method, we carefully have to select the right specialization to fit with the signature of the method. This is something compilers do for a living, and humans should not translate any program that is larger than "Hello World" themselves.

- Varying basic types are incompatible. The following (configurable) translation table is used by C2J:

C++ basic type	Java basic type
char *	java.lang.String
const char *	java.lang.String
unsigned int	int
unsigned long	int
unsigned char	char
unsigned	int
long	int

- C++ has nested classes; Java does not. The solution implemented by C2J is to put the nested class at global scope, and prepend the enclosing class's name to the nested class's name. Here is an example:

C++ classes	Java classes
`class Parent {`	`class ParentChild {`
`    class Child {`	`    int x, y;`
`        int x, y;`	`}`
`    }`	`class Parent {`
`}`	`}`
`...`	`...`
`Parent::Child *child;`	`ParentChild child;`
`...`	`...`

- Java has no pointers and makes no distinction between reference variables and pointer variables, unlike C++. Therefore, all pointer references (->) need to be translated into references (.). That is the case for the declaration and for actual usage of the variables:

C++ pointers	Java references
`Widget *widget;`	`Widget widget;`
`widget = new Widget();`	`widget = new Widget();`
`widget->x = 0;`	`widget.x = 0;`
`*widget = *other;`	`???`
`Widget onStack;`	`Widget onStack = new Widget();`

The latter two (by-value assignment and declaration on the stack are not correctly covered by C2J, because not enough analysis is done on the underlying C++ code. As a matter of fact, the by-value assignment gets translated into a reference assignment, which is clearly incorrect. The declaration on the stack is unmodified resulting in just a declaration of a *reference* in Java not the allocation of any memory for it. Usage of the variable after this declaration will be flagged by the compiler with a warning that onStack may not be initialized.

- Member access control (such as public, protected, and private) is done by region in C++, while it is done per individual method in Java.

C++ access control	Java access control
`class Example {`	`public class Example {`
`public:`	
`    void foo1();`	`    public void foo1() { ... }`
`    void bar1();`	`    public void bar1() { ... }`
`private:`	
`    void foo2();`	`    private void foo2() { ... }`
`    void bar2();`	`    private void bar2() { ... }`
`}`	`}`

Actually, I personally prefer the Java model of access control. It is very easy to lose focus in a large C++ class and determine in what kind of section a certain method is declared. It is not uncommon to finding oneself scrolling up the editor to find the closest access keyword. In Java, the keyword is added to the type specification; a more natural location. It still is a good programming style to keep methods of the same access type together (first a public section, then a protected section, and a private section at the end). The javadoc tool correctly arranges the methods in the generated documentation, but a lot of people still use the implementation as their source of information.

- In C++ programs, it is very common to insert print statements that use overloaded operators to print to `cerr` and `cout`. Those calls need to be translated into calls to `System.err.print`, and `System.out.print`, respectively:

C++ output	Java output
`cout << "x = " << x`	`System.out.print( "x = " + x`
`    << "y = " << y`	`    + "y = " + y`
`    << endl ;`	`    + "\n" );`
`cerr << "error";`	`System.out.print( "error" );`

- Java has garbage collection and hence needs (and has) no mechanism for explicitly deleting objects. Therefore, statements containing `delete object` may need to be translated into another form. In general, when the variable is an instance variable, `object=null` would render a similar effect. When the variable is a local variable in a method, leaving the scope will make the system lose all references to the object, and no assignment is necessary. Similarly, note that these assignments are also not necessary in a destructor (i.e., the `finalize` method), as we will lose the reference to the object automatically.

- C++ has multiple inheritance; whereas, Java has single inheritance and interfaces. In the case of multiple inheritance, we need to make a decision. The algorithm used by C2J is such that in the case of multiple inheritance, we extend from the first class, and the other classes are referred to as interfaces. An example is the following:

multiple inheritance in C++	single inheritance in Java
`class A : public B, C, D`	`class A extends B`
	`implements C, D`

A problem is that classes C and D will have to be implemented as interfaces in this example. Section 9 in Chapter 1 discusses in detail all the implications of implementing multiple inheritance in Java.

- Java has no global variables nor globally scoped functions. All variables and functions have to be attached as static fields or methods to a specific class. Variables that play the role of global variables in C++ could be placed in one special Java class (for instance called `Global`). Instead of creating a special global class, C2J collects all global variables it finds and adds them to the first located class. Access to these fields from other classes needs to be changed now to include the name of the class where the global variable now resides. That aspect is currently not handled by C2J. Furthermore, global functions are ignored, also, although it is trivial to also collect those.

- Comments. When generating a Java class out of its C++ equivalent, all the appropriate `javadoc` style comments are generated. That includes a general comment section for the class including something similar to a copyright notice. Furthermore, each generated method has its own javadoc comment, mentioning the return type of the method, and the name of each parameter passed. An example is given below, in Section 0.

- The difference between *static* methods and *instance* methods, is another problem tackled by the parser.

3. Features Not Covered by C2J

In principle, a full translation from C++ to Java is impractical, for the list of features not covered by C2J would be endless. Therefore, for practical reasons, this section describes some aspects and idioms used in C++ that are important enough to be mentioned here:

- Variable declarations on the stack are not recognized and handled. In Java and in C++ objects are created on the heap. In C++, however, objects can also be created and managed on the stack. An example is given here:

C++ variable on the stack	Java variable on the heap
| ```
if (someCondition) {
  Type t(123);
  t.doSomething();
}
``` | ```
if (someCondition) {
  Type t = new Type(123);
  t.doSomething();
}
``` |

The declaration `Type t(123)` creates an object, allocates its memory on the stack, and calls the appropriate constructor for the object. At the end of the scope of the variable (in this case the closing brace of the if-statement block), it is destructed, and its destructor is called, accordingly. For the Java equivalent, an explicit call to new has to be made. At the end of the loop, there are no more references to the object, and it is a candidate for garbage collection at a later stage. When an array is declared on the stack, things get a little more complicated:

C++ array on the stack	Java array on the heap
| ```
Type t[32];
``` | ```
Type[] t = new Type[32];
t[0] = new Type();
t[1] = new Type();
...
...
t[30] = new Type();
t[31] = new Type();
``` |

In C++, the statement Type t[32] creates 32 objects, initializes them, and uses the address of the first one to access them. The Java equivalent needs an explicit object for the array itself and needs an explicit creation statement for each element.

- Overloaded operators in the code. Although Java does not support overloaded operators, a smart translation tool could do type analysis of expressions and generate functionally equivalent, though perhaps less readable, Java code. An example is given here:

C++ overloaded operators	Java, using methods
`class Type {`	`class Type {`
`  void operator+(const& Type t);`	`  void add(Type t) {...}`
`  void operator=(const& Type t);`	`  void assign(Type t) {...}`
`  ...`	`  ...`
`}`	`}`
`Type t1, t2, t3;`	`Type t1 = new Type(),`
	`     t2 = new Type(),`
	`     t3 = new Type();`
`t3 = t1 + t2;`	`t3.assign(t1.add(t2));`

Class `Type` implements two overloaded operators, which can be used in an expression (as is done in the assignment to `t3`). In the equivalent Java code, the parser has to give sensible names to each of the operators, and it has to replace all infix uses of the operators by appropriate method calls.

- Java does not support templates. See Section 19 in Chapter 1 for a discussion of using a crude form of templates in Java.

- Automatic casting to boolean expression. In C++, any integral expression automatically casts into a boolean expression (by comparing it with zero). Pointers to objects cast into an integer; as a result, conditional statements in C++ very often use an integer or a pointer value for the conditional expression. For instance, the following construct is a very common idiom to traverse all elements in a linked list

```
for (Element *e=list; e; e=e->next) { ... }
```

The condition uses the value of variable e, casts the address that it currently points to, an integer value, and results in *true* when it is not equal to zero (the null pointer). In Java, there is no automatic type conversion between any type and the type boolean. Therefore, the equivalent Java for-loop requires a comparison with `null`

```
for (Element e=list; e!=null; e=e.next) { ... }
```

C2J does not create the comparison with `null`, as that would require full type and expression analysis, something that *real* C++ compilers are much better equipped at doing.

C2J is not a complete C++ parser. In order to do more interesting automatic C++ to Java translation, it would be interesting to use the front-end of a C++ compiler, such as the GNU C++ compiler, to do the analysis of the C++ code. Instead of generating executable code, the back-end of the compiler could just as well generate Java.

4. C2J In Action

C2J has been used to translate a large amount of code from C++ to Java. It has been proven very successful for "clean" C++ code. The following example is translated completely (except for the main function, because global functions are not handled). Note the automatic translation of types like unsigned, the initializer lists, the distribution of the public keyword, the automatic generation of comments, the translation of iostream classes, and the weaving of the C++ member functions into the class definition in Java. First of all, here is the C++ header file

```
class Rectangle {
public:
    Rectangle(int x_, int y_, unsigned w_, unsigned h_) :
    x(x_), y(y_), w(w_), h(h_) { }
    void move(int x_, int y_);
    void resize(unsigned w_, unsigned h_);
    void print();
protected:
    int x, y;
    unsigned w, h;
};
```

Below is the corresponding .C file

```
#include "test.h"
#include <iostream.h>

void Rectangle::move(int x_, int y_) { x = x_; y = y_; }
void Rectangle::resize(unsigned w_, unsigned h_) { w = w_; h = h_; }
void Rectangle::print() {
    cout << "Rectangle " << x << " " << y <<
                    " " << w << " " << h << endl;
}
void main() {
    Rectangle *rect = new Rectangle(10,10,100,100);
    rect->print();
}
```

The following Java file is automatically generated. The only changes made to it are formatting and the addition of a main method

```
package SomePackage ;

/**
 * class Rectangle
 *
 * This code has been generated using c2j.
 * Courtesy of Morgan Stanley & Co., Inc.
 * Read general disclaimer distributed with c2j before using this
 * code. For information about c2j, send mail to laffra@ms.com
 *
 * Copyright 1995/1996, SomeCompany All rights reserved
 * @author SomeBody
 */
public class Rectangle {

/**
 * Rectangle
 * @param x_
 * @param y_
 * @param w_
 * @param h_
 */
public Rectangle(int x_, int y_, int w_, int h_) {
    x=x_;
    y=y_;
    w=w_;
    h=h_;
}

/**
 * move
 * @param x_
 * @param y_
 */
public void move(int x_, int y_) { x = x_; y = y_; }

/**
 * resize
 * @param w_
 * @param h_
 */
public void resize(int w_, int h_) { w = w_; h = h_; }

/**
 * print
 */
public void print() {
```

```
        System.out.print("Rectangle " + x + " " + y +
                    " " + w + " " + h + "\n");
    }
    int x;
    int y;
    int w;
    int h;

    /**
     * This main routine has been added manually.
     */
    public static void main(String args[]) {
     Rectangle rect = new Rectangle(10,10,100,100);
     rect.print();
     }
    };
```

Both programs execute and generate the correct output.

5. How C2J Works

C2J is a C++ to Java translator. The input must consist of:

- one .H file containing one or more C++ class definitions.

- one .C file containing all method bodies referenced in the .H file.

C2J is basically a shell-script that calls *sed*, followed by a C++-to-Java translator, and the C preprocessor to do all the weaving of moving methods into one Java class definition. It runs on all platforms that support the standard Unix utilities. In particular it has been tested on various Unix and Linux systems using various C++ compilers (such as the Lucid C++ compiler and the GNU g++ compiler). It also runs on PC platforms that have the MKS toolkit installed on it.

References

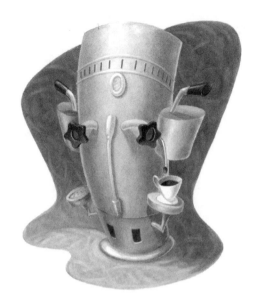

[De Pauw et.al., 1993]
  Wim De Pauw, Richard Helm, Doug Kimelman, and John Vlissides.
  Visualizing the behavior of object-oriented systems.
  In Object-Oriented Programming Systems, Languages and Applications
  Conference (OOPSLA'93), 1993.

[De Pauw et.al., 1994]
  Wim De Pauw, Doug Kimelman, and John Vlissides.
  Modeling object-oriented program execution.
  In European Conference on Object-Oriented Programming, (ECOOP'94), 1994.

[Ellis & Stroustrup, 1991]
  Margaret Ellis and Bjarne Stroustrup.
  C++ Annotated Reference Manual.
  Addison-Wesley, 1991.

[Gamma et.al., 1995]
  Erich Gamma, Richard Helm, Ralph Johnson, John Vlissides.
  Design Patterns: Elements of Reusable Object-Oriented Software.
  Addison-Wesley, 1995.

[Laffra & Malhotra, 1993]
  Chris Laffra and Ashok Malhotra.
  HotWire — A Visual Debugger for C++.
  USENIX 1994 C++ Technical Conference, Cambridge, Massachusetts, 1994.

APPENDIX

A

Contents of Diskette

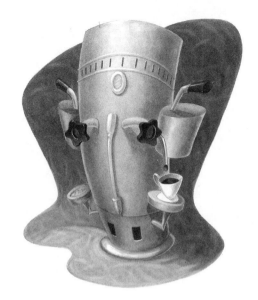

The enclosed diskette is a standard DOS diskette. The software on the diskette runs best on Windows 95, Windows NT, Macintosh (System 7.5), and various UNIX® systems. The software can be run directly off the diskette, or copied from a zip file.

WINDOWS 3.1 IS NOT SUPPORTED

Diskette Includes

Development tools for advanced Java(TM) developers. Source code designed to raise your Java programming skills to a higher level...

c2j	A C++ to Java translator for Windows® 95, Windows NT™, and various UNIX(TM) systems, including Linux. Takes your existing C++ code and automatically translates most of the language incompatibilities. A must for C++ developers.
LTK	The little toolkit. Shows how the Java AWT could have looked like, how to do double buffering, how to implement structured graphics, and how to plan for look-and-feel independence. The LTK complements the AWT with flexible layout managers and easy-to-enhance components, such as a table widget and a notebook widget.
Tracer	A new visual debugger for Java programs. Uses instrumented Java code or a specially enhanced Java VM to visualize the objects in your Java project. The debugger itself is written in Java and can be customized to show those aspects you are interested yourself!

INDEX

Index

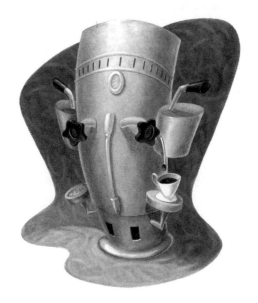

LICENSE AGREEMENT AND LIMITED WARRANTY

READ THE FOLLOWING TERMS AND CONDITIONS CAREFULLY BEFORE OPENING THIS SOFTWARE MEDIA PACKAGE. THIS LEGAL DOCUMENT IS AN AGREEMENT BETWEEN YOU AND PRENTICE-HALL, INC. (THE "COMPANY"). BY OPENING THIS SEALED SOFTWARE MEDIA PACKAGE, YOU ARE AGREEING TO BE BOUND BY THESE TERMS AND CONDITIONS. IF YOU DO NOT AGREE WITH THESE TERMS AND CONDITIONS, DO NOT OPEN THE SOFTWARE MEDIA PACKAGE. PROMPTLY RETURN THE UNOPENED SOFTWARE MEDIA PACKAGE AND ALL ACCOMPANYING ITEMS TO THE PLACE YOU OBTAINED THEM FOR A FULL REFUND OF ANY SUMS YOU HAVE PAID.

1.   **GRANT OF LICENSE:** In consideration of your payment of the license fee, which is part of the price you paid for this product, and your agreement to abide by the terms and conditions of this Agreement, the Company grants to you a nonexclusive right to use and display the copy of the enclosed software program (hereinafter the "SOFTWARE") on a single computer (i.e., with a single CPU) at a single location so long as you comply with the terms of this Agreement. The Company reserves all rights not expressly granted to you under this Agreement.

2.   **OWNERSHIP OF SOFTWARE:** You own only the magnetic or physical media (the enclosed SOFTWARE) on which the SOFTWARE is recorded or fixed, but the Company retains all the rights, title, and ownership to the SOFTWARE recorded on the original SOFTWARE copy(ies) and all subsequent copies of the SOFTWARE, regardless of the form or media on which the original or other copies may exist. This license is not a sale of the original SOFTWARE or any copy to you.

3.   **COPY RESTRICTIONS:** This SOFTWARE and the accompanying printed materials and user manual (the "Documentation") are the subject of copyright. You may not copy the Documentation or the SOFTWARE, except that you may make a single copy of the SOFTWARE for backup or archival purposes only. You may be held legally responsible for any copying or copyright infringement which is caused or encouraged by your failure to abide by the terms of this restriction.

4.   **USE RESTRICTIONS:** You may not network the SOFTWARE or otherwise use it on more than one computer or computer terminal at the same time. You may physically transfer the SOFTWARE from one computer to another provided that the SOFTWARE is used on only one computer at a time. You may not distribute copies of the SOFTWARE or Documentation to others. You may not reverse engineer, disassemble, decompile, modify, adapt, translate, or create derivative works based on the SOFTWARE or the Documentation without the prior written consent of the Company.

5.   **TRANSFER RESTRICTIONS:** The enclosed SOFTWARE is licensed only to you and may not be transferred to any one else without the prior written consent of the Company. Any unauthorized transfer of the SOFTWARE shall result in the immediate termination of this Agreement.

6.   **TERMINATION:** This license is effective until terminated. This license will terminate automatically without notice from the Company and become null and void if you fail to comply with any provisions or limitations of this license. Upon termination, you shall destroy the Documentation and all copies of the SOFTWARE. All provisions of this Agreement as to warranties, limitation of liability, remedies or damages, and our ownership rights shall survive termination.

7.   **MISCELLANEOUS:** This Agreement shall be construed in accordance with the laws of the United States of America and the State of New York and shall benefit the Company, its affiliates, and assignees.

8.   **LIMITED WARRANTY AND DISCLAIMER OF WARRANTY:** The Company warrants that the SOFTWARE, when properly used in accordance with the Documentation, will operate in substantial conformity with the description of the SOFTWARE set forth in the Documentation. The Company does not warrant that the SOFTWARE will meet your requirements or that the operation of the SOFTWARE will be uninterrupted or error-free. The Company warrants that the

media on which the SOFTWARE is delivered shall be free from defects in materials and workmanship under normal use for a period of thirty (30) days from the date of your purchase. Your only remedy and the Company's only obligation under these limited warranties is, at the Company's option, return of the warranted item for a refund of any amounts paid by you or replacement of the item. Any replacement of SOFTWARE or media under the warranties shall not extend the original warranty period. The limited warranty set forth above shall not apply to any SOFTWARE which the Company determines in good faith has been subject to misuse, neglect, improper installation, repair, alteration, or damage by you. EXCEPT FOR THE EXPRESSED WARRANTIES SET FORTH ABOVE, THE COMPANY DISCLAIMS ALL WARRANTIES, EXPRESS OR IMPLIED, INCLUDING WITHOUT LIMITATION, THE IMPLIED WARRANTIES OF MERCHANTABILITY AND FITNESS FOR A PARTICULAR PURPOSE. EXCEPT FOR THE EXPRESS WARRANTY SET FORTH ABOVE, THE COMPANY DOES NOT WARRANT, GUARANTEE, OR MAKE ANY REPRESENTATION REGARDING THE USE OR THE RESULTS OF THE USE OF THE SOFTWARE IN TERMS OF ITS CORRECTNESS, ACCURACY, RELIABILITY, CURRENTNESS, OR OTHERWISE.

IN NO EVENT, SHALL THE COMPANY OR ITS EMPLOYEES, AGENTS, SUPPLIERS, OR CONTRACTORS BE LIABLE FOR ANY INCIDENTAL, INDIRECT, SPECIAL, OR CONSEQUENTIAL DAMAGES ARISING OUT OF OR IN CONNECTION WITH THE LICENSE GRANTED UNDER THIS AGREEMENT, OR FOR LOSS OF USE, LOSS OF DATA, LOSS OF INCOME OR PROFIT, OR OTHER LOSSES, SUSTAINED AS A RESULT OF INJURY TO ANY PERSON, OR LOSS OF OR DAMAGE TO PROPERTY, OR CLAIMS OF THIRD PARTIES, EVEN IF THE COMPANY OR AN AUTHORIZED REPRESENTATIVE OF THE COMPANY HAS BEEN ADVISED OF THE POSSIBILITY OF SUCH DAMAGES. IN NO EVENT SHALL LIABILITY OF THE COMPANY FOR DAMAGES WITH RESPECT TO THE SOFTWARE EXCEED THE AMOUNTS ACTUALLY PAID BY YOU, IF ANY, FOR THE SOFTWARE.

SOME JURISDICTIONS DO NOT ALLOW THE LIMITATION OF IMPLIED WARRANTIES OR LIABILITY FOR INCIDENTAL, INDIRECT, SPECIAL, OR CONSEQUENTIAL DAMAGES, SO THE ABOVE LIMITATIONS MAY NOT ALWAYS APPLY. THE WARRANTIES IN THIS AGREEMENT GIVE YOU SPECIFIC LEGAL RIGHTS AND YOU MAY ALSO HAVE OTHER RIGHTS WHICH VARY IN ACCORDANCE WITH LOCAL LAW.

ACKNOWLEDGMENT

YOU ACKNOWLEDGE THAT YOU HAVE READ THIS AGREEMENT, UNDERSTAND IT, AND AGREE TO BE BOUND BY ITS TERMS AND CONDITIONS. YOU ALSO AGREE THAT THIS AGREEMENT IS THE COMPLETE AND EXCLUSIVE STATEMENT OF THE AGREEMENT BETWEEN YOU AND THE COMPANY AND SUPERSEDES ALL PROPOSALS OR PRIOR AGREEMENTS, ORAL, OR WRITTEN, AND ANY OTHER COMMUNICATIONS BETWEEN YOU AND THE COMPANY OR ANY REPRESENTATIVE OF THE COMPANY RELATING TO THE SUBJECT MATTER OF THIS AGREEMENT.

Should you have any questions concerning this Agreement or if you wish to contact the Company for any reason, please contact in writing at the address below.

Robin Short
Prentice Hall PTR
One Lake Street
Upper Saddle River, New Jersey 07458